6/04

Police Brutality

Other books in the Current Controversies series:

Police Brutality

Louise I. Gerdes, *Book Editor*

Bruce Glassman, *Vice President*
Bonnie Szumski, *Publisher*
Helen Cothran, *Managing Editor*

CURRENT CONTROVERSIES

GREENHAVEN
PRESS ®

THOMSON
GALE

San Diego • Detroit • New York • San Francisco • Cleveland
New Haven, Conn. • Waterville, Maine • London • Munich

LIBRARY OF CONGRESS CATALOGING-IN-PUBLICATION DATA

Police brutality / Louise I. Gerdes, book editor.
    p. cm. — (Current controversies)
    Includes bibliographical references and index.
    ISBN 0-7377-1627-4 (lib. bdg. : alk. paper) —
    ISBN 0-7377-1628-2 (pbk. : alk. paper)
    1. Police brutality—United States. I. Gerdes, Louise I., 1953– . II. Series.
    HV8141.P564 2004
    363.2'32—dc21   2003060738

Printed in the United States of America

Contents

Chapter 2: What Factors Contribute to Police Brutality?

faith in the criminal justice system, police departments must discontinue the practice of racial profiling.

Chapter 4: Is Police Brutality Adequately Punished?

civilian oversight systems that allow citizens a hand in making sure that investigations of abuse are impartial and objective.

Foreword

By definition, controversies are "discussions of questions in which opposing opinions clash" (Webster's Twentieth Century Dictionary Unabridged). Few would deny that controversies are a pervasive part of the human condition and exist on virtually every level of human enterprise. Controversies transpire between individuals and among groups, within nations and between nations. Controversies supply the grist necessary for progress by providing challenges and challengers to the status quo. They also create atmospheres where strife and warfare can flourish. A world without controversies would be a peaceful world; but it also would be, by and large, static and prosaic.

The Series' Purpose

The purpose of the Current Controversies series is to explore many of the social, political, and economic controversies dominating the national and international scenes today. Titles selected for inclusion in the series are highly focused and specific. For example, from the larger category of criminal justice, Current Controversies deals with specific topics such as police brutality, gun control, white collar crime, and others. The debates in Current Controversies also are presented in a useful, timeless fashion. Articles and book excerpts included in each title are selected if they contribute valuable, long-range ideas to the overall debate. And wherever possible, current information is enhanced with historical documents and other relevant materials. Thus, while individual titles are current in focus, every effort is made to ensure that they will not become quickly outdated. Books in the Current Controversies series will remain important resources for librarians, teachers, and students for many years.

In addition to keeping the titles focused and specific, great care is taken in the editorial format of each book in the series. Book introductions and chapter prefaces are offered to provide background material for readers. Chapters are organized around several key questions that are answered with diverse opinions representing all points on the political spectrum. Materials in each chapter include opinions in which authors clearly disagree as well as alternative opinions in which authors may agree on a broader issue but disagree on the possible solutions. In this way, the content of each volume in Current Controversies mirrors the mosaic of opinions encountered in society. Readers will quickly realize that there are many viable answers to these complex issues. By questioning each author's conclusions, students and casual readers can begin to develop the critical thinking skills so important to evaluating opinionated material.

Current Controversies is also ideal for controlled research. Each anthology in the series is composed of primary sources taken from a wide gamut of informational categories including periodicals, newspapers, books, United States and foreign government documents, and the publications of private and public organizations. Readers will find factual support for reports, debates, and research papers covering all areas of important issues. In addition, an annotated table of contents, an index, a book and periodical bibliography, and a list of organizations to contact are included in each book to expedite further research.

Perhaps more than ever before in history, people are confronted with diverse and contradictory information. During the Persian Gulf War, for example, the public was not only treated to minute-to-minute coverage of the war, it was also inundated with critiques of the coverage and countless analyses of the factors motivating U.S. involvement. Being able to sort through the plethora of opinions accompanying today's major issues, and to draw one's own conclusions, can be a complicated and frustrating struggle. It is the editors' hope that Current Controversies will help readers with this struggle.

Greenhaven Press anthologies primarily consist of previously published material taken from a variety of sources, including periodicals, books, scholarly journals, newspapers, government documents, and position papers from private and public organizations. These original sources are often edited for length and to ensure their accessibility for a young adult audience. The anthology editors also change the original titles of these works in order to clearly present the main thesis of each viewpoint and to explicitly indicate the opinion presented in the viewpoint. These alterations are made in consideration of both the reading and comprehension levels of a young adult audience. Every effort is made to ensure that Greenhaven Press accurately reflects the original intent of the authors included in this anthology.

Studies show that women police officers possess better communication skills, are more effective at defusing potentially violent confrontations, and use excessive force far less often that their male counterparts.

Introduction

"I'd much rather talk somebody out of something before I have to put my hands on them," explains Deputy Bonnie Kalboskopf of the Richmond County sheriff's office in Georgia. "There's no sense in escalating the situation and causing problems that wouldn't have arisen if it didn't become physical," she says. Research of police departments nationwide reveals that Kalboskopf's attitude is typical of many female law enforcement officers. Studies show that women police officers possess better communication skills, are more effective at defusing potentially violent confrontations, and use excessive force far less often that their male counterparts. Some analysts have therefore concluded that increasing the number of female officers in police forces will reduce incidents of police brutality.

Police brutality can have a significant impact on the community. Incidents of brutality can so divide a community that in some cities riots have erupted after abusive encounters between police and citizens are made public. The resulting loss of trust between citizens and the police can make it difficult for police officers to be effective. Police brutality is costly for taxpayers as well, particularly in large cites where payouts for police brutality lawsuits can be substantial. In its 2002 study *Men, Women, and Police Excessive Force: A Tale of Two Genders*, the National Center for Women and Policing (NCWP) discovered that Los Angeles paid out $63.5 million between 1990 and 1999 for judgments or settlements in civil liability lawsuits involving excessive force by a male officer. Only $2.8 million was paid out for cases involving female LAPD officers. Since male officers outnumbered female officers on patrol by a ratio of 4:1 during this period, the payouts for excessive force by males exceeded those for female offices 23:1. When payouts for only assault and battery are examined, the ratio increases to 32:1. If only fatalities are considered, the ratio is 42:1. Penny Harrington, former chief of police of Portland, Oregon, and director of NCWP concludes, "This new study shows that increasing women on the force holds the key for substantially decreasing police violence and its costs to taxpayers."

One reason the payouts for female officers are so much lower than those for male officers, analysts argue, is that women have fewer sustained allegations of excessive force decided against them. When compiling data from participating departments, the NCWP study found that female officers comprised only 2 percent of sustained allegations of excessive force. Although male officers represented 82.6 percent of the force, they accounted for 98 percent of its sustained allegations of excessive force. The study concluded, "Male officers are over eight and a half times more likely than their female counterparts to have an allegation of excessive force sustained against them."

Female officers also have fewer citizen complaints filed against them. Although women comprise 25 percent of the Washington D.C. Metropolitan Police Department, during 2001 only 13.2 percent of complaints received named female officers while 86.8 percent named male officers; thus male officers were twice as likely as female officers to receive a complaint for excessive force. These numbers were even more dramatic in San Jose, California, where males were over three times more likely than females to be named in an excessive-force complaint.

Commentators who support adding more women to police forces dispute critics' claims that women are less likely to be named in excessive force incidents because they avoid potentially dangerous situations that might require the use of force. In 1999 the National Institute of Justice found that there was no difference in the extent of routine use of force by male and female officers during patrol duties. Unlike excessive force, routine force—the force necessary to subdue a suspect who is resisting arrest, for example—is considered legally justified. Moreover, according to Richmond, Georgia, County Sheriff's Colonel Gary Powell, the use of force is not dependent on gender but on the individual working in the particular situation. "We have some [women] that are as tough as any male you'll ever run into," says Powell.

Some analysts claim that the ability to defuse a potentially violent situation is often preferable to the use of force. Coolness and people skills are considered by many to be more important than strength in conflict situations. In his research summary "Why Policemen Don't Like Policewomen," Joseph Balkin explains that female officers are more likely to have these qualities than male officers. Researcher Carol Ann Martin maintains, for example, "Women have proven that they have excellent communication skills which can be extremely helpful in police-citizen encounters where there may be potential violence. Quite often if the male officer is of the John Wayne–type he will provoke a fight or violence, instead of calming down the situation."

Female officers are also less hostile and aggressive than their male counterparts, some analysts argue. "The experience of street policing is deeply steeped in a masculine culture of brotherhood that rests on the division between 'us' and 'them,'" law professor Angela Harris maintains. "The hypermasculinity of policing leads to a culture in which violence is always just below the surface," she argues. According to law professor Robert W. Benson, "the practical results of this police machismo are that male officers get themselves involved in hostile confrontations with the public, use of excessive force, shootings, drug dealing, and . . . framing of suspects through deceit and lies." This hostile attitude on the part of male officers, he argues, may lead to incidents of police brutality. "The silver lining in this cloud," Benson claims, "is that female officers are rarely involved in such misconduct, precisely because they rarely share the value system of machismo." Researcher Balkin adds, "Policemen see police work as involving control through authority, while policewomen see it as a public service. The women's orientation is more likely to result in better relations with the public and a better image of police departments."

The fact that women are less likely to use excessive force and often have skills to diffuse potentially dangerous situations has led many to conclude that having more female officers would reduce police brutality. According to Peter Bloch and Deborah Anderson, "A department with a substantial number of policewomen may be less aggressive than one with only men. Women act less aggressively and they believe in less aggression. The presence of women may stimulate increased attention to the ways of avoiding violence and cooling violent situations without resorting to the use of force." In 1991 the Christopher Commission, created to investigate the use of force in the LAPD, made just such a recommendation to the department. The commission's report concluded, "Female officers are not reluctant to use force but they are not nearly as likely to be involved in use of excessive force."

Despite such recommendations, however, women are still underrepresented in most police departments. According to Katherine Spillar, executive vice-president of the Feminist Majority Foundation, "our research shows that the increase of women in law enforcement remains stuck at an alarmingly slow rate. Women comprise only 13.8% of all sworn law enforcement positions nationwide—a paltry increase of one-half of one percent from 1997 and only 3.2 percentage points from 1990 when women made up 10.6% of officers."

The NCWP argues that "widespread bias in police hiring, selection practices and recruitment policies keeps the numbers of women in law enforcement artificially low." Entry exams over-emphasize upper body strength even though physical prowess is less related to job performance than communication skills, the NCWP argues. Female officers also face harassment and intimidation that discourages them. In addition, officer Wendy Austin of the New South Wales police service in Australia claims that male police officers try to keep female officers away from hostile confrontations. "Is it an act designed to be protective of women Police," she asks, "or is it designed to protect male Police from seeing women in displays of competence?" Citing the theories of psychologist Harry Stack Sullivan, Austin claims that the very presence of women undermines the masculinity of male police officers. "The women do their work perhaps not with equal physical strength, but with equal courage and competence," Austin contends. "If the male police officer recognizes the worth of women [in] police work, it would make him fell less manly, so he distorts his view of them to perceive them as not as strong, competent or courageous." Perpetuating these attitudes and discouraging female police officers, reasons former police chief

Harrington, is not only "unfair to women who are seeking law enforcement careers, but [the NCWP] study shows that depriving women of jobs in policing is costly to taxpayers and results in more police brutality."

The authors of the viewpoints in *Police Brutality: Current Controversies* examine the nature and scope of police brutality and the various strategies being tried to reduce and punish police misconduct.

Chapter 1

Is Police Brutality
a Serious Problem?

Chapter Preface

In the wake of the terrorist attacks of September 11, 2001, the U.S. government increased the powers of law enforcement to identify, detain, and interrogate suspected terrorists. Some analysts argue that these policies could lead to increased incidences of police brutality. What particularly troubles some civil rights advocates is that in their zeal to prevent another tragedy, government leaders might conclude that brutal police interrogation techniques such as torture are appropriate tools to obtain information from suspected terrorists. While some believe torture may be necessary to protect Americans from terrorist attacks, others believe torture is never appropriate in a democratic society.

Those who support the use of torture argue that traditional interrogation techniques are not sufficient. These commentators claim, for example, that traditional techniques have not worked on terrorists being held as suspects in the September 11 terrorist attacks. FBI sources indicate that suspected terrorists Zacarias Moussaoui, Mohammed Jaweed Azmath, Ayub Ali Khan, and Nabil Almarabh have refused to talk. The FBI believes them to be members of al-Qaeda, a network of terrorists led by expelled Saudi Arabian millionaire Osama bin Laden, who is also believed to be the mastermind behind the September 11 attacks. Law enforcement agents have offered the suspects the prospect of lighter sentences, money, jobs, and a new identity and life in the United States for them and their family members, but attempts to obtain information have failed. According to *Washington Post* staff writer Walter Pincus, "FBI and Justice Department investigators are increasingly frustrated by the silence of jailed suspected associates of Osama bin Laden's al-Qaeda network, and some are beginning to say that traditional civil liberties may have to be cast aside if they are to extract information about the September 11 attacks and terrorist plans."

Another argument put forward by analysts who support the use of torture is that extreme measures may be necessary to prevent terrorism. Torture, they argue, may be necessary when trying to extract information from a prisoner who has knowledge of imminent violence against American citizens. In Israel, for example, interrogators from the Shin Bet, Israel's counter-intelligence and internal security service, tortured tens of thousands of alleged Palestinian terrorists, some of whom died in custody. In 1987 the Supreme Court of Israel outlawed these practices but left open the possibility that torture could be justified in "ticking bomb" situations—when obtaining information could save Israeli lives.

Critics of torture argue, however, that the "ticking bomb" justification assumes, sometimes wrongly, that those in custody have the needed information. David Walsh, who writes for the World Socialist Web Site, argues, "The assumption of . . . 'torture advocates' is that the American state and its police agencies do not lie and are infallible, that those alleged to be guilty of crimes are indeed guilty of crimes, and that the FBI, CIA, and police forces in general should be given an entirely free hand." Walsh maintains that in numerous cases U.S. law enforcement has arrested and imprisoned innocent citizens, which proves that the police are not infallible and thus could end up torturing innocent people.

Those who oppose the use of torture also claim that the laws of the United States protect those suspected of crimes by regulating police interrogation practices. According to law professors John Parry and Welsh White, "The prohibition of torture is a fundamental aspect of our system of government. All citizens, whether innocent, suspected or actually guilty, receive the benefit of this protection." U.S. law, Parry and White maintain, expressly prohibits the use of torture when interrogating suspects. "For more than half a century," they contend, "it has been established that the police are absolutely prohibited from using force, threats of force, excessively protracted questioning, and other forms of physical or mental torture to produce a confession."

Opponents of torture also argue that interrogators have other techniques at their disposal to obtain information from terrorists. According to Parry and White, "In America, skilled interrogators have generally concluded that the harsh practices associated with the third degree [torture] are less effective in obtaining truthful statements than psychologically oriented techniques that are designed to reduce the suspect's resistance by first gaining his rapport and then probing his psyche to find the best means of inducing his cooperation." Robert M. Blitzer, former chief of the FBI counterterrorism section, maintains that offers of reduced sentences worked to obtain testimony from Ahmed Ressam, caught bringing explosives into the United States for millennium attacks that never took place, and from Ali Mohammed, who pleaded guilty in the 1998 embassy bombings of U.S. embassies in Africa. Mohammed, says Blitzer, provided valuable information about al-Qaeda.

Opponents of torture also argue that torture should never be permissible in a democratic society. Americans should not fight those who oppose liberty by sacrificing liberty, they claim. "We certainly should give greater leeway to interrogating officers when they seek to protect public safety," Parry and White reason. "But law enforcement officials should not be allowed to decide for themselves that desperate times call for desperate measures. The cost of adhering to fundamental safeguards may be high in some situations, but it is the price of upholding the constitutional values that distinguish us from our opponents. In order to uphold those values, we must make it clear to the police that they are not permitted to employ abusive interrogation practices including any form of torture."

Whether law enforcement agents should be allowed to torture terrorist suspects remains controversial. The authors in the following chapter examine whether or not police brutality is a serious problem.

Police Brutality Is a Serious Problem

by the *Progressive*

About the author: *The* Progressive *magazine advocates peace and social justice.*

Police brutality is a fact of American life. In major cities across the country, officers are abusing their authority in the most flagrant ways.

New York City and Los Angeles are the epicenters of this crisis.

When the New York City officers who shot and killed Amadou Diallo[1] were acquitted . . . February [25, 2000], [former] Mayor Rudolph Giuliani responded to the verdict with the words, "Probably until the day I die, I will always give police officers the benefit of the doubt."

Imposing Law and Order

But what about giving other people the same benefit?

Diallo, an African immigrant, was unarmed, but the police said they acted in self-defense when they unloaded forty-one shots at him. Two days after the verdict, Malcolm Ferguson, also unarmed, was killed while struggling with a police officer in the same Bronx neighborhood where Diallo was shot.

Throughout his time as mayor, Giuliani has shown his disdain for civil rights and his eagerness to impose law and order at all costs. When Giuliani took office in 1994, he instituted his "zero tolerance" policy, which led to a huge increase in arrests for such crimes as playing music too loudly, biking on the sidewalk, and public drinking. Some officers got the message that it was OK to rough people up—especially people of color.

"Many of the people allegedly kicked or beaten by police were not criminal suspects but people who had simply questioned police authority or had minor disagreements with officers," Amnesty International said in a 1996 report "Police Brutality and Excessive Force in the New York City Police Department."

---

1. Diallo, a West African immigrant, was killed after New York City police officers fired forty-one shots while he stood in his Bronx doorway on February 4, 1999.

"Nearly all the victims in the cases of deaths in custody and police shootings reviewed by Amnesty International were from racial minorities—particularly African Americans, Latinos, and Asians."

Diallo's murder and the grotesque abuse of Haitian immigrant Abner Louima[2] in 1997 are only the most notorious examples of the brutality behind the N.Y.P.D. badge. Other incidents have occurred with alarming regularity.

The Abuse of Power

In Los Angeles, infamous for the Rodney King case,[3] a new, smoldering scandal has singed an elite anti-gang unit and threatens to consume the entire police department. The L.A.P.D. had a unit called Community Resources Against Street Hoodlums, or C.R.A.S.H. Formed in the late 1970s, it patrolled the Ramparts section of Los Angeles, a low-income area with a large immigrant population, and a home to gangs.

Ramparts officer Rafael Perez—who was accused of stealing eight pounds of cocaine in police custody—cooperated with authorities. He claimed that his fellow officers frequently framed suspects and hid wrongful shootings.

In 1998, when investigators searched Perez's house, they saw a plaque that was decorated with a playing card imprinted with a red heart that had two bullets through it. "Uh, that plaque that you probably saw at my house. . . . Do you know what that plaque is even about?" Perez said to the internal police investigators, according to a transcript obtained by the *Los Angeles Times*. "[A sergeant] gave me that plaque for the Ovando shooting. That's what that is. We give plaques when you get involved in shootings. Uh, if the guy dies, the card is a black No. 2. If he stays alive, it's a red No. 2." (Perez had admitted to shooting, then framing, Javier Ovando, an unarmed man, with another officer. The victim was paralyzed as a result of the shooting and sentenced to twenty-three years in prison as a result of the frame-up.)

> *"In major cities across the country, officers are abusing their authority in the most flagrant ways."*

"Is it more prestigious to get one that is black than red?" Detective Mark Thompson asked Perez.

"Yeah. I mean, you know, the black one signifies that a guy died," he answered.

According to the *Los Angeles Times*, "So-called shooting parties at which officers drank beer and were awarded plaques for wounding or killing people

2. Louima, a Haitian immigrant, was beaten and sodomized in a New York City police precinct house, on August 9, 1997.   3. King was beaten by three Los Angeles police officers as their supervisor watched after King led police on a high-speed chase on March 3, 1991. After the officers were acquitted of excessive force on April 29, 1992, rioting broke out in Los Angeles. On April 16, 1993, a federal jury convicted two of the officers of violating King's civil rights.

were quasi-official events sometimes held at the Los Angeles Police Academy and attended by supervisors, according to four officers who worked in the Ramparts Division's anti-gang unit. The officers—all of whom asked not to be identified—said similar plaques were awarded to anti-gang officers in the L.A.P.D.'s 77th Street Division, and to officers in other units."

But police brutality is not confined to New York and Los Angeles. In 1998, Human Rights Watch published a 440-page report "Shielded From Justice: Police Brutality and Accountability in the United States." It examined fourteen U.S. cities (Atlanta, Boston, Chicago, Detroit, Indianapolis, Los Angeles, Minneapolis, New Orleans, New York, Philadelphia, Portland, Providence, San Francisco, and Washington) from 1995 to 1998. It concluded that "police brutality is persistent in all of these cities; that systems to deal with abuse have had similar failings in all the cities; and that, in each city examined, complainants face enormous barriers in seeking administrative punishment or criminal prosecution of officers who have committed human rights violations."

A National Pattern

The evidence of excessive force is all around us:

In Houston in July 1998, Pedro Oregon was shot during a drug raid on his home. He was an unarmed Mexican national. The police officers were fired following protests from the Hispanic community.

In Kansas City, Missouri, in November 1998, thirteen-year-old Timothy Wilson, a black child, died from a gun wound after six officers saw him driving recklessly and chased him.

In Hartford, Connecticut, in April 1999, fourteen-year-old Aquan Salmon, an unarmed suspect in a robbery, and also African American, died after being shot in the back by a police officer.

And in early March of [2000] . . . , Louisville, Kentucky, was reeling from days of community protests and counter-protests by the police department after Mayor David L. Armstrong fired police chief Eugene Sherrard. Chief Sherrard had approved medals of valor for two police officers who used twenty-two bullets to shoot at and kill an unarmed black man suspected of stealing a car. The officers were later cleared in a grand jury inquiry, but their action was denounced by black leaders.

Human Rights Watch makes the following sensible recommendations:
- federal aid to police departments should be contingent on regular reports concerning excessive force "and on improvements in oversight and discipline";
- police and political leaders should create "a policy of zero tolerance for abuse";
- police departments should establish means of identifying officers who are at risk of using excessive force and should remove those who commit abuses;
- civilian review agencies should have adequate power to rein in the police;

• each state should hire a special prosecutor for police cases.

Not all, not most, police officers are brutal. And many cities, from Boston to San Diego, have reduced crime by taking an enlightened approach, one that stresses community policing and good relations with the citizenry. They have had as much success reducing crime as New York City has, without trampling on civil liberties. Departments around the country should be looking to this civilized approach—and discard the N.Y.P.D. and L.A.P.D. models.

Police cannot become a law unto themselves. Those who act illegally must be forced, through criminal prosecution, to pay for their crimes. And we must hold the officials in charge accountable: the police chief, the mayor, the district attorney.

We deserve to be treated as citizens, not as subjects—or suspects.

Police Officers Use Deadly Force Too Frequently

by Amnesty International

About the author: *Amnesty International is an international human rights organization.*

> "This was a person who did not have to die. I don't understand why law enforcement always says 'we have to make split decisions'. Why is the decision always to kill? The black life is so expendable". Sister of unarmed motorist Stanton Crew, shot dead by New Jersey police officers in June 1999 (quoted in the New Jersey Record, June 6 1999)

Unjustified Police Shootings

There continue to be frequent disturbing reports of unjustified police shootings, with officers firing on unarmed suspects fleeing non-violent crime scenes, during traffic stops, at the end of pursuits or in other questionable circumstances. In some cases suspects have been hit with multiple police gunfire. In most of the cases reported, the victims were African American or other minorities, and some were children. For example:

- *Kansas City:* In November 1998 a 13-year old black child, Timothy L. Wilson, driving a friend's pick-up truck, was shot dead after a brief chase. Six officers had pursued the truck for several minutes after seeing Timothy driving erratically. All six surrounded the truck when it came to a halt in mud. Four white officers opened fire after, they said, he tried to reverse then drove towards them, a version disputed by an attorney for the Wilson family. The officers were cleared of criminal wrongdoing by a local grand jury. . . .

- *California:* In August 1999, in an early morning narcotics raid, a SWAT team from the El Monte police department burst into the home of a Mexican immigrant family and shot dead an unarmed elderly man, Mario Paz, in his bedroom. He was reportedly shot twice in the back. No drugs were found in the raid and a different name to that of the residents was on the search warrant. Many other questionable police shootings have been reported in California, several of which are cited below.

- *Connecticut:* In April 1999, a 14-year old unarmed African American. Aquan Salmon, a suspect in an attempted street robbery, was fatally shot in the back by Hartford, Connecticut, police officers during a foot chase. The officer was cleared of criminal wrongdoing but a separate investigation by the state attorney was pending at the beginning of September 1999.[1]

- *Chicago:* In June 1999, La Tanya Haggerty, a 19-year-old passenger in a car pulled over by Chicago police after a short chase, was shot dead when officers mistook the cell-phone in her hand for a gun. In September 1999, the Chicago Police Board (a police adjudicatory body) opened a hearing to decide on a recommendation by the police chief that the officers should be dismissed from the force. A day after the Haggerty shooting, Chicago police officers shot dead Robert Russ, a former college football player, after he refused to get out of his car after a pursuit. He was shot when an officer smashed the car window and pointed his gun directly into the car. The case was still under investigation at the time of writing. Both Haggerty and Russ were black.

> *"There continue to be frequent disturbing reports of unjustified police shootings, with officers firing on unarmed suspects fleeing non-violent crime scenes."*

- *New York City:* In May 1999 unarmed 16-year old Dante Johnson (black) was shot and critically injured after running away from three police officers who had stopped to question him and a friend while they were standing in the street. The officers were from the same street crime unit which had shot and killed Amadou Diallo in February 1999.[2] . . .

- *New Jersey:* In June 1999 Stanton Crew, an unarmed African American, was shot dead in New Jersey, after he tried to manoevre his car out of the way of two police cars which had boxed him in after a car chase. The officers fired 27 shots at his vehicle, as he tried to drive back and forth. A female passenger in the car suffered police gunshot wounds to her leg. . . .

- *Philadelphia:* In October 1998, 19-year-old Donta Dawson, an unarmed African American youth, was shot dead by a police officer who approached him after seeing him sitting in a stationary car with the engine running. The officer opened fire, shooting Dawson in the eye, after he said Dawson leaned forward and raised his arm. The officer was twice charged with manslaughter (voluntary and involuntary) but city judges dismissed the charges each time. He was fired from the force but is currently seeking to

1. State Attorney Kevin Kane ruled that Hartford Police Officer Robert Allan complied with state law in the use of deadly force.   2. Diallo, a West African immigrant, was killed after New York City police officers fired forty-one shots while he stood in his Bronx doorway on February 4, 1999.

get his job back through arbitration. In July 1999 the city agreed to pay Donta's family $712,500 in settlement of a civil action.

• *Texas:* In July 1998 Pedro Oregon, an unarmed Mexican national, was fatally shot by six Houston police officers during a drugs raid on his home. He reportedly died in his bedroom with six gunshot wounds to the back, two to the head and another in his hand. Only one officer was indicted, on a criminal trespass charge. However, after an outcry from the Hispanic community, a police internal inquiry found the officers guilty of "egregious misconduct" and they were fired.

When Should Deadly Force Be Used?

The above cases appear to grossly violate international standards which provide that force should be proportionate to the threat faced—and that firearms should be used only in self defence or the defence of others against an imminent threat of death or serious injury and "only when less extreme measures are insufficient to achieve these objectives."

Most US police departments also stipulate that officers should use deadly force only when their lives or the lives of others are in direct danger—and the majority of police officers do not fire their weapons or do so only in response to armed confrontations. However, dozens of cases similar to those described above occur annually, causing devastating loss to the families as well as costly payouts by cities in civil lawsuits. Many police departments have guidelines specifically restricting the use of deadly force in certain common situations, such as in the case of unarmed suspects in moving vehicles. Officers have frequently been exonerated, however, after claiming they feared for their lives, despite having failed to take basic avoidance procedures (such as moving out of the path of an oncoming vehicle). Others have been only mildly disciplined even after being found to have breached guidelines. Furthermore, lax training or supervision have led to systematic problems in some areas.

For example, an eight-month investigation into police shootings in Washington, DC, carried out by the *Washington Post* in 1998 found a pattern of "reckless and indiscriminate" shootings by officers in the 1990s, the extent of which had been hidden from public scrutiny through inadequate investigations and oversight. DC police shootings doubled between 1992 and 1995, even though homicides in the city had fallen from a record peak in

> *"Firearms should be used only in self defense or the defense of others against an imminent threat of death or serious injury."*

1991. Shootings since mid-1993 included 54 cases in which police had fired at vehicles (none of whose occupants had shot at officers), killing nine unarmed motorists and wounding 19. The *Washington Post* study looked at court records and police files and found that many internal investigations were riddled with omissions and errors. Most of the 422 police shootings examined by an internal police review board from 1993 to early 1998 were ruled to be justified, and only two cases resulted in criminal charges against police officers. One case was pending at the time of the *Post*'s report. In the other case, two officers were convicted of making false statements about a shooting: one was sentenced to 15 days in jail and the other received probation.

A Rise in Police Shootings

Although DC had a higher rate of police shootings than other cities, police shootings have reportedly risen in some other jurisdictions as well, . . . going against the general downward trend noted in earlier studies. For example, in Chicago police officers are reported to have shot 71 people in 1998, the highest annual total in a decade, despite a fall in homicides in the city. Other cities where police shootings are reported to have risen include San Jose in California, where six fatal shootings from January to July 1999 was the highest annual total in ten years; San Francisco, where shootings (fatal and nonfatal) reportedly rose from 2 in 1996 to 6 in 1997 and 12 in 1998; and Tulsa, Oklahoma, where the 7 armed people shot by police in 1998 was reported to be the highest in the force's history.

Police shootings in other areas have also caused concern. The US (federal) attorney's office in Los Angeles is investigating at least a dozen police shootings in seven Southern California jurisdictions, including Los Angeles County and has increased the number of civil rights lawyers to deal with an increase in complaints. The US Justice Department is also conducting a detailed inquiry into the Riverside Police Department, California, following several controversial shootings and other allegations of mistreatment of minorities in the past year. Cases include the December 1998 shooting of Tyisha Miller, a 19-year-old African American woman shot 12 times by four white Riverside police officers after they found her apparently unconscious in her locked car with a gun on her lap. (The officers fired a total of 23 shots into the car after breaking the window.) Allegations were also made that, after Miller was shot, other officers sent to the scene uttered racial slurs. The officers who shot Miller were cleared of criminal wrongdoing by the local District Attorney but were fired by the police chief for violating departmental policy after sustained local protests. (They are reported to be appealing against their dismissal.)[3]

Eight fatal police shootings in the small northeastern state of Connecticut since September 1998 (mainly of minorities) have led to widespread protests by the black community. Cases of concern include the Aquan Salmon shooting (above) and the fatal shooting of an unarmed Jamaican immigrant, Franklyn

---

3. In May 2002 a Culver City arbitrator exonerated two Riverside police officers in the shooting of Tyisha Miller and awarded them full back pay and benefits but refused to order the city to restore them to full-time duties, although the arbitrator concluded it was an "abuse of administrative discretion" to fire the officers.

Reid, in December 1998. Reid, who was wanted for a parole violation, was shot in the back of the neck at close range by a white police officer from the New Milford Police Department, after a brief chase. He had been apprehended and was on his knees when he was shot. The officer said he fired after Reid made a quick movement and he could not see his hands. He has been charged with murder in the case (with the trial due to start in November 1999), but is reported to be back on active duty. Another disturbing case was the fatal shooting by a West Haven officer of unarmed motorist Victoria Cooper as she tried to drive away from a routine traffic stop in July 1999. The officer said she tried to run him down. In May 1999, the Governor of Connecticut asked a state law enforcement commission to study police shooting investigations by looking at practice in other jurisdictions, and to make recommendations. The commission is due to report its findings in November 1999.

Looking for Explanations

Although the reasons for a rise in shootings are not always clear, community and civil rights groups have expressed concern that some officers may be using over-aggressive tactics. There is also concern that the introduction of powerful semi-automatic weapons which, unlike revolvers, fire many rounds in rapid succession, can increase the risk of unjustified shootings as well as deaths from multiple police gunfire, as in the Diallo and other cases. The *Washington Post* study found that the rise in police shootings in DC coincided with an influx of new recruits who were inadequately trained or supervised in use of the powerful Glock 9mm semi-automatic handgun, introduced by the department in 1988 to replace the revolver. The *Post* study found there had been 120 accidental discharges of the weapon by DC police since 1988 and that 75% of DC officers in 1996 had failed to comply with twice-yearly retraining requirements. Many other US police forces, including the NYPD, have reportedly introduced the Glock or similar semi-automatic weapons in recent years. The use of such weapons underscores the need for thorough training both in the handling of the weapons and in broader tactics to minimise the need to use firearms.

"The introduction of powerful semi-automatic weapons which, unlike revolvers, fire many rounds in rapid succession, can increase the risk of unjustified shootings."

Police shootings resulting in death or injury are routinely reviewed by local prosecutors in many US jurisdictions to see whether criminal laws have been violated. However, few officers are criminally charged and little public information is given out if a case does not go to trial. Police administrative inquiries into officer-involved shootings are rarely open to public scrutiny and even decisions on whether or not a shooting contravened policy are not always made public. Thus, systemic problems may remain hidden, as shown in DC. A few police departments have increased outside oversight of the review process in police shootings. Following the rise in police shootings in San Jose, the city announced in April 1999 that a new panel would review all police shootings, which would include the civilian complaints auditor and the city attorney, as well as police personnel. The findings in individual cases, however, were to remain internal, although any resulting policy changes would be made public. LAPD shootings are reviewed by the civilian Board of Police Commissioners who informed Amnesty International in August 1999 that "Following the final adjudication of each incident, the Board's findings and the report of the Chief of Police become public documents." However, in many departments, including the NYPD, the shooting review process as well as the findings in individual cases are completely internal.

The Media Underestimate Police Brutality

by Michael Novick

About the author: *Michael Novick, a Los Angeles public school teacher, is an antiracist activist, author of* White Lies White Power: The Fight Against White Supremacy and Reactionary Violence, *and editor of the antiracist journal,* Turning the Tide.

"Don't trust everything you read in the papers." This expression has become a proverb. Nowhere is it more true than in dealing with media reports of police killings. For several years, I've been browsing mainstream news media websites for stories about police killings, beatings, racism, and corruption. What I've learned is that the media report the *fact* of police killings, but not *the facts.*

Police Brutality Is Not an Aberration

Killings and shootings by the police are considered newsworthy on a par with traffic fatalities or yesterday's weather. Many reports are word-for-word transcripts of press statements by the police department involved. Few reporters bother to talk independently with witnesses, or to interview the family of the victim as they do with victims of other crimes. If they do report on the victims, it's often to dehumanize and criminalize them. To the mainstream media, with rare exceptions, police killings are an unfortunate necessity. Victims of police violence generally have only themselves to blame. Police abuse is an aberration.

But the beating of Rodney King, the torture of Abner Louima were no aberrations. The killings of Amadou Diallo in NY, Tyisha Miller in Riverside, [California], Malice Green in Detroit, Jonny Gammage in Pittsburg, Margaret Mitchell in LA, LaTanya Haggerty in Chicago were not aberrations. Police brutality is not an aberration—it's an epidemic, and its systemic! In failing to treat it as such, the media are failing in their responsibility to the truth and to their communities. But they are carrying out their responsibilities to their corporate owners, to the same economic and political elites that the police themselves serve and protect.

The role of the media in this regard is well-illustrated in the coverage of three . . . killings—the shooting deaths of Tyisha Miller in Riverside, Ricardo Clos by LA sheriff's deputies, and Margaret Laverne Mitchell by LAPD [Los Angeles Police Department]. We should also consider the treatment of extremely high profile cases, championed by community-based demonstrators, such as those of Abner Louima and Amadou Diallo in New York.[1]

A Character Assassinated by the Media

Tyisha Miller, a young Black woman, was fired on dozens of times, and pierced by at least 11 bullets, killed by four members of the Riverside police just before New Year's. After months of foot dragging, the District Attorney ruled the killing "justifiable," an unfortunate tragedy in which there was no criminal behavior by the police, only "errors of judgment." Thereby, the DA prevented jurors from determining if the cops were criminally responsible in the shooting death of a semi-conscious woman they had been called to help. In response, the *Riverside Press Enterprise* ran a story that was practically written by the police. It made Tyisha, the victim, appear the villain of the incident.

AP headlined the story, "Report: Teen killed by Riverside police was a gun-toting street tough." The opening paragraph states: "The teenager whose killing by Riverside police stirred racial tensions was a gun-toting street tough with a violent reputation, according to police documents." Note how the headline and the opening paragraph carefully refer to Tyisha Miller only as a "teen" and a "street tough," and her gender is studiously ignored. In fact, she is left name-less, to drive home the dehumanizing cop propaganda message that she was just another gang-banger who deserved what she got from the cops. This is further evidence that, as noted by [comedian and human rights activist] Dick Gregory, Tyisha's killing was about adding Black Women to the 'justifiable homicide' target list along with young Black men.

The story goes on to say, "Tyisha Miller, portrayed by her family as a care-free, outgoing choir girl who died unjustly in a hail of police bullets, actually played the part of a gang member who intimidated and brawled with others, according to the documents." The evident implication is that the family's portrait of Tyisha is a falsehood, and the police are telling the real story. Thus her death in a hail of police bullets was not unjust, after all!

The newspaper report goes on, "In the documents, police and school officials said she dressed and acted like a gang-banger, that she had some connection to the West Side Project Crips, and that she was suspected of beating two girls in the past year." This blatant, unsubstantiated character assassination is hardly

---

1. Louima, a Haitian immigrant, was beaten and sodomized in a New York City police precinct house, on August 9, 1997. Diallo, a West African immigrant, was killed after New York City police officers fired forty-one shots while he stood in his Bronx doorway on February 4, 1999.

worthy of analysis except that it's being used to portray four killer cops as community saviors, saving innocent victims from the scourge of Tyisha Miller! "Dressed like a gang-banger!" Strike one! "Connection to the Crips!" Strike two! "Suspected of a beating!" Strike three! Come the cops as judges, jury and executioners—bang, you're dead!

At this point in the article it states, "The Rev. Bernell Butler, a cousin of Ms. Miller's who has acted as an unofficial spokesman for her family, was angry about some information in the Police Department report." Implicitly, this says that the family, which is angry about "some" of the information, does not and cannot challenge "most" of the "information."

"In January 1998, Ms. Miller was charged with battery," the story goes on, "after a student told police she was jumped on her way home from Rubidoux High by Ms. Miller, seven other females and one male." Was there any disposition or adjudication of this charge filed a full year before Tyisha's execution? Did Tyisha ever go to court, or were the charges dismissed? As nothing more is said, we can conclude the charges were probably dropped (but they'd rather not say so openly to preserve the case against Tyisha). The newspaper goes on, "In September, Assistant Principal Sharon Dimery said Ms. Miller came in to enroll another girl in the school. But Dimery believed Ms. Miller was there to beat up a student and had Ms. Miller and the girl escorted off campus." Of course, Tyisha herself is no longer with us to defend herself against Ms. Dimery's 'belief,' for which no supporting evidence is offered. Even if all these allegations are true, what's their relevance, except to cast Tyisha, *post mortem*, beyond the pale of human concern?

"Last August," the story continues, "a 17-year-old girl told police Ms. Miller beat her with a Club—a metal anti-auto theft device . . . , police said." Were charges filed? Was Tyisha arrested, let alone convicted? Apparently not. But these unsubstantiated rumors, while not sufficiently sound to be the basis of criminal charges, are handy ammunition for the police to use to paint Tyisha as the criminal, not the victim of police criminality, and for the media to dutifully reprint and broadcast.

> *"Police brutality is not an aberration. . . . In failing to treat it as such, the media are failing in their responsibility to the truth."*

In a court, Tyisha would have had a chance to confront and cross-examine her accuser. In the court of public opinion, orchestrated by the police with the connivance of the media, the accuser is nameless and unchallenged, while Tyisha is vilified.

The Coalition Against Media Exploitation noted that the DA and the press reports "said virtually nothing about the behavior or background of the four officers who shot Miller." According to Earl Ofari Hutchinson, the Coalition called on the Press-Enterprise to print a balanced story on Miller's life based on complete interviews with friends, family members, school officials, and co-workers.

They also demanded that the newspaper request that police release full details on the background and behavior of the four officers involved in the Miller shooting and publish the details in a feature story. Neither of these demands has been met.

Ignoring a Tragedy

If the media treatment of Tyisha Miller's killing. . . . December [1999] requires a close reading and analysis to understand the propaganda techniques being used, the coverage of the killing of Ricardo Clos by L.A. Sheriff's deputies in February [1999] is more easily handled. Clos was a mentally distressed Mexicano man, whose wife called 911 for police help when he cut himself on the neck. The deputies arrived on the scene, and confronted the agitated and possibly suicidal man with a knife. When he threw the knife at them—in other words, after he was disarmed—the deputies fired 38 times at Clos, killing him instantly.

This killing happened after those of Miller in Riverside and Amadou Diallo in New York, in which multiple-gunshot killings of people of color by white cops were making big national and local headlines. How did the *LA Times*, the local newspaper of record, treat this story of yet another multiple-gunshot killing by law enforcement officers in their own local bailiwick? They ignored it! Not one word—no headline, no briefs, no photo with a caption, appeared in the *Times*. The Associated Press wires carried a one paragraph story, essentially a press release from the sheriff's department, which carefully said only that "the number of shots that hit [Clos] was not yet ascertained by the coroner's office." No mention was made of the number of shots that had been fired! What could be more newsworthy than another killing by law enforcement locally, firing 38 times at a distressed man in response to a call for help by his wife? Yet amazingly, this story did not merit a single line of type in the *LA Times*. Only *La Opinion*, LA's Spanish-language daily, 50% owned by the *Times*, carried an account of the killing, and only in any depth after a march and rally conducted by the Brown Berets to the East LA Sheriff's station.

> *"It is this vast majority of under-reported cases that allow the press to treat the few exceptional cases deemed news-worthy as 'aberrations.'"*

Could this glaring lack of coverage by LA media be related to the fact that Clos was not Black, but Mexicano, and that the powers-that-be were intent upon keeping a lid on things in LA when NY, the country's other media capital, was being wracked by demonstrations and civil disobedience over the killing of Diallo? How else to account for the complete silence about this story? Perhaps the media will claim that the killing did not provoke the kind of public protest that made it an on-going story, as the Diallo and Miller killings did. But if so, the press would stand condemned by its own excuses, acknowledging that in fact it never independently covers police abuses, and that—as is in fact the case—most police killings go virtually unreported.

Clos's death, which stands out because it missed even the single obligatory paragraph or two on the page of metro briefs in the *LA Times*, is thus much closer to the rule than the exception represented by Diallo and Miller. It is this vast majority of under-reported cases that allow the press to treat the few exceptional cases deemed news-worthy as "aberrations." For example, the same week that Abner Louima, a Haitian immigrant, was tortured by the NYPD, six other Black men, mostly unarmed, were shot and killed by police in Bell Gardens near LA, in Chicago, Baltimore, and several other cities around the U.S. But even though a mini-rebellion greeted the Baltimore police killing, these killings were not even mentioned in the extensive press coverage around the Louima atrocity. This allowed his torture to be treated as an isolated case, rather than a window into on-going police racism, abuse and criminality.

Stilling the Voice of Dissent

The third killing whose coverage we should consider is the police shooting of Margaret Laverne Mitchell, a Black homeless woman in her 50's, by the LAPD. The *LA Times*, in seeking to explain why the killing did not galvanize Los Angeles as the Amadou Diallo shooting had roused New York City, printed a commentary by Joe Domanick. He's a police critic, an alternative journalist, and the host of a public affairs show on KFPK-FM, the local Pacifica affiliate. Domanick proposed there was less social tinder to ignite in LA than NY. He wrote that "shootings have been going down [in L.A.], not up, since 1992, most radically since [Black police chief Bernard] Parks [who had strongly defended the cops in the Mitchell killing] became chief in 1996. In 1992, the year of the riots," Domanick went on, "21 people were killed and 54 wounded by police gunfire. A year later, the number was 15 killed, 48 wounded. In 1998, it dropped to 11 killed . . . and for the first five months of this year, only four people have been killed and four wounded by police fire."

"Only four people killed" in five months! What a wonderful improvement! This bit of statistical flummery is astounding, more so because it comes from a journalistic 'critic' of the police, rather than a more typical apologist for them. 1992 was one of the worst years for police killings in recent LA history, almost double the "normal" average over many years of about one killing a month. Yet only by taking this high water mark as a base point is Domanick able to argue that killings have "fallen." So in fact eleven shooting deaths by the cops [in 1998], and "only four in five months" in 1999 is about one killing off the city's 'normal' average! And this is over several years that the crime rate and arrest rate have been dropping dramatically overall! Not to mention the killings by the sheriff's department, and the numerous other police agencies in the vicinity.

It's bad enough that the city politicos treat these killings as the "cost of doing business." It's worse when even the "anti-brutality" forces and the media demonstrate the same complacency. There were in fact a string of rallies and meetings, drawing out diverse constituencies, over the Mitchell killing, admittedly not on the level of the protests over the killing of Amadou Diallo. The real problem in LA has always been unifying the communities that do come out. Gays and lesbians demonstrate about police harassment of gay bars. Latinos protest the killings or beatings of Chicanos and Mexicanos. Blacks come out over police abuse and shootings of Black folks. There was a homeless rally over the Mitchell killing. Rarely if ever does everyone come out at the same time in the same place about the same case. And the media, by refusing to draw out the systematic connections, by in fact suppressing even the report of cases like Ricardo Clos that might outrage Mexicanos at the same time that Blacks are burning over the case of Amadou Diallo, serve to perpetuate this divide and conquer strategy.

> *"The news media tend to portray opponents of police brutality as grand-standing opportunists, professional agitators with no concern for the facts, or clowns."*

Joe Domanick also reports in his *LA Times* piece, as a "positive sign" that "[i]n the early 1990s, pepper spray was used about 30 times a year to subdue combative suspects. More recently, its use has risen sixteenfold. At the same time, baton use is way down. In the early 1990s, batons were used about 500 times a year. Today, they are employed about 30 times a year. That's a positive sign in terms of reducing injuries."

Again, remarkably, a 'police critic' seems to be lauding the police use of pepper spray 480 times a year! Unbelievable—all the cops have done, by these exact statistics, is to swap pepper spray for night-sticks, and pepper spray is probably responsible for more fatalities than batons have been. Yet this is a "positive sign" to Domanick! And remember, this is not a police puff piece by a media flack for the LAPD—this is a critique by a Pacifica public affairs broadcaster, published author of a book critical of the LAPD's history of militarism, and a regularly published alternative journalist, who appears in *LA Weekly* more often than in the *LA Times*.

Serving the Same Master

The mainstream media consider these killings yesterday's fish-wrap, or perhaps, like the *Washington Post*, will report on a pattern of abuse years after the fact. That's because they serve the same corporate interests as the police do. The police function as an occupying army in communities of color and an internal border guard in more privileged neighborhoods, based on the realities of capitalism and colonialism. The problem is not only police misconduct, but police conduct, as enforcers of a racist and sexist status quo. Corporate news media serve the same masters and the same system by providing diversion and propaganda to lull people into acquiescence.

One final aspect of media coverage of police abuse issues should be noted. The news media tend to portray opponents of police brutality as grand-standing opportunists, professional agitators with no concern for the facts, or clowns. As Rev. Al Sharpton noted when NYPD Officer Volpe pleaded guilty to shoving a stick up Abner Louima's rectum and then down his throat, "Do you [reporters] still think we are exaggerating?" Simultaneously, of course, the media promote these self-same spokes-people, while silencing more radical or grassroots voices. [Civil rights leader] Jesse Jackson is sure to get coverage for a march, but the people doing community organizing on the ground, the people doing CopWatch projects as direct vigilance against police abuse on a street level, the outraged families of the victims who are reaching out to each other, are rarely heard from.

Years ago, a progressive radio journalist in San Francisco used to sign off by saying, "If you didn't like today's news, go out and make some of your own." This is the real answer to the problem of slanted media coverage, not only of police brutality, but of all issues of oppression and exploitation. We need to make our own news, and create our own news media.

Some Prisons Condone Guard Brutality

by Douglas Dennis

About the author: *Douglas Dennis, an editor of* Angolite, *an uncensored prison journal, is serving a life sentence at Louisiana State Penitentiary at Angola for murder.*

Isolated incidents of brutality occur often in the nation's prisons. As with police brutality, they violate written policy—a guard loses his temper and punches out a prisoner, an inmate is "touched up" after injuring or cussing out a guard, and so on. Official, systemic brutality, an entire corrections department gone out of control, is rare—but it happens.

Georgia prisoners had long complained of systemic guard brutality, but no one listened—or cared. Not until a black-clad tactical team led by corrections Commissioner Wayne Garner (also in black) conducted a "sweep" for drugs and weapons through Hays State Prison on July 10, 1996, leaving broken and bloodied prisoners in its wake. What made this incident different was that 15 employees, including guards and a tact-team lieutenant, corroborated the inmates' claims in sworn depositions a year later, as part of a federal lawsuit brought by brutalized prisoners. After that, investigative reporters from the *Atlanta-Journal Constitution* and the *New York Times* wrote exposés, and a network-TV newsmagazine gave it a full hour.

Employee depositions described "guards walking behind inmates, kicking and punching them when they didn't move fast because their ankles were chained. Inmates were dragged along concrete floors and tossed over railings to a lower-level floor. Injured inmates were refused medical treatment." Ordinarily, prison guards, like police, do not testify against their "buddies." That blue wall of silence cracked this time, and their testimony couldn't be dismissed as easily as "whining" by prisoners.

Guard Phyllis Tucker, on duty that day in July, stated she saw "a lot of inmates" lined up against a wall. "Their hands were cuffed behind their backs and

Douglas Dennis, "News Briefs: Out of Control," *Angolite*, vol. 23, March/April, 1998, pp. 7–9. Copyright © 1998 by *Angolite*. Reproduced by permission.

about half were naked. There was blood coming from their faces. There was blood on the floor, the walls." She described how another guard had shoved an inmate's face into a concrete wall: "He screamed. Blood went up the wall. Blood went all over the inmate. I heard it. It had a sickening, cracking sound." When a lawyer asked her why she had not reported the abuse to her superiors, she replied, "Because the superiors were there."

Linda Hawkins, another guard on duty, testified that after Garner's men in black battered their way through the prison, "I went to my office and I cried. Then I went to the restroom and threw up. When you go snatching them out of bed for nothing . . . beating them while they are shackled, that is wrong."

> *"Once the model for state penal systems, the California corrections department has degenerated into barbarity."*

Lt. Ray McWhorter testified that the bloody attack began when an aide to the commissioner grabbed an unresisting inmate by the hair and dragged him across the floor. "When Mr. [Jerry] Thomas did that," McWhorter said, "we were all under the impression that it was OK to do it. If Mr. Thomas can slam one, then we can slam one, too. That is just the dad-gum way it was. Folks were still getting forced to the floor and slammed into the wall and flexi-cuffed and all that stuff. It was a dad-gum shark frenzy in G-Building. It was a free-for-all."

That same day, according to McWhorter, Commissioner Garner watched in another cellblock while they punched, kicked and stomped inmates, some handcuffed and lying on the floor, until blood streaked the walls. Later, Garner applauded the guards at a "celebratory" chicken dinner. "Everybody was high-fiving and shaking hands and congratulating each other and patting each other on the back and bragging about how much butt you kicked," McWhorter stated in his deposition.

He said guards walked up to inmates and beat them. Some stepped on inmates' heads after they were lying on the floor. "We have to put up with a lot," McWhorter explained. "In the years I've been working, I have been spit at. I have had urine thrown on me. I have been kicked. I have been punched. When you are dealing with that and all of a sudden they are saying, 'Get them, boys,' well, hell, you go in there and you get them.

"I got caught up just like everybody else," he continued. "If I have to suffer the consequences for that, that is fine." He said he would rather lose his job for telling the truth than lie in a trial about what happened.

A Sadistic Assault

Stephen Bright, director of the Southern Center for Human Rights, which represented the prisoners, stressed that the men who were beaten had broken no rules and were not resisting. "These were people who were handcuffed," he said. "Some were stripped completely naked. They had no ability to resist and were not engaged in any unlawful behavior. This was just old-fashioned brutality for the sadistic pleasure of it."

According to the lawsuit, Garner created the flying tactical squad that descended on prisons without warning, dressed in black, with black berets and high-top black paratrooper boots. They do not wear name tags. Garner, wearing the same garb, traveled with them from time to time. Syndicated columnist Bob Herbert wrote that Garner is "a former undertaker who left that profession to become a full-time political hack. Appointed by his good buddy, Governor Zell Miller, Garner likes to play the bureaucratic macho man, joining his riot squads for their so-called prison sweeps. He also likes to travel the state bragging about how tough he is on inmates. One-third of the inmates, he has said, 'ain't fit to kill.'". . .

[In] February [1998], the Georgia corrections department agreed to pay $283,000 to 14 inmates. In the settlement, the state admits no wrongdoing or liability. For the state to settle financially but refuse to admit liability is not unusual in these lawsuits. Garner steadfastly denied the allegations and received the governor's continuing support. Governor Miller said the settlement confirmed his belief that Garner had nothing to do with any use of excessive force. Although flying-squad sweeps supposedly have stopped, Garner remains in his post as commissioner.

A Return to the Dark Ages

Rough as it is, Georgia's "corrections" department is not in the same league as California's. Once the model for state penal systems, the California corrections department has degenerated into barbarity. Its super-max prison at Pelican Bay has been the object of scathing denunciation by print and TV journalists, including segments on *60 Minutes*. A federal judge placed it under court order three years ago to correct the worst of its brutalities. Prominent among a long litany of documented complaints, guards there had forced a prisoner under steaming hot water until his skin peeled off. Guards at Corcoran State Prison went that one better. They staged "gladiator" battles among rival gang members in maximum security, and bet on the outcome. In April 1994, during one of those fights, a guard shot a participant to death. . . .

> *"Give individuals power over a despised class of people, remove accountability, and it tends to bring out the worst in them."*

[In] February [1998], according to news media, a federal grand jury indicted eight Corcoran guards (a lieutenant, two sergeants and five correctional officers) with violating the inmates' constitutional protection against cruel and unusual punishment. One guard was also charged with perjury. "These defendants used their authority to sponsor blood sport," said federal prosecutor Paul Seave in Sacramento. "They violated the civil rights of individuals and abused their power and public trust."

"The defendants sent inmates from rival groups into the [tiny] exercise yard together, knowing that a fight would be the likely result," added James Maddock, special agent in charge of the FBI's Sacramento office. "It appears the fights were staged, and even provoked, for the amusement of correctional officers or as retribution against inmates. That this activity could be allowed to occur, and did occur, with the knowledge and participation of prison management personnel is particularly troubling."

The indictments came more than a year after the *San Francisco Chronicle* reported that high-ranking prison officials tried to block the FBI investigation into the abuses. Simultaneously, corrections director James Gomez was citing the violence to support his request for billions of dollars in new prison construction. Gomez resigned two months after the *Chronicle* report.

Dan Lungren, the state's hard-line attorney general, investigated the abuses and . . . [in] August [1997] declared: "After a thorough review that included interviewing more than 100 inmates and correctional officers, [we] have concluded [our] investigation and determined that no criminal charges can be sustained based on obtainable evidence." In other words, a whitewash.

FBI investigators, as happened in Georgia, found the prisoners' allegations credible through corroboration by guards and videotape. Guards had filmed some fights, including the April 1994 rifle slaying of inmate Preston Tate, for their later viewing pleasure. That tape was later broadcast nationwide on TV news programs.

On the heels of the Corcoran indictments, the FBI announced it had begun civil rights investigations into the possible role of guards in beatings and killings of prisoners at Susanville and Pelican Bay penitentiaries. The decision came after recent assaults and deaths at the two Northern California maximum-security prisons.

Eight Pelican Bay prisoners since 1996 were killed by other inmates in their two-man cells, seven strangled and one stabbed to death. Prison guards are suspected of "setting up" the victims, and prison managers of trying to cover it up. At Susanville, the FBI is probing the death of inmate David Torres, gunned down by a guard . . . [in] February [1998]. Torres was engaged in a "stand-up fist fight" with another prisoner at the time.

Why this return to the dark ages of penal management? Georgia attorney Stephen Bright said prison brutality is a by-product of "get-tough-on-crime-politics. While it may be a great way to play to the crowd, it's a disastrous way to run a corrections institution." Give individuals power over a despised class of people, remove accountability, and it tends to bring out the worst in them. Prison officials are not demons. Like prisoners, they're just human.

The Extent of Police Brutality Is Exaggerated

by Arch Puddington

About the author: *Arch Puddington is vice president for research at Freedom House, an organization that advances democratic values and opposes dictatorships worldwide.*

[In July 1998], Human Rights Watch issued a report claiming that police brutality is "one of the most serious, enduring, and divisive human rights violations in the United States." The report is startling in at least two respects. First, Human Rights Watch usually trains its sights on the world's most vicious governments, not the domestic social problems of the United States. Second, while the report echoes previous investigations by civil libertarians of police-abuse cases, it goes an important step further by urging the widespread application of international law as a weapon against what it deems an epidemic of police violence against the American people.

A careful reading of the report, titled "Shielded From Justice: Police Brutality and Accountability in the United States," suggests that the group got things backwards. America does not have a human-rights problem. Human Rights Watch, on the other hand, does seem to have an America problem: It neither understands nor appreciates the workings of democracy in its own backyard.

A Shifting Focus

Human Rights Watch emerged out of Helsinki Watch, perhaps the most prominent of the private organizations established during the 1970s to monitor Soviet compliance with the 1975 Helsinki accords. Human Rights Watch began its work without ideological bias, and it earned a reputation as a sharp critic of the Soviet Union's failures to live up to its international obligations. It later became a fierce opponent of the Reagan administration's Central America policies, in particular its support of the government of El Salvador, then involved in a civil war against Marxist insurgents, and of the Nicaraguan contras, the anti-

Communist group that was attempting to overthrow the leftist Sandinista regime.

Since the end of the Cold War, Human Rights Watch has actually expanded its mission. The organization maintains separate projects to monitor the observance of human rights in every part of the world, and continues to issue meticulously researched and often quite powerful reports on such diverse subjects as repression in Kashmir, atrocities in East Timor, and the inhumane treatment of handicapped children in China. At the same time, the group has ventured into several new areas: It has devoted more attention to the persecution of minority groups and launched ambitious projects to publicize violations of the rights of women and homosexuals. Recent reports have thus dealt with such issues as the enforced prostitution of young girls in Asia and discrimination against homosexuals in Romania.

> *"Considerable anecdotal evidence in the [Human Rights Watch] report suggests that in some cities police abuse is declining."*

A further sign of the organization's shifting focus is the criticism it now directs at alleged patterns of human-rights violations in the United States. To be sure, from the beginning Human Rights Watch has been a vociferous critic of aspects of American foreign policy, a tradition it carries forward today through its pointed attacks on the Clinton administration for its refusal to sign various international treaties. . . . The group also publishes regular reports on such issues as the treatment of women in U.S. prisons, the death penalty, and alleged misconduct of Border Patrol agents along the U.S.-Mexican border.

But the report on police abuse is the organization's most ambitious such investigation, and the most tendentious. As Human Rights Watch notes, police abuse is something over which Americans are deeply divided, especially along racial lines. But does police misconduct amount to a human-rights violation, a phrase that suggests crimes perpetrated by the state, sanctioned by the state, or tolerated by the state? The report conveys no doubts on this score. It carries a message of rampant police violence and official indifference. It contends that police brutality is "pervasive," that police racism is undiminished, and that abuse goes "unchecked" by higher authorities. Besides being exaggerated and sometimes downright wrong, these conclusions are contradicted by the facts in the report itself.

Questioning Contradictory Evidence

There is, to begin with, the question of whether police abuse has become more prevalent in recent years. Although the report's language often suggests that police brutality has reached epidemic proportions, the truth is that national statistics on police abuse are not compiled. The considerable anecdotal evidence in the report suggests that in some cities police abuse is declining. Nor does the report sustain the charge that police officials are passive towards misconduct in the ranks or, as was sometimes true in the past, actually encourage the worst instincts of law-enforcement officers. American cities no longer hire Frank Rizzos[1] to run their police departments. Indeed, as the report indicates, police departments in a number of cities have implemented reform measures, such as improved training of recruits to reduce the chances of abusive behavior, and have stiffened disciplinary procedures to punish abusive officers.

The individual cases of alleged police brutality cited throughout the report—including the high-profile Rodney King episode in Los Angeles[2]—are apparently intended to demonstrate the barriers to justice in the current system. Here again, however, the careful reader might reach the opposite conclusion. In case after case, offending officers were in fact brought to justice, often even imprisoned. Sometimes, it's true, these cases extended over years and required several trials. But in this, police-abuse cases are not so different from other criminal cases where the accused make effective use of procedural protections to delay or evade punishment. What's more, as the American system has evolved through the years, an abusive police officer faces the prospect not merely of an investigation by his own department's internal affairs unit, but of state or federal criminal prosecution and punishment leading to years in prison. The victims of police abuse also have the option of seeking justice through civil lawsuits; as Human Rights Watch notes, millions of dollars have been paid to abuse victims in recent years.

> *"Police departments in a number of cities have implemented reform measures, such as improved training of recruits to reduce the chances of abusive behavior."*

Not surprisingly, the report gives special emphasis to the racial dimension of conflict between police and the public. "Race continues to play a central role in police brutality," the report alleges. "Indeed, despite gains in many areas since the civil rights movement of the 1950s and 1960s, one area that has been stubbornly resistant to change has been the treatment afforded minorities by police."

This is the kind of sweeping, superficial, and ultimately inaccurate assertion that one might expect from a domestic cause group, but not from a human-rights organization that prides itself on disentangling reality from conventional wisdom. For example, to buttress its claim of massive police racism, the report on more than one occasion notes that abuse claims by minority citizens are proportionately higher than their presence in the overall population. For purposes of comparison, however, the relevant statistic is not the minority presence in the

---

1. During the 1970s, Rizzo, who had a reputation for aggressive policies, was mayor and police commissioner of Philadelphia.   2. King was beaten by three Los Angeles police officers as their supervisor watched after King led police on a high-speed chase on March 3, 1991. After the officers were acquitted of excessive force on April 29, 1992, rioting broke out in Los Angeles. On April 16, 1993, a federal jury convicted two of the officers of violating King's civil rights.

local population, but the frequency with which minorities come in contact with the criminal-justice system. When this comparison is employed, the results suggest that complaints by black persons of police abuse are only slightly disproportionate or not disproportionate at all. Furthermore, there is the fact, not mentioned by Human Rights Watch, that minorities comprise a majority or near-majority of police officers in a number of the cities investigated for the report, and that black chiefs of police run the departments of an even larger number of big cities, including Los Angeles, Houston, Atlanta, Detroit, and New Orleans. Such developments do not ordinarily occur in systems that are "stubbornly resistant to change."

Where the report gives a distorted picture of police-minority relations, it skirts the role of police unions and civil-service rules in thwarting the expeditious and fair resolution of abuse cases. Most states have adopted laws intended to protect police officers and other civil servants from arbitrary or politically motivated reprisal. In practice, though, these measures also severely restrict the authority of a police chief to discipline abusive officers. Even in cases where department officials have dismissed officers for repeated acts of brutality, the officers have sometimes won reinstatement through legal appeals or the arbitration process. Yet while the report explains the impediments to effective discipline posed by certain civil-service procedures, it refrains from calling for major changes, an uncharacteristically cautious approach in a report that otherwise demands thorough-going change.

Urging Federal Control

Many of the remedies Human Rights Watch proposes are so unexceptional they might as well have been copied out of an old ACLU fund-raising letter. No reasonable person opposes improving the recruitment of police, or the weeding out of habitually abusive officers, or the goal of preventing police abuse before it occurs.

Unfortunately, Human Rights Watch also advocates a substantial increase in state and federal oversight of local police matters. The report urges that each state establish a special prosecutor's office to deal exclusively with police-abuse cases. It expresses unhappiness with the Justice Department's reluctance to bring charges against police officers for violating the civil rights of alleged victims; in addition to advocating more aggressive federal prosecution of individual policemen, it asks for an expansion of Justice Department investigations into the policies of municipal police forces. And the report proposes that Congress adopt legislation denying federal grants to any police department that "fails to fully respect human rights."

In justifying this proposal, Human Rights Watch cites as precedent the U.S. policy of tying assistance to foreign countries to their governments' compliance with human-rights standards. It cannot have escaped the notice of Human Rights Watch that the countries on which human-rights sanctions have been placed tend to be brutal dictatorships that routinely murder political opponents, persecute opposition parties, muzzle the press, and commit other heinous acts that clearly qualify as human-rights violations. The authors of "Shielded From Justice" thereby demonstrate both a serious misreading of the extent of police abuse in this country and a cavalier willingness to extend to the federal government extraordinary supervisory powers over a traditional responsibility of localities.

Globalizing Social Problems

In its most important, and disturbing, recommendation, Human Rights Watch urges that the authority of international law be invoked in police-abuse cases in the United States. Specifically, the report asserts that citizens should have the right to cite three international agreements to strengthen legal action in abuse cases: the International Covenant on Civil and Political Rights, the Convention Against Torture or Other Cruel, Inhuman or Degrading Treatment or Punishment, and the International Covenant on the Elimination of All Forms of Racial Discrimination.

Although the United States has signed all three agreements, it did so only after adding reservations and understandings that effectively nullify their impact on American law. Indeed, such international covenants cannot become the basis for lawsuits in American courts without legislation passed by Congress. And successive administrations have declined to send implementing legislation to Congress on grounds that American law generally conforms to international standards.

Human Rights Watch is highly critical of this unwillingness to incorporate international law as part of the country's domestic law, and looks forward to the day when U.S. citizens can claim that police abuse violates international standards against torture or racial discrimination. As the report points out, the standards inscribed in international covenants sometimes differ in important respects from American law. This is certainly true of the international agreement against racial discrimination. Under American law as interpreted by the Supreme Court, for an act to be judged discriminatory usually requires that it have both a discriminatory intent and effect. By contrast, under international law, it is sufficient to demonstrate effect. In other words, under international law the very fact of a racial disparity in police-abuse cases might be sufficient to "prove" racial bias by a city's police department.

> *"Police departments pay more attention to the prevention of abuse in their recruitment and training policies than ever before."*

Human Rights Watch not only places more faith in international law than in American law, it places unwarranted confidence in the human-rights mechanisms of the United Nations. The U.N.'s record in dealing with the world's most serious human-rights crises has historically been unimpressive (to put it mildly). Nevertheless, in recent years the U.N. has conducted a number of human-rights investigations in the United States; among the subjects of investigation have been the treatment of women in state prisons and allegations of racial discrimination in the application of capital punishment. Although couched in the cautious phrases of diplomacy, these reports have expressed dissatisfaction with American policies.

Condemning American Policies

The timing of the Human Rights Watch report suggests a similar desire to dress up as an appeal to human rights—and to international law—what is in fact a condemnation of American policies with which the report's drafters find themselves in political disagreement. Although the United States has recently experienced a number of well-publicized police-brutality cases, the same could be said for any period since the 1960s. If anything, police departments pay more attention to the prevention of abuse in their recruitment and training policies than ever before.

At the same time, police departments in many cities have recently adopted more aggressive law-enforcement tactics, notably in cracking down on so-called quality-of-life crimes, such as public urination, the open use or sale of drugs, subway fare-beating, and similar non-violent offenses.

The emphasis on quality-of-life enforcement began in New York at the instigation of Mayor Rudolph Giuliani in 1994 and has been credited by many New Yorkers with making the city safer, more civil, and in general a better place to live. Although some minority spokesmen have complained that the new policy has led to an increase in police abuse, others have credited the new tougher line with having contributed to the revival of declining neighborhoods, including Harlem. Other cities have taken note of the steep decline in crime rates in New York, and have instituted similar policing tactics.

Human Rights Watch takes a dim view of quality-of-life policing, is disturbed by its popularity with the public, and objects to Giuliani's law-and-order policies. In this, it echoes the views of the New York Civil Liberties Union.

The NYCLU's parent organization, the American Civil Liberties Union, [ACLU] has, of course, played a central role in the ongoing debate over American law enforcement for decades, and is best known for having spearheaded the legal effort to broaden the rights of criminal defendants. In recent years, the ACLU perspective has suffered a series of legislative setbacks, of which New York state's decision to reinstate the death penalty is the most vivid example. And where in the past the civil-liberties movement often won change in criminal-law procedures through the courts, in recent years the pendulum has swung in the opposite direction, as the federal judiciary has issued decisions that have restricted the rights of criminal defendants.

There is a considerable overlap of personnel between the ACLU and the lawyers and scholars who served as consultants to the Human Rights Watch report on police abuse. This is consistent with a pattern in which liberal and left-ish cause organizations, having failed to win change through the normal channels of American democracy, "go global" to press their issues through international treaties and institutions, especially the U.N. With an American public strongly supportive of the kind of stepped-up crime-fighting techniques undertaken in New York, it is understandable that civil libertarians and groups like Human Rights Watch might turn in frustration to international law for a solution that they cannot now win domestically.

They are, however, seriously mistaken in believing that reform can be promoted by "globalizing" the social problems of democracies. Indeed, the very suggestion betrays an astonishing lack of faith in the American democratic system and a misunderstanding of the process of winning political change in this country. More so than any other system, American democracy is flexible and open to adjustment. But Americans quite rightly resist change that is imposed by institutions not subject to popular control. They are certain to resist the notion that specialists in international law are better equipped to pass judgment on the system's shortcomings than Americans themselves.

"Shielded From Justice" never explains why the United States should recognize the authority of international law and global institutions. The report's authors presumably thought the answer to be self-evident. This in itself explains why Human Rights Watch, despite its impressive record in publicizing and protesting the crimes of the world's dictators, is not likely to exert a similar influence in the debate over social reform in the United States.

The Use of Deadly Force Is Sometimes Necessary

by Randy Tedford

About the author: *Randy Tedford, a sergeant with the Oak Ridge, Tennessee, Police Department, writes a weekly column for the* Oak Ridger.

For the sixth time [in 2001], law enforcement personnel in Knoxville or Knox County have found themselves in incidents where the situation, their training and job experience has compelled them to shoot a suspect.

Rehashing Common Misconceptions

This time, as has happened before, a person who is untrained, non-police, and not a witness to what led up to the shooting has felt equally compelled to make condemning comments to the news media. This type of person usually speaks with an emotional response and not with a factual, reasoned evaluation.

Such condemning persons will frequently rehash unsubstantiated, fictional, urban legends they've heard wherein police brutality is the rule and not the exception. In many cases, they'll readily admit they didn't witness the incident being discussed, but they "just know" it had to happen in the worst case scenario they can imagine.

As I write this, I don't have much of the factual information about what led up to the shooting by Knoxville police officers Tuesday [August 7, 2001]. Therefore, I can't reasonably declare that they were justified in using deadly force. For their sake, the suspect/victim's sake and for the sake of the families of the officers and the person they shot, I hope there was no alternative.

One comment, attributed to a bystander, was typical of what I've heard reported before. This person seemed surprised that officers would have to use a firearm to subdue a female whom he had deemed as obviously suffering from ill health.

First of all, don't you think for one second that a person who isn't in the best of mental or physical health can't hurt you seriously or even kill you. Secondly, gender does little to determine someone's fighting capability. (Are you having a buildup of brain methane or did you forget about such things as karate and kung fu?)

The Right to Live Another Day

I don't know what weapon the woman in this incident had, but no one, I repeat, NO ONE, has any more right to threaten a police officer with, or wave, point or brandish a lethal weapon at a cop than they do any other citizen. Just because we choose to work in this profession, there is no obligation to allow someone to harm us before we take the action necessary to end the threat. Wearing a uniform, a badge and all the other equipment associated with policing doesn't mean we have surrendered the common right to live and not be injured.

No government or its law enforcement agency pays well enough for any of us to surrender those rights. Each cop out there has the right to defend others and him or herself against threats of physical violence, regardless of the mental or physical health of the person making the threat.

Let's suppose the woman had a gun and was "merely" waving it around. While randomly pointing it at officers or other people with a finger on the trigger, she could be verbally, or through body language, threatening to shoot. And haven't you ever heard of a weapon "accidentally" discharging? There are times, unfortunately, when force must be used preemptively for the public's and the cops' safety.

> *"There are times, unfortunately, when force must be used preemptively for the public's and the cops' safety."*

And, if you think for one moment that the way television and movies depict cops as being elated or physically pumped up after a shooting is anything like real life, it's time for you to have another "think." Over the past several years, I've become involved in a Critical Incident Stress Debriefing cooperative effort across the state of Tennessee and elsewhere. There has not been even one debriefing involving officers having to shoot a suspect where there has ever been any indication that the police officer was anything but emotionally and physically drained after having had to shoot.

There's one other thing you ought to remember. Cops don't shoot to kill. If we have to shoot, we are shooting to survive. We've promised our families, co-workers and friends that we're going to do what is necessary to come home intact and unhurt at the end of each shift.

And you'd do the same thing, too.

The Police Rarely Use Excessive Force

by the International Association of Chiefs of Police

About the author: *The International Association of Chiefs of Police is a non-profit organization that guides policy and provides direction for law enforcement.*

The International Association of Chiefs of Police (IACP) National Police Use of Force Database is the first substantial aggregation of state, county and local law enforcement use of force data. What follows are some of the recent and noteworthy findings from the data. Information in this report is based on years 1991–2000 representing a composite population of 149,940,551; 45,913,161 calls for service (CFS); 177,215 use of force incidents, and 8,082 use of force complaints. In some cases single data years are represented to show current levels of use of force. In other cases, multiple years are grouped to provide a larger sample of incidents.

Examining the Findings

- How often do police use force?
  Data for 1999, the last year for which complete data from participating agencies is available, shows that police used force at a rate of 3.61 times per 10,000 calls-for-service. This translates to a rate of use of force of 0.0361%. Expressed another way, police did not use force 99.9639% of the time. . . .
- How much force is used?
  IACP tracks the most commonly used force by both subjects and police. The street continuum tracks the actual progression of type of force, employed by either officers or subjects. From 1999–2000, physical force was the most common force used by officers, followed by chemical force and then impact. The use of chemical force, primarily OC products (i.e., pepper spray), was greater than the combined totals for electronic, impact and fire-arm force.
- Are police using force differently today than in years past?

Data from years 1995–2000 shows that the historical street continuum for officers was physical force, chemical force and firearm force. At that time, the ratio between the frequency of physical force incidents to chemical force incidents was about 13 to 1, while the ratio between physical and firearm was 16 to 1. Between 1999–2000, the ratio of physical to chemical was about 2 to 1, while the ratio of physical to fire-arm was about 22 to 1. Thus, as officer use of chemical force has increased, firearm use has decreased.

> *"Excessive force was not used in 99.583% of all reported . . . [force-related complaints]."*

• Can "excessive" force be measured?

The IACP has created a measure of excessive force that assumes a force-related complaint, sustained as alleged equals an incident of excessive force. Between 1994 and 2000, of the 7,495 force-related complaints reported to the project, 750 were sustained. This total number of sustained force-related complaints was produced by a total of 174,820 total reported incidents. Expressed as a percentage of total incidents, excessive force was used 0.42% of the time. Again looking at this another way, excessive force was not used in 99.583% of all reported cases. . . .

• In what circumstance is force used?

Arrests were the most frequent circumstance of use of force in data years

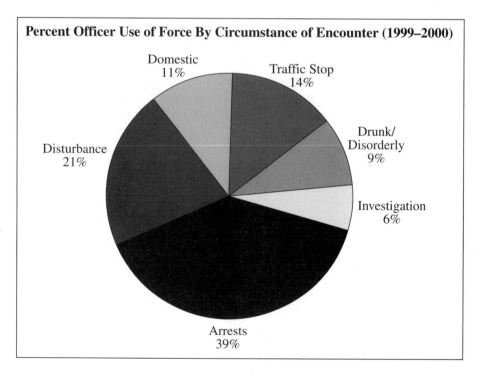

Percent Officer Use of Force By Circumstance of Encounter (1999–2000)

Domestic 11%

Traffic Stop 14%

Drunk/ Disorderly 9%

Disturbance 21%

Investigation 6%

Arrests 39%

1999–2000. Of the reported incidents for these years, which included circumstance descriptors, 39% were arrest related. The next largest category was disturbance with 21% of use of force incidents, and traffic stops with 14%. . . .

• What are the racial characteristics of use of force incidents?
From 1995 to 2000 there were 8,148 reported incidents in which the contributors included racial descriptors for both the involved officers and subjects. Of this total, 3,169, or 39% involved white officers using force on white subjects, 3,622, or 44% involved white officers using force on African American subjects, 585, or 7% involved African American officers using force on African American subjects and 277, or 3.4% involved African American officers using force on white subjects. . . .

• Subject Use of Drugs/Alcohol as a Use of Force Indicator During Traffic Stops
Subject intoxication appears to be a substantial predictor of police use of force during traffic stops. Where both force and intoxication information is available (838 incidents during the period 1995 to 2000) 46% of all use of force incidents occurred where the subject was intoxicated or under the influence of drugs.

• Subject Use of 'Other' Types of Force During Traffic Stops
Intoxicated drivers are almost three times as likely to engage officers in use of force other than physical, chemical, electronic, impact or firearm, than subjects

> *"Overall levels of police use of force are extremely low."*

who are either not intoxicated or whose state of intoxication is unknown. The predominant subject weapon in such encounters is the automobile used in 43% of such cases, followed by knives and baseball bats, each used in 11% of all such reported cases. . . .

• Who gets injured—and how seriously—when force is used?
Between 1999 and 2000, 3,577 incidents were reported that included data on force-related officer injuries. During this period, the majority of officers, some 87%, suffered no injuries from their encounters. Minor injuries were reported by 12% of these officers and less than one percent of these officers reported major injuries. No officer deaths during this period were reported.
Subject injury outcomes were reported for 2,427 incidents between 1999 and 2000. Uninjured subjects accounted for 60% of the total. Subjects with minor injuries comprised 38%; subjects with major injuries were reported at less than one percent. Five subject deaths were reported.

- Officer injuries related to the use of chemical and impact force substantially exceed subject injuries during the same time period. . . .

• What is the involvement of emotionally disturbed (EDS) subjects?
Based on 111 incidents involving emotionally disturbed subjects, between 1995 and 2000, a full 58% of female EDS were involved in use of force incidents relating to their arrest, as opposed to only 52% of male EDS. This is

particularly of interest because in general, male EDS outnumbered female EDS by over 2 to 1. Second only to arrests were disturbance-related calls, in which the intra-gender percentages for male and female EDS was roughly equal, at 41% to 39% respectively. Again this was despite the fact that the actual number of male subjects for this circumstance exceeded the numbers for female subjects by almost 3 to 1. Overall, calls related to EDS attempted suicides accounted for 31% of the total specific incident circumstances for all genders (including unreported genders). . . .

Applying the Data

The first two data reporting years of the National Use of Force Database Project (1996–1997; supported by a joint grant from the National Institute of Justice and the Bureau of Justice Statistics) allowed the IACP to create a national advisory group, create standardized definitions for all applications of force, and design a software package to facilitate use of force data collection.

Since 1998 this project has been supported exclusively by the IACP. During this period, staff focused on gathering state level support for the database, implementing the software in the field, and creating a prototype national use of force report using data contributed by local agencies. Specific accomplishments include:

• Local Level

From 1996 to 2000, over 2,500 state, county and local law enforcement agencies have requested the IACP software to gain clearer understanding of use of force trends and issues. The software captures information on subject force, officer force, use of force outcomes/injuries, a number of pertinent officer and suspect demographics, and related complaint data.

• State Level

State Associations of Chiefs of Police (SACOP) in Arkansas, the District of Columbia, Illinois, Kentucky, Maryland, Missouri, New Jersey, New York, Rhode Island, Virginia, Vermont, Washington, and West Virginia are serving as the lead agency in their state to expand the number of local agencies achieving full participation in the use of force project. Local agencies within these states receive guidance and support from these associations as they sign on to the database program.

• National Level

Since project inception (1995), a total of 564 agencies have provided anonymous and voluntary use of force incident/complaint data to the IACP. This data consists of 45,913,161 calls-for-service, 177,215 use of force incidents and 8,082 use of force-related citizen complaints. The IACP utilizes this data to craft annual use of force updates for the law enforcement community, the media, and the public. . . .

The IACP Use of Force reporting software has been recognized by CALEA as meeting or exceeding the current CALEA standards for police use of force reporting and is in use by many departments seeking accreditation.

Chapter 1

Independent Corroboration of Principle Findings

In March 2001, the Department of Justice, through its Bureau of Justice Statistics (BJS) released the results of its *1999 National Survey on Contacts Between the Police and the Public.* In this comprehensive analysis of police/citizen contacts, BJS reported that less than one percent of all such contacts involved either use of force or the threat to use force.

IACP has previously released the results in 1996 and 1999 of the ongoing National Police Use of Force Database survey, which showed similar values for the frequencies of police use of force. The current baseline figure for the rate of police use of force is 3.61 for every 10,000 dispatched calls-for-service. This results in a rate of police use of force of less than one percent, consistent with BJS findings.

Despite the significant differences in study methodology, the fact that both sets of results converge on the same low values for frequencies of police use of force provides a convincing argument that overall levels of police use of force are extremely low.

The Force Used Against Political Demonstrators Is Appropriate

by James J. Fotis

About the author: *James J. Fotis is executive director of the Law Enforcement Alliance of America, a coalition of law-enforcement professionals, crime victims, and concerned citizens.*

Whether police are using inappropriate force is a question that cannot be answered without frankly acknowledging the anti-police atmosphere promoted by the media that has been steadily evolving; this is a frightening phenomenon which should be a source of great concern. It leads to low morale among police officers, lack of respect for law enforcement by the public and increasing fear by police officers of being accused of doing too much or being too proactive in preventing crime before it occurs. Police officers are fearful of unwarranted criticism, harsh disciplinary action or loss of employment; accusations of police misconduct before the facts have even been uncovered; rampant lawsuits; and the omission of due process and fairness.

Inflaming Anti-Police Attitudes

Take, for instance, the inflammatory comments made by Hillary Rodham Clinton regarding a tragic shooting in New York City involving four police officers which resulted in the death of Amadou Diallo.[1] Here we have the first lady of the United States, a senatorial candidate and an attorney, no less, publicly calling the officers "murderers" before the facts of the case were even known. Whatever happened to "innocent until proven guilty"? Does this premise not apply to police officers? [On February 25, 2000], a jury of their peers found the officers innocent of all charges. This kind of attack on our men and women in

1. Diallo, a West African immigrant, was killed after New York City police officers fired forty-one shots while he stood in his Bronx doorway on February 4, 1999.

James J. Fotis, "Are Police Using Inappropriate Force on Political Demonstrators? No: 'Over the Line' and 'Out of Hand' Describe the Critics of the Police—Not Police Conduct at the Political Conventions," *Insight*, vol. 16, October 16, 2000, pp. 41–43. Copyright © 2000 by News World Communications, Inc. All rights reserved. Reproduced by permission.

blue seems to be a regular occurrence these days and the media, as well as opportunistic politicians, fuel that fire. Often, actions taken by police are scrutinized and magnified by the media. This close inspection frequently proves to be one-sided, ignorant of key factors and sorely misinterpreted.

The trend is quickly shifting toward law-enforcement policies and regulations being guided by politics, the media, political correctness and plain ignorance of the facts.

A[n] incident in Philadelphia involving a police chase exemplifies this perspective: Although the perpetrator in this case eluded police for hours, what the public was privy to was a 25-second video clip shot from a hovering helicopter, showing a

> *"When demonstrators begin to act violently or criminally, they have become criminals, not demonstrators exercising their rights."*

number of officers appearing to kick a man on the ground, endlessly played time and again in agonizing slow motion.

Many viewers were outraged. But they were missing most of the facts and left with an erroneously skewed perception of the truth. There was no mention of the fact that the suspect had allegedly been involved in two car chases (crashing the first stolen car and then stealing a police car) and a foot pursuit. The suspect also had been shot by police yet continued to resist arrest until he finally was wrestled to the ground and apprehended.

How much force should be used to control an individual who clearly is out of control, has harmed others and damaged personal and public property? Are we willing to accept the consequences which may result from a lack of action, a lack of applying necessary force? Are we ready to accept harm to innocent bystanders for the sake of preserving a perpetrator's unchecked "freedom of expression" even if it means harm to innocents?

Collections of Criminals

What about incidents involving larger collections of criminals? Much more is at stake: more individuals involved, greater risk of disruptions and criminal activity erupting. Take the so-called public demonstrations against the World Trade Organization (WTO) in Seattle and those less intense activities staged during the Republican National Convention in Philadelphia and the Democratic Convention in Los Angeles. When demonstrators begin to act violently or criminally, they have become criminals, not demonstrators exercising their rights. Invariably things will go wrong, emotions can run high and anger can escalate. Isn't it appropriate, then, to use the means necessary to quell the disruption, overcome resistance and restore peace? That's a primary purpose and goal of law enforcement.

The threats demonstrators pose to preservation of life—and, to a lesser degree, damage or theft of property—are non-negotiable premises that dictate much of the behavior of law enforcement (something rarely discussed or brought forth by the media or critics of law enforcement). We also need to remember that an officer is in constant fear for his or her own life. This is no idle concern when you look at the statistics: One out of every 10 officers is assaulted or killed every year. That's an astounding figure which seems to get little or no attention.

Here's another astounding figure which gets little notice: According to a U.S. Justice Department report, an estimated 45 million U.S. residents (one in five) have some sort of face-to-face contact with law-enforcement officers annually. Only about 1 percent of those who came in contact with police say police used any kind of force or threatened to use force against them, although a majority of those respondents say their own actions may have provoked the police.

In most cases, an officer is reacting to the situation or threat at hand and, once that threat has been eliminated, the officer ceases to apply the force he or she deemed necessary. If one or two people in a crowd decide to act violently or criminally, it's the officer's job to put a stop to that behavior. The force continuum allows that officer to use adequate force to overcome resistance and prevent danger or harm to innocent people or damage to property. An officer must be allowed and trusted to use his training, knowledge, judgment and tools available to perform his duties.

By extension, the valuable input of rank-and-file law enforcement should be included when it comes to creating meaningful use-of-force policies—but it almost never is. While demanding that police officers successfully fulfill their responsibility to protect the public, we continually strip them of necessary tools and options available to them to accomplish such a task. Such is the case in the controversy over whether police departments should allow the use of less-lethal weapons. Some say that to use such devices on criminal demonstrators is contrary to our core belief in our freedom of speech and constitutes a civil-rights violation. The fundamental rights guaranteed every citizen of this country do not protect those who make threats of bodily harm and disrupt the peace.

> *"If one or two people in a crowd decide to act violently or criminally, it's the officer's job to put a stop to that behavior."*

Using Appropriate Force

Police had every right to use the appropriate force necessary to overcome resistance, restore law and order and prevent loss of life and property at the WTO demonstration. This also applies to other well-publicized (or not so well-publicized) incidents where rubber bullets or other less-lethal devices are used to overcome someone resisting arrest or posing harm to others or to self. I'm not suggesting that use of less-lethal weapons is the only way to handle such situations, but clearly, in some instances, these are good alternatives to more-lethal force.

Less-lethal weapons may include batons, pepper spray, rubber bullets, electronic shockers, doughnut-shaped projectiles and even Spiderman-style net guns known as WebShots (which wrap and immobilize a suspect). They provide police officers with more choices in handling the various situations they face daily.

Training is a key component in any officer or department's ability to gauge the degree of force appropriate to the circumstance. I guarantee most law-enforcement critics quickly will change their tune if they experience the training scenarios required of the typical officer. Regardless of the situation, "stopping the threat" is the primary goal. Sometimes the mere presence of one or more law-enforcement officers is sufficient. Sometimes circumstances require measures viewers of the 6 o'clock news may easily misinterpret.

The question of what is appropriate in a specific context, then, is one that requires on-site information and is colored by the quality of the individuals tasked with keeping order, as well as the training they've received, overlaid on their real-world experiences and fears. It's also important to emphasize here the need to allow individual police departments the authority, without unnecessary interference, to decide what is or isn't appropriate for their own communities. Local law enforcement understands better than anyone the specific needs for their communities whether that means chasing a suspect in a stolen car, using rubber bullets to stop a deranged individual intent on "suicide by cop," or containing a large crowd of demonstrators.

The laws officers swear to uphold include those embodied in the Constitution as well as those codified by city councils, state legislatures or Congress. A good cop is the first person to abhor any infringement of basic rights guaranteed by the Constitution and Bill of Rights. The idea of law enforcement is to help ensure that all citizens enjoy their rights free from infringement by those who seek to deny or deprive them of those rights. There is no greater infringement upon individuals' rights than a threat to deprive them of their life via criminal violence.

Evaluating the Options

If a child's life or a visiting foreign dignitary is threatened by a would-be assassin, the appropriate use of force is whatever it takes to keep that person's finger from pulling the trigger. Ask any parent what is the appropriate amount of force necessary to prevent physical harm to his or her child. Then ask a cop.

The degree of emotion will be the same, only the cop, due to his or her training, will do an instant visual inventory of the threat and calculate the response necessary to deter the threat. It may be a shout, a punch in the nose or a call for two or more officers to subdue an out-of-control assailant. The options may be extensive, but the time to decide is not. Second-guessing the officer involved seems to have become a cottage industry, particularly among quick-to-litigate lawyers and those seeking political gain by scapegoating the cops.

Regardless of whether the incident is the political tantrums staged by the criminally irresponsible at the WTO meetings in Seattle, or the highly controversial attempt by Philadelphia police to subdue an alleged violent carjacker who assaulted an elderly woman, stole a police car and tried to battle every uniformed officer in sight, appropriate force is directly proportional to that which halts the threat. That's a fact of life wether you are a cop or a parent protecting your own.

Chapter 2

What Factors Contribute to Police Brutality?

Chapter Preface

"I used to be the kind of person, when I see an officer, I smile," said Nancy Tong, a Hong Kong immigrant and documentary filmmaker who was taken into custody for speaking disrespectfully to a New York City police officer. "I'm not that kind of person anymore." When Tong got out of her car to see why she was trapped in a New York City traffic jam, she heard a voice behind her shout, "Get back in that car." "What's the big deal? It's a free country," she responded. Unfortunately, Tong had inadvertently talked-back to a police officer. When she was unable to produce her driver's license, the officer handcuffed her and took her into custody. At the precinct house Tong was strip-searched and locked in a holding cell until early the next morning. She was released with a ticket for driving without a license and for failure to comply with an order. Both charges were dismissed, and Tong later won a $35,000 settlement.

According to some analysts, police officer overreaction to sarcasm, insults, and other challenges to their authority is one of several factors that contribute to police brutality. Police officers, particularly in large cities, are subject to a lot of verbal abuse. "Many officers experience rampant disrespect and view it as undermining their authority," claims Stuart London, a lawyer who defends officers accused of misconduct. "Every day, throughout [New York City], you have officers who are routinely turning the other cheek. But sometimes they feel they have to take a stand in order to patrol effectively, and then something minor can really escalate." Challenges to police authority vary from asking for a badge number to leading the police on a chase. While some police officers ignore these challenges, others react inappropriately. These reactions also vary, ranging from vindictive arrests such as Tong's to the infamous fifty-six blows that Rodney King received from three Los Angeles police officers when King resisted arrest after having led the police on a high-speed chase.

To justify the use of excessive force, some police officers try to shift the blame to their victims, charging them with resisting arrest, disorderly conduct, or the obstruction of governmental administration. The city of Los Angeles tracks these charges to identify problem officers. "You find clearly that often those contempt-of-cop arrests are filed by the police officer as a way to cover a use of force that may be questionable," claims Merrick Bobb, special counsel to the city of Los Angeles. "You also find that these charges get dropped because they are not valid."

Defenders of the police argue that overreaction is the exception rather than the rule. These commentators claim, for example, that every year in New York City the police department makes approximately 330,000 arrests and issues 1.5 million summonses for moving violations. Thousands of police misconduct claims are made each year in New York City, defenders acknowledge; however, in view of the enormous number of summonses and arrests, clearly the great majority of citizen–police encounters are handled without violence. Officer Michael F. Wilson, a thirteen-year veteran of the New York Police Department who teaches sociology at the police academy explains, "Initially, when someone gives you major grief, you're stunned. It's like the first time you get punched as a kid. You're shocked, and your body wants to react. In the best of cases, though, there is this little person inside your head saying, 'It's not worth it. I put my hands on this person, I lose.'"

In an effort to prepare officers for the abuse they will encounter, police academies attempt to train them to react appropriately. Officers are taught that their role is to end, not win, confrontations. Dr. James O'Keefe, director of training at the New York Police Academy, says the academy works to instill in officers a wary respect for the public and to convey the lesson that emotion should never overtake reason. For years, academies operated like a military boot camp. Academy directors reasoned that the verbal abuse experienced in police academies would prepare recruits for the streets. Officials later concluded, however, that the approach taught officers to treat citizens like their abusive instructors had treated them. After trying several other unsuccessful techniques, academies nationwide began using a martial arts paradigm known as "Verbal Judo," developed by George Thompson, a former police officer. The program teaches police officers techniques to defuse their anger and frustration when dealing with difficult people in critical situations.

Whether or not police brutality is a result of officer's overreacting to challenges to their authority is subject to debate. The authors in the following chapter argue about what other factors contribute to police brutality.

Racism Promotes Police Brutality

by Salim Muwakkil

About the author: *Salim Muwakkil is a senior editor at* In These Times, *a liberal biweekly publication.*

On October 24 [1997], Officer James Knight shot and killed 18-year-old Tyrone Lewis, an unarmed black man, during a routine traffic stop in St. Petersburg, Florida. Lewis apparently failed to respond when Knight and his partner ordered him out of the car after pulling him over for speeding in the city's predominantly black south side. When Knight's partner broke one of the car windows, the car lurched forward, bumping Officer Knight, who then threatened to shoot. Lewis' car then reportedly lurched forward again, this time striking Knight forcefully. Knight fired his gun three times, shooting Lewis twice in the arm and once in the chest. Police later learned the car was stolen and that Lewis was wanted on three arrest warrants. But community residents who witnessed the incident insist that the police were never threatened.

Lewis' death sparked a riot in the resort city's African-American neighborhood. The disturbance covered a 20-square-block area; 29 buildings and many cars were set on fire. Eleven people were injured. The grand jury decision not to indict the police officer provoked another round of civil unrest three weeks later.

While so far only the black community in St. Petersburg has responded with such destructive rage, black neighborhoods across the country are seething with anger at the impunity enjoyed by police officers who kill black men.

Relations between African-Americans and the police have been antagonistic throughout U.S. history. The first organized police forces in this country were slave patrols created to keep enslaved Africans in check. The troubled relationship between blacks and the police has erupted sporadically in violence: Most of the "long hot summer" riots during the '60s were sparked by charges of police brutality. The urban unrest in Miami during the '80s was associated with allegations of police violence. And the nation's largest urban explosion occurred in Los Angeles following the 1992 acquittal of the police who brutalized motorist Rodney King.

Stories of Deadly Force

The police are using deadly force more and more frequently these days—and getting away with it. The stories are eerily similar:

- July 30, 1995: Joseph Gould, an unarmed homeless black man, is shot to death outside a downtown Chicago nightclub by Gregory Becker, an off-duty white cop. The officer is initially charged with official misconduct, but vigorous protests convince the Illinois state attorney to increase the charge to armed violence. The city now anxiously awaits Becker's February trial [Becker was sentenced to fifteen years in prison in May 1997].
- October 3, 1995: Jorge Guillen, a Honduran immigrant, dies of suffocation in police custody in Chicago. The state attorney's office declines to prosecute the officers, citing lack of evidence of any criminal conduct. The Office of Professional Standards (OPS), an independent agency of civilian staffers considered by many to be in the pocket of the police, nevertheless concludes that the three officers involved used excessive force. The agency recommends that they receive short suspensions. The recommendation, however, is overruled on December 11, 1996, by the Chicago Police Board, which cites conflicting medical evidence and inconsistent witness statements.

> *"Relations between African-Americans and the police have been antagonistic throughout U.S. history."*

- June 13, 1996: Aswan Keshawn Watson, an unarmed 21-year-old black man, is killed when three plainclothes officers fire 24 bullets into him during a drug raid in Brooklyn's Flatbush section.
- October 17, 1996: Aaron White, the black owner of a television repair shop in the west-central Mississippi town of Leland, is shot to death by a white policeman. Initially, police say the 29-year-old White was trying to escape from the scene of a traffic accident and fired first on Officer Jackie Blaylock, who successfully returned fire. The police later revise their story, saying White accidentally killed himself in the escape attempt.
- November 19, 1996: James Cooper, a black 19-year-old, is shot to death by Officer Michael Marlow during a traffic stop in Charlotte, North Carolina. The white officer tells investigators he fired because he thought Cooper was reaching for a gun. No gun is found, but Marlow is not charged.

Examples of blacks and other minorities killed by police officers with near impunity could fill three times this space. Unfortunately, the list is still not long enough to convince political leaders to effectively confront the racism responsible for these crimes.

Escalating police violence reflects a growing fear of black criminality among the broader population. The skyrocketing rate of black imprisonment and the profits to be made from the prison industry suggest that the criminal justice system and young African-Americans are increasingly becoming each other's sworn enemies.

A History of Racism

"Racist assumptions are built into the very foundation of American policing," says William Geller, associate director of the Police Executive Research Forum, a Washington-based group that studies law enforcement issues. Geller, the author of several books on police abuse, is not surprised by the ratcheting up of tensions between police and black men. The widening gap between the rich and the poor combined with the absence of well-paying jobs in urban America have placed these two populations at loggerheads, he says.

Amnesty International released a report in late June 1996 that documented a disturbing pattern of police violence in America's largest police force. Entitled "Police Brutality and Excessive Force in the New York City Police Department," the 72-page report found that the New York Police Department routinely violates international human rights standards as well as its own guidelines governing the use of deadly force. The 18-month investigation found that charges of police brutality in New York climbed from 977 in 1987 to more than 2,000 in 1994. Deaths in police custody rose from 11 in 1991 to 24 in 1994. According to the report, most of the victims were minorities, while most of the offending police officers were white. Amnesty International concluded that excessive use of force has probably led to many more deaths in police custody than the New York Police

"Placing the black community under police siege will do little to facilitate the struggle for enlightened solutions."

Department is willing to acknowledge. The report cited several cases in which men in custody subjected to choke holds or sprayed with capsicum pepper died of apparently related seizures or asphyxiation.

Shooting Black Undercover Cops

The report also noted a troubling new development: black undercover police officers being shot by their white colleagues. New York City transit officers Derwin Pannell and Desmond Robinson both were mistaken for criminals and shot by white officers. On November 18, 1992, Pannell was attempting to arrest a farebeater in a dark subway station in the Canarsie section of Brooklyn, when he was confronted by white transit officers who mistook him for a mugger because he was rifling through the woman's handbag with his gun drawn. In later testimony, Pannell said his fellow officers did not identify themselves before opening fire. A Brooklyn grand jury cleared Pannell's assailants of all charges.

Officer Robinson had his gun drawn and was in pursuit of a suspect on August 24, 1994, when he was mistaken for a criminal and shot by Peter Del Debbio, an off-duty police officer on his way home. Testimony and evidence in the case suggest that Del Debbio stood over Robinson as he lay helpless on the subway platform and shot him three times in the back. Del Debbio was convicted in March 1996 of second-degree assault and sentenced to 200 hours of community service and five years' probation.

New York City, of course, is not the only place where white cops have mistakenly shot black cops. In Nashville, Reggie Miller, a black cop, was working on an undercover prostitution sting when five white police officers pulled him over for a traffic violation and forced him to the ground. The officers didn't give Miller the opportunity to identify himself, and within minutes they began beating him for no apparent reason. The offending officers were initially dismissed from the police force, but were later reinstated by the city's civil service commission.

The Amnesty International report may cause a temporary spasm of civic embarrassment in New York, but if previous experience in Chicago and Los Angeles is any indication, don't expect much to change. Amnesty International issued a 1990 report describing police torture and brutality in Chicago and an equally scathing 1992 report on the Los Angeles Police Department. Neither the police nor their political overseers in either city have moved to address the concerns raised in those reports.

"All of this is part of a larger crackdown on African-Americans," says political scientist and author Andrew Hacker. "White Americans have decided that enough is enough. They want longer prison sentences, and welfare mothers to go out and work. White America is tired of hearing about racism and says 'We've done enough.'"

In these times of racial and economic polarization, police officers are increasingly in the line of fire, called upon to quell the growing antagonisms. Criminal justice solutions, however, are woefully inadequate to heal the deep social wounds that plague contemporary America.

Placing the black community under police siege will do little to facilitate the struggle for enlightened solutions. Instead, police violence "in the line of duty" will stir up more black anger. When that anger reaches the boiling point, we can expect to see more St. Petersburgs. That would mark the beginning of a downward spiral whose repercussions, rest assured, will not be limited to the inner cities.

The Police Are Not Racist

by Michael Levin

About the author: *Michael Levin is a contributing editor of the* Journal of Libertarian Studies.

The script is always the same. A black does something bad—by driving recklessly, robbing a candy store, assaulting someone or in some other way getting involved in an altercation. White policemen appear. The perpetrator or someone mistaken for him fails to heed an order to stop/show his hands/pull over/display his license. Often he draws a gun or, if in a car, tries to run over one of the cops. The police attempt to subdue him by force, injuring or killing him.

Exaggerating Police Action

Within hours community leaders—translation: no visible means of support—organize demonstrations against "police brutality," complete with a telegenic chorus of black women wailing "they've got to stop killing our babies" even though the deceased was 6'2" and weighed 250 pounds. These small protests acquire a life of their own under media magnification. Well-known blacks suddenly remember how often they have been hassled by the police for no reason, allegedly, other than their color. Politicians, to show "racial sensitivity," declare that a grave wrong was done.

After meeting with [civil rights activist] Jesse Jackson, the US attorney general announces "possible civil rights violations," a guarantee that the cops will face federal charges should they escape local ones. All sides agree that the only cure for the racism inherent in the police department is a double dose of race preference: more blacks on the force at all levels—necessitating easier qualifying exams—and fewer white cops in black neighborhoods.

Cases in point: Eleanor Bumpers, shot to death by a policeman she attacked with a knife when he tried to mediate a family dispute; Kiko Garcia, shot to death attempting to grab a cop's gun from his holster; Abner Louima, beaten during a 3 AM brawl outside a homosexual bar; Johnny Gammage, shot by highway patrolmen he attempted to run down; and of course Rodney King,

Michael Levin, "Much Ado About Amadou," *Rothbard-Rockwell Report*, vol. 10, July 1999, pp. 8–10.

stopped for speeding and drunken driving.

One of the two most recent incidents involves Amadou Diallo, a Guyanese immigrant. At 1:00 AM . . . [on February 4, 1999], four plainclothesmen from the elite Street Crimes Unit spotted a man (Diallo) fitting the description of a wanted rapist as he loitered on a Bronx street. Leaping from their unmarked car they asked Diallo to stand still and show identification, triggering an unfortunate chain reaction. Instead of complying immediately, Diallo backed up and reached into his pocket; at that very moment one of the SCU men stumbled while another yelled "Gun!," causing all four to open fire with their service automatics. In a few seconds Diallo was dead.

> *"So long as society either privately or collectively is justified in using force against criminals, . . . blacks will be disproportionately discomfited."*

A few seconds later community leader Al Sharpton was on the scene, demanding the cops be indicted for murder. A day or two later the usual suspects began marching in front of police headquarters—when someone had the bright idea of engaging in "civil disobedience." Pretty soon a dozen people had been arrested and taken a few feet to be booked (remember, the scene was police headquarters). Suddenly getting arrested at One Police Plaza became the In thing, and second-rate celebs began making the scene as if it was the latest hot restaurant. Ossie Davis, Susan Sarandon, Dick Gregory, and the redoubtable Jesse himself, along with more than a thousand others, were duly led away in handcuffs.

Things went less well for the four policemen. New York's Mayor Rudy Giuliani initially pleaded for suspension of judgment until the facts were in, but the media ridiculed his circumspection for "insensitivity" to blacks. As Diallo's parents thanked him on TV, the Bronx District Attorney indicted the policemen on charges of 2nd degree murder, punishable by life in prison.[1]

Examining the Facts

The facts? For one, Diallo spoke little English and probably did not grasp the orders given him. More suggestive was the revelation, a few days after the shooting, that he was in the United States illegally; he had told the Immigration and Naturalization service that he was a Mauritanian fleeing political persecution (a magic formula that opens all immigration doors).

So imagine his guilty thoughts when four white representatives of officialdom suddenly confronted him. "They know I lied; they're going to deport me. Maybe I can get away. [The cops tell him to stand still.] Uh-oh; maybe shoving my wallet at them will convince them I'm on the up-and-up." The cops, already fearful that they are dealing with an armed robber-rapist, think he is going for a gun. One yells, one falls, and all open fire.

---

1. All four officers were acquitted of any wrongdoing on February 25, 2000.

But the particulars offer a too narrow view of the Diallo case. To understand it fully, consider a second racial melodrama now playing itself out, the charge of "racial profiling" currently being made against the New Jersey Highway Patrol. It seems that, while only 35% of the vehicles on NJ roads are driven by blacks, more than 70% of the drivers stopped by state troopers are black. This statistical "discrimination"—to liberals. the worst sin—has prompted the usual commotion and calls for investigation.

To check up on troopers in future, patrol cars are being equipped with videocams to record all traffic stops. (Consider the waste in having policemen watching tapes at headquarters instead of being out protecting life and property, their proper function.) A more immediate result was the firing by New Jersey's governor, at the behest of the NAACP [National Association for the Advancement of Colored People] and "Black Ministers Council of New Jersey," of the State Police Superintendent, Carl Williams. The reason: he did not go along with the feeble defense other NJ officials were offering of NJHP tactics.

These other officials had mostly led with their chins, making up lame excuses or denying the obvious. At first the NJHP kept insisting that its troopers did not single out blacks, and that cars are stopped for minor infractions like malfunctioning tail-lights—which hardly explains why blacks are stopped more often, unless (what nobody had the guts to say) blacks are more neglectful of their cars. A TV station then produced an embarrassing patrolman's guide for a NJ township in which cars flying Ethiopian flags were described as likely to be transporting drugs.

> *"Cops associate blacks with potential violence, so, out of sheer self-preservation, are more prepared to use violence in dealing with them."*

Seeking to inject a note of realism into the debate, Williams called it "naive" to separate the race issue from crime. "Two weeks ago the president of the United States went to Mexico to talk to the president of Mexico about drugs. He didn't go to Ireland. He didn't go to England. [Today] the drug problem is cocaine or marijuana. It is most likely a minority group that's involved with that."

A Reasonable Response

Certainly, drugs should be legal, trafficking is so lucrative and the cause of so much crime only because drugs are now illegal. State troopers shouldn't be stopping anyone for drug searches. But this is beside the larger point, which is that *racial profiling is a perfectly proper response* to what even the staunchest libertarian will regard as criminal. Blacks commit a disproportionate amount of all forms of violence against persons and property. So long as society either privately or collectively is justified in using force against criminals (as of course it is), blacks will be disproportionately discomfited.

Per capita, blacks commit about ten times as many robberies, murders, and rapes as do whites. This disparity, usually chalked up to bias in the justice system, is also found in victim reports. And this disparity is one that all policemen are aware of. They are more suspicious of a black than they would be of a white in identical circumstances—driving oddly on the highway, being out in the wee hours—and it is perfectly reasonable for them to be so. As it turned out, the robber-rapist Diallo was mistaken for was subsequently apprehended a few blocks from where Diallo was shot, and looks rather like him.

Nor is this a purely intellectual judgment that entitles the police to be more suspicious of blacks. Cops have also learned to be more apprehensive and more prepared for trouble when confronting blacks in a tense situation. In any confrontation violence is always close to the surface. And it is this general atmosphere rather than any particular gesture on Amadou Diallo's part which explains his death. Cops associate blacks with potential violence, so, out of sheer self-preservation, are more prepared to use violence in dealing with them. "Police racism" will diminish precisely as fast as the black crime rate does.

An immediate and entirely predictable consequence of the hysteria about the Diallo shooting was police paralysis. In the weeks after the incident arrests fell by 250 percent and the murder rate, down to 650 per year, began to creep back up to the 2000+ per year level it had reached under Giuliani's black predecessor, David Dinkins. The police were inhibited in their dealings with blacks by fear that one misstep could lead to *their* arrest. And, needless to say, most of the victims of the preventable murders that occurred as a result were themselves black.

Given that blacks are the main beneficiaries of an aggressive local constabulary, why do black leaders oppose it so frenziedly? Part of the answer may be different levels of tolerance for disorder; measures regarded by whites as necessary for social life are perceived by blacks as impositions. Part of the answer may be a failure to link cause to effect: a black sees white cops handcuffing other blacks, and simply fails to realize that he is safer as a result.

But the main reason for the opposition is tactical: it keeps whites off balance. It lets whites everywhere know that if they harm a black, their lives are over. This intimidation has its uses, the most conspicuous of which is making justice impossible. The LA riots[2] demonstrated to juries everywhere that blacks will run amok if they don't get the verdict they want. That is why OJ Simpson[3] got off, and why the NY cops will spend at least twenty years in jail.

---

2. The riots occurred in response to the acquittal of the officers accused of beating Rodney King.
3. Simpson was accused of killing his wife Nicole Brown Simpson and her friend Ron Goldman.

Aggressive Policing Encourages Police Brutality

by Joseph D. McNamara

About the author: *Joseph D. McNamara, a former police chief in Kansas City, Missouri, and San Jose, California, is a research fellow at the Hoover Institution at Stanford University.*

Police credibility in the United States should be extremely high: . . . Crime has decreased [since 1992], and the number of shootings by police has also diminished. But in many areas, police credibility is down. Questionable shootings by officers across the nation have led to doubts: A police officer in Connecticut shot a motorist he believed was reaching for a gun, which turned out to be a cell phone. Four Riverside, California, officers and a sergeant have been fired after fatally shooting a young African American woman dozing in her locked car with a gun on her lap. Two Los Angeles officers are under investigation for shooting a 105-pound homeless woman to death.

In this context, public concern about police shootings is understandable. It is wrong, however, to decide that there is an established number of times that cops can shoot people and then condemn officers for exceeding some "quota." Although even one unnecessary shooting is too many, police officers have no way of controlling the number of life-threatening incidents to which they respond.

Instead, each case must be evaluated by this criterion: Did the officers fire as a last resort, in the reasonable belief that they or others faced imminent danger of death or serious injury? Answering this question, although not easy, is the way to distinguish between police shootings that are necessary in the line of duty and those that are warning signs of deeper problems. The truth is, bad police shootings and instances of police brutality do not take place in a vacuum. They ferment in negative police cultures thriving on overheated rhetoric that describes cops as "soldiers" in "wars" against crime and drugs.

In San Jose, California, where six people were killed in police shootings in the first half of [1999], Chief Bill Lansdowne has ordered a review of training and procedures and increased the use of crisis-intervention teams specially trained in nonlethal methods. These steps send a strong message of restraint to officers, and they should reassure citizens that the police department is committed to minimizing the use of force.

The Wrong Way

[In February 1999], New York mayor Rudolph Giuliani responded quite differently to the police shooting of Amadou Diallo. Diallo, an unarmed African immigrant with no criminal record, died in his own hallway after four white New York City police officers fired forty-one shots at him. Giuliani called the subsequent protests and demonstrations "silly." The police officers did not testify before a grand jury or publicly justify their actions; they have been indicted for murder.[1] Trust in the department has plummeted: Almost 80 percent of minority citizens said, in a . . . poll, that New York cops are biased against them. Even most whites polled thought that cops treated minorities unfairly.

The mayor and his police commissioners are experiencing the results of creating a zero-tolerance police culture. New York has adopted the "broken windows" model of policing, which holds that urban decay, littering, and graffiti send encouraging signals to criminals. Therefore, police are ordered to crack down on even minor violations. Amid this climate of a "war" on crime and drugs, many New York cops do not see local citizens as allies against crime but rather as individuals needing to be firmly controlled by the police. There is no evidence, of course, that such conditions signify anything other than an impoverished and segregated area. The ugly confrontations between police and minorities set in motion by "broken windows," however, have led to broken trust in the police.

It reminds me of what I saw when I came to San Jose as police chief in 1976. Before my arrival, a San Jose officer pursuing a black man for a traffic violation had fatally shot him in front of his home. Another policeman had fatally wounded a young Latino, thinking he was reaching for a gun. The boy was sitting in a car with his girlfriend in front of her home, and no weapon was ever found. The police department reacted with much the same insensitivity Giuliani displayed in the Diallo case. The San Jose mayor and city council, however, did not. Their desire for improvement led to my appointment.

"[Instances of police brutality] ferment in negative police cultures thriving on overheated rhetoric that describes cops as 'soldiers' in 'wars' against crime and drugs."

As a result of the shootings and generally bad relations between the police

1. All four officers were acquitted of all charges on February 25, 2000.

and minority communities, the San Jose mayor and city council had asked the U.S. Civil Rights Commission to monitor the department. Three years later, the commission praised San Jose police for greatly improving relations and recommended that the department be used as a national model for large cities.

Those shootings, tragic as they were, were part of a more serious problem. Like Giuliani's officers, . . . San Jose police back then believed it was their job to keep the citizens in line. They saw themselves as tough cops and believed that confronting

> *"A police culture embracing zero tolerance can also encourage biased officers to use unnecessary force."*

everyone—especially minority males—as potential criminals would scare people into being law abiding. In reality, police disrespect made citizens reluctant to report crime, help gather evidence, or come forward as witnesses. Paradoxically, the police were discouraging the very citizen cooperation they needed to fight crime.

With the help of San Jose supervisors and leaders from community organizations, we were able to change the police culture and bring cops back into contact with the people they served. Both crime and police use of force declined as trust was renewed.

A War Mentality

Reasonable people accept that a cop's job is difficult and dangerous, and most people understand that sometimes an officer will have to shoot someone. State penal codes and juries everywhere support an officer's right to use reasonable force, including deadly force, when necessary. But the police are not and should never be allowed to think of themselves as soldiers or to believe they face the same level of danger.

General Colin Powell during the Persian Gulf war bluntly reminded the nation that a soldier's duty was to kill the enemy. Because of that, the military accepts certain civilian casualty levels in dealing with the enemy. Police, however, are public servants who maintain order and enforce the law. They are never right in viewing any group in society as the enemy. Police training should emphasize that officers are not justified in shooting motorists reaching for drivers' licenses or cell phones.

In many cities today, overbearing policing has greatly reduced police credibility—worsening the tendency to view police shootings as racially biased even when they are not. A police culture embracing zero tolerance can also encourage biased officers to use unnecessary force. Philadelphia police commissioner John Timoney, former first deputy commissioner in New York, recently said: "Frankly, there is a problem with race in policing. To solve it, we have to deal openly with it."

New York police justify their aggressive style of policing and the resentment it causes by saying they are a necessary price to pay for reducing crime. But that claim does not hold up. Crime had begun to decline in New York before Giuliani's election. Moreover, crime has declined nationally—including in areas such as San Jose and San Diego, where police pursued cooperative partnerships with neighborhood groups. Crime also declined in Los Angeles following the police beating of Rodney King, when cops did little more than answer calls because they feared complaints. Furthermore, during the 1980s—when crime was increasing nationally—San Jose became the safest large city in America. Crime dropped as the department followed a community-policing model and as the computer-driven economy provided ample jobs.

The latest reports indicate homicides in Manhattan are up 27 percent compared with last year and up 19 percent in Brooklyn. Of course, the police commissioner and mayor who took credit for the previous declines are not attributing the increases to their own ineptness.

My dad, older brother, and I all worked as policemen for many years in New York's highest-crime areas. None of us would have fired at Amadou Diallo. We were conditioned to believe that cops were part of the neighborhood—not an occupation force put there to maintain our own image of what the neighborhood should look like. In my ten years as a policeman in Harlem, I, like other cops, frequently experienced tense moments, only to find out later that things were not what they appeared to be. And even a police chief can face split-second decisions.

About 9 o'clock one evening in San Jose, as I was driving home from headquarters, I saw the passenger in the car in front of me point a gun at youngsters in a park. I radioed a description and requested backup. A uniformed officer quickly arrived and went to the driver's side of the car, not realizing that it was the passenger who had the gun. I rushed to the car and pointed my weapon at the suspect's head, ordering him to freeze. Instead, he reached under the seat. I had seen him pointing a gun at other people. I would have been morally and legally justified in shooting, and he certainly would have been killed. But like almost every cop I've known, I didn't want to shoot anyone. I grabbed him by the neck and hauled him out of the car. It turned out he wasn't drawing the gun but sticking it under the seat. It was a poor-quality weapon and probably would not have done much damage if it had been fired. I could have killed a confused seventeen-year-old playing out a fantasy with his girlfriend, the driver. He had no intention of shooting anyone.

The point is that, every day, cops refrain from shooting even when justified. Of course, we never see these cases in the news. When we analyze officers' split-second decisions later, we don't owe them a blank check. But we do owe them a calm and fair verdict reached under due process of law, not a judgment based on partial media reports.

Equally important, the cops deserve reasoned political leadership—not the all-too-common belligerent demagoguery delivered by ambitious politicians declaring phony wars on crime and drugs.

Aggressive Policing Does Not Encourage Police Brutality

by George L. Kelling

About the author: *George L. Kelling, a professor at Rutgers University, coauthored with Catherine M. Coles* Fixing Broken Windows: Restoring Order and Reducing Crime in Our Communities.

The New York City Police Department [NYPD] is under fire in the wake of [the February 4, 1999], killing of Amadou Diallo, an unarmed immigrant from Guinea, whom officers shot 41 times. Both the Justice Department and the state attorney general have launched investigations of alleged police abuse, and the U.S. Commission on Civil Rights will hold hearings in the city in May [1999]. Even President [Bill] Clinton used his national radio address . . . to denounce police abuse, and . . . New York Gov. George Pataki joined the fray, criticizing the NYPD and Mayor Rudolph Giuliani.

Diallo's killing was a horrible tragedy. But the offensive against the NYPD should be seen for what it is: an ideological attack on a successful philosophy of policing. The astonishing crime reductions in New York during the 1990s came about because the city administration rejected the reigning doctrine that if crime was to be reduced, its "root causes"—poverty, racism and social injustice—had to be abolished. Mr. Giuliani and his first police commissioner, William Bratton, stunned the "experts" by predicting they would cut crime, telling how and then doing it.

Two Different Incidents

Now, the root-cause liberals are mounting a second assault. Perhaps police can reduce crime, they concede, but only at the cost of abusing citizens, especially the poor and minorities. They link Diallo's shooting with the 1997 police attack on Haitian immigrant Abner Louima, claiming to prove that the NYPD's crime-reduction activities rest upon violating civil rights.

The Louima and Diallo incidents were in fact quite different. Mr. Louima was brutally assaulted and tortured in a precinct station house. The attack was inexcusable, and few doubt that it was motivated by racial bigotry. The officers involved are, properly, being prosecuted.[1] Obviously, a police department should do all it can to combat such virulent racism, should recruit minorities and should improve training and supervision. But corruption and depravity are facts of life, and any system designed to control them will sometimes fail. When they do, the community and police department must rally together to condemn and contain such evil conduct.

The Diallo case, by contrast, was a street encounter gone awry. Four officers were searching for a serial rapist of black and Hispanic women, in a high-crime area where edgy youths carry heavy-duty weapons. We don't know for certain what happened, but the hypothesis of racist police seems far-fetched. A more likely scenario is that in the chaos of a shooting that lasted only a few seconds, a stum-

> *"There's no evidence that . . . shootings are made more likely by the [order maintenance] philosophy of policing."*

bling officer, ricocheting bullets or reflected gunfire flashes disoriented officers, confirming the misperception that Diallo was shooting at them and leading them to keep firing.[2] Street contacts between police and citizens in such situations are complex; police are understandably frightened; interactions take place in an instant and may result from inaccurate perceptions. Under such circumstances, police are bound to make occasional mistakes, some of which will prove deadly.

Taking Action Against Crime

Remember that cops are not soldiers; they rarely draw their weapons and even more rarely fire them. Clearly, police should improve weapons training and reconsider how special units are deployed and used. But accidental shootings by police are a tragic fact of life. Even so, there's no evidence that such shootings are made more likely by the philosophy of policing the NYPD has adopted—in which police do not wait for crime to occur and then respond, but instead take action to prevent crime.

In fact, [in 1998] New York had 0.48 fatal shootings per 1,000 officers, the lowest figure since 1985 and the second lowest since 1973, when data collec-

---

1. Officer Justin Volpe pleaded guilty to the assault. Officer Charles Schwarz was found guilty of assisting Volpe. Schwarz, Thomas Wiese, and Thomas Bruder were subsequently convicted of obstruction, for attempting to cover up the facts of the case, though these convictions were put aside on February 28, 2002. The city of New York and a police union settled with Louima by giving him $8.75 million.
2. All four officers were acquitted of any wrongdoing on February 25, 2000.

tion began. This rate puts New York below Philadelphia (0.72), Dallas (1.05), Miami (2.01), and Washington (312). (These numbers, however, are not directly comparable and thus paint only a rough picture.) It's true that the number of complaints against police has risen, but this must be understood within the context of an increasing number of officers on the street, their widening activity and growing antipolice activism.

In 1992, when David Dinkins was mayor, more than 2,200 people were murdered in New York City—a high proportion of them minorities. In 1998, the city had just 600 murders—fewer than in Chicago, whose population is barely one third of New York's. Sixteen hundred more New Yorkers would have died [in 1998] alone had crime remained at Dinkins-era levels. Calculate the number of lives saved, families spared grief, youths not imprisoned, and we are talking about thousands of New Yorkers whose lives have been immeasurably improved thanks to the Giuliani administration's crime-fighting efforts.

These dramatic changes did not result from "business as usual" in the NYPD. Readied with a theory of action, leadership, sophisticated planning and crime analysis, and an accountability structure that riveted precinct commanders' attention on neighborhood problems, the NYPD revolutionized itself and made clear just how much police can accomplish. The wholesale attacks on the NYPD are especially worrisome because policing's gains are reversible. The continuity provided through Mr. Giuliani's five years in office, and through Commissioner Howard Safir's continued focus on order maintenance, can create a false confidence that the NYPD will never revert to the "stay out of trouble" mentality that ruled for the previous 20 years. In fact, if a new commissioner backtracked on maintaining order and on the careful precinct-by-precinct analysis of problems that characterizes the department today, control of public spaces could easily and quickly be lost.

A Political Strategy

Politics certainly plays a role here: Mayor Giuliani's political foes can be expected to do their best to discredit him and the police department and to neutralize his greatest achievement—crime reduction. But more is on the line than a mayor's political future.

The root-cause liberals are outraged; no longer can they hold crime-control policy hostage to an agenda of massive social change. So now, making political hay of the Louima and Diallo tragedies, they falsely accuse police of systematic abuse. And they wanted to have it both ways: When complaints against police go up, critics like Norman Siegel of the New York Civil Liberties Union argue that police brutality is increasing; when complaints decline, it means that citizens do not trust the complaint process.

Attacks on order maintenance and indiscriminate charges of racism are not limited to the current discussion over New York; they appear in court, in elite law journals, in other cities. For example, in Seattle, City Attorney Mark Sidran has been called a racist because of his attempts to close a "nightclub" owned by an African-American couple. Never mind that it is a drug dealing center threatening the entire community.

A Delicate Matter

Public policy dealing with race and crime is a delicate matter. But if charges of racism and threats of riot follow every disagreement, conflict or tragedy, as we are seeing in New York now, we are in a hopeless situation. In addition to minority recruitment, improved supervision and better weapons training, other issues need sober and thorough discussion. One example is the tendency of police departments to rely on large special units that have few links to neighborhoods. And we must remember that there are no panaceas: Washington, D.C., has a large percentage of minority officers, yet has had such a serious problem with police violence that the new chief there, Charles Ramsey, has asked for an outside investigation.

No matter how successful police are, mistakes inevitably will be fair game for political opponents in a democracy. That makes it all the more important that police seek the high moral ground. In the hurlyburly of urban politics, operating within the law and being successful are necessary but not sufficient; police must aggressively and constantly pursue the consent, cooperation and collaboration of citizens, never taking their support for granted. Only such an approach can provide the cushion of good faith that will allow citizens to tolerate and learn from mistakes, move forward and not retreat.

Antiterrorism Measures Encourage Law Enforcement Agencies to Harass Immigrants

by Jane Bai and Eric Tang

About the author: *Jane Bai is executive director and Eric Tang is associate director of Citizens Against Anti-Asian Violence.*

Within hours of the collapse of the World Trade Center [as a result of the terrorist attacks of September 11, 2001], President [George W.] Bush appeared on national television to offer his first promise to the American public: "We will smoke these barbarians out of their caves." A cleansing was in order. The world was to be decontaminated of every last trace of Islamic fundamentalism. Yes, a nation that is ruptured and speechless in the wake of terror can still find comfort in a trustworthy colonial logic: cleanse, decontaminate.

We braced ourselves for the very worst. Hundreds of reported incidents of brutal beatings of Arab, South Asian, and multinational Muslims flowed in. Before long, we learned of the first, second, and then third racist killings. Bush vaguely told the American public to "cut it out." But in reality the president was fast making good on his extraordinary promise of a permanent war at home linked to the war abroad.

In the name of fighting terrorism, Bush is expanding and redirecting the ongoing attacks on people of color. A qualitative shift has taken place wherein the prison industrial complex is being reorganized to fully serve the war program. Two changes stand out: positioning immigrants at the forefront of racist state violence and increased control of law enforcement by the federal government. These changes pose grave new dangers. But they also provide opportunities for deepening and unifying struggles for racial justice and immigrant rights.

Immigrants in the Crosshairs

Prior to September 11, state violence was often viewed through the lens of the African American experience. Post–September 11, immigrants are the new face of racial profiling, racist laws, and deprivation of civil liberties. As the state and some of the public have quickly made Arabs and South Asians new targets of racism, can we incorporate these new racialized groups into a more inclusive vision of racial justice?

Today the language and imagery are "terrorist," "immigrant," and "Arab," but the infrastructure established in the process is a potent source of increased racism and repression against all peoples of color and indeed all who live in the U.S. The fight for immigrant rights must become a centerpiece of efforts to build a broad national front to reverse Bush's attempt to permanently deprive all people of color of civil and constitutional rights.

Police chiefs from around the country who, only a year ago, were being scrutinized by the Department of Justice for their "racial profiling" of African Americans are now being summoned by Attorney General [John] Ashcroft to "interview" tens of thousands of immigrants merely because they are of Middle Eastern descent. Meanwhile, INS [Immigration and Naturalization Service] detention centers, many of them run by private prison corporations, function as today's internment camps.

The INS has become a lead enforcement agency in the nation. With an already exponentially growing budget, it has been transformed into two agencies, one to deal with "services" and the other to focus on enforcement.

The Bureau of Immigration Enforcement (BIE) will oversee border patrol, detention centers, and deportation proceedings, as well as the new forms of immigrant policing already occurring in the interior. In addition, the INS added the names of more than 300,000 immigrants scheduled for deportation to the FBI's criminal database. Thus, state violence—in the form of policing, detention, and prisons—has become a crucial political arena for the immigrant rights movement. The immigrant rights movement can ill-afford to view state violence as peripheral to its longtime core issue, legalization of the undocumented.

Increasing Federal Control

Indeed, the draconian USA-PATRIOT Act passed by congress [in Fall 2001] stripped away much of the protection formerly provided by legalization. Under the Act, all non-citizens, documented or not, are deemed potential terrorists and subject to the newly expanded powers of local and state police, the FBI, and INS. Before September 11, a green-card holder could get a traffic ticket, pay a $50 fine, and their case was closed. Today, that same person can be racially profiled, stopped, turned over to the FBI and INS, and detained for up to six months without being charged with any crime or violation. They may be deprived of attorney-client confidentiality and, if brought to court, convicted by secret evidence. The "war at home" has shifted the dividing line from documented vs. undocumented to citizen vs. non-citizen.

This may create division among people of color along citizenship lines. But the extensive history of violence against African Americans proved long ago that citizenship for people of color is never bulletproof. Thus, the "war at home" also provides a strong basis for unity among immigrants, citizens of color, and indigenous peoples in the fight against the prison industrial complex. It is critical that the racial justice and immigrant rights movements seize this opportunity.

Prior to September 11, there was anecdotal evidence of collusion among the different law enforcement agencies, and local anti-police brutality struggles had framed racism as a central factor in shaping policing policies and practices in the U.S. Now such collusion is official policy and is being institutionalized at a rapid pace.

> *"Post–September 11, immigrants are the new face of racial profiling, racist laws, and deprivation of civil liberties."*

The Bush administration has erected entirely new national policing institutions like Homeland Security, federalized airport security, and military tribunals. The USA-PATRIOT Act, gravely undermines the rights of Americans, especially noncitizens, and frees law enforcement to broaden and deepen spying, harassment, imprisonment, and sentencing.

The administration is unburdening the FBI and the CIA of former constraints and refocusing them away from traditional crimes to political "crimes" and spying. It is eliminating the already woefully weak guidelines against political spying and harassment that were erected after the exposure of COINTELPRO[1]— the program that undermined the black liberation movements of the 60s and 70s. And bureaucratic barriers between and among different agencies—local police, state police, FBI, INS, and CIA—are being reduced or eliminated. The Bush Administration has made it clear that it plans to create a nationally unified and politicized policing command.

A Need for Unity

Prior to September 11, struggles against police brutality had been most effective on the local level in raising public consciousness of institutionalized racism and engendering small reforms, such as civilian review boards. This is because local police departments are controlled by local governments, not by states or the national government. This localism was an important obstacle to creating a national movement against police brutality. Even major political explosions, like the riots following the Rodney King verdict or the street actions after the Amadou Diallo case in New York, remained largely localized.[2]

1. COINTELPRO was a secret FBI program that involved the use of surveillance, fraud, and force to sabotage the constitutionally protected political activity of specific groups and individuals.   2. King was beaten by three Los Angeles police officers as their supervisor watched on March 3, 1991. Diallo, a West African immigrant, was killed after New York City police officers fired forty-one shots while he stood in his Bronx doorway on February 4, 1999.

Now that Bush has seized increased national control over policing policies, the fight against various elements of the prison industrial complex can and must be linked into a national movement.

The immigrant rights and racial justice movements face a critical juncture. With the advent of the "war on terrorism," immigrant rights and anti-racist violence organizing can no longer be thought of as separate spheres within the broader social justice movement.

The immigrant rights movement must give increased priority to the issue of state violence. And the fight against the prison industrial complex—while correct in the view that prisons serve as a means of confining and/or disappearing a generation of black and brown youth—must include in its analysis the pivotal role immigrants play in the expansion of the big business of law enforcement and prisons.

There is much to be shared between those who have been taking on border patrol and INS raids, and those who have been fighting urban police. And both are now indelibly linked to the fight against the Bush administration's program of permanent war at home and abroad.

Antiterrorism Measures Target Only Terrorists

by John Ashcroft

About the author: *John Ashcroft is the U.S. attorney general.*

Editor's Note: The following viewpoint is taken from testimony given before the Senate Committee on the Judiciary on December 6, 2001.

On the morning of September 11, [2001], as the United States came under attack, I was in an airplane with several members of the Justice Department en route to Milwaukee, in the skies over the Great Lakes. By the time we could return to Washington, thousands of people had been murdered at the World Trade Center. 189 were dead at the Pentagon. Forty-four had crashed to the ground in Pennsylvania. From that moment, at the command of the President of the United States, I began to mobilize the resources of the Department of Justice toward one single, over-arching and over-riding objective: to save innocent lives from further acts of terrorism.

America's campaign to save innocent lives from terrorists is [as of December 6, 2001] 87 days old. It has brought me back to [the Senate Judiciary Committee] to report to you in accordance with Congress's oversight role. I welcome this opportunity to clarify for you and the American people how the Justice Department is working to protect American lives while preserving American liberties.

Since those first terrible hours of September 11, America has faced a choice that is as stark as the images that linger of that morning. One option is to call September 11 a fluke, to believe it could never happen again, and to live in a dream world that requires us to do nothing differently. The other option is to fight back, to summon all our strength and all our resources and devote ourselves to better ways to identify, disrupt and dismantle terrorist networks.

Under the leadership of President [George W.] Bush, America has made the choice to fight terrorism—not just for ourselves but for all civilized people. Since September 11, through dozens of warnings to law enforcement, a deliber-

John Ashcroft, testimony before the Senate Committee on the Judiciary, Washington, D.C., December 6, 2001.

ate campaign of terrorist disruption, tighter security around potential targets, and a preventative campaign of arrest and detention of lawbreakers, America has grown stronger—and safer—in the face of terrorism.

Thanks to the vigilance of law enforcement and the patience of the American people, we have not suffered another major terrorist attack. Still, we cannot—we must not—allow ourselves to grow complacent. The reasons are apparent to me each morning. My day begins with a review of the threats to Americans and American interests that were received in the previous 24 hours. If ever there were proof of the existence

> *"The Justice Department is working to protect American lives while preserving American liberties."*

of evil in the world, it is in the pages of these reports. They are a chilling daily chronicle of hatred of America by fanatics who seek to extinguish freedom, enslave women, corrupt education and to kill Americans wherever and whenever they can.

Who Is the Enemy?

The terrorist enemy that threatens civilization today is unlike any we have ever known. It slaughters thousands of innocents—a crime of war and a crime against humanity. It seeks weapons of mass destruction and threatens their use against America. No one should doubt the intent, nor the depth, of its consuming, destructive hatred.

Terrorist operatives infiltrate our communities—plotting, planning and waiting to kill again. They enjoy the benefits of our free society even as they commit themselves to our destruction. They exploit our openness—not randomly or haphazardly—but by deliberate, premeditated design.

This is a seized al Qaeda[1] training manual—a "how-to" guide for terrorists—that instructs enemy operatives in the art of killing in a free society. Prosecutors first made this manual public in the trial of the al Qaeda terrorists who bombed U.S. embassies in Africa. We are posting several al Qaeda lessons from this manual on our website today so Americans can know our enemy.

In this manual, al Qaeda terrorists are told how to use America's freedom as a weapon against us. They are instructed to use the benefits of a free press—newspapers, magazines and broadcasts—to stalk and kill their victims. They are instructed to exploit our judicial process for the success of their operations. Captured terrorists are taught to anticipate a series of questions from authorities and, in each response, to lie—to lie about who they are, to lie about what they are doing and to lie about who they know in order for the operation to achieve

---

1. Al-Qaeda is a network of extremists organized by expelled Saudi Arabian millionaire Osama bin Laden, the leading suspect in the terrorist attacks of September 11, 2001, although he has denied involvement in the attack. The principal aims of al-Qaeda are to drive Americans and American influence out of all Muslim nations.

its objective. Imprisoned terrorists are instructed to concoct stories of torture and mistreatment at the hands of our officials. They are directed to take advantage of any contact with the outside world to, quote, "communicate with brothers outside prison and exchange information that may be helpful to them in their work. The importance of mastering the art of hiding messages is self-evident here."

The Campaign Against Terrorism

Mr. Chairman and members of the committee, we are at war with an enemy who abuses individual rights as it abuses jet airliners: as weapons with which to kill Americans. We have responded by redefining the mission of the Department of Justice. Defending our nation and its citizens against terrorist attacks is now our first and overriding priority.

We have launched the largest, most comprehensive criminal investigation in world history to identify the killers of September 11 and to prevent further terrorist attacks. Four thousand FBI agents are engaged with their international counterparts in an unprecedented worldwide effort to detect, disrupt and dismantle terrorist organizations.

We have created a national task force at the FBI to centralize control and information sharing in our investigation. This task force has investigated hundreds of thousands of leads, conducted over 500 searches, interviewed thousands of witnesses and

> *"Action taken by the Department of Justice . . . is carefully drawn to target a narrow class of individuals—terrorists."*

obtained numerous court-authorized surveillance orders. Our prosecutors and agents have collected information and evidence from countries throughout Europe and the Middle East.

Immediately following the September 11 attacks, the Bureau of Prisons acted swiftly to intensify security precautions in connection with all al Qaeda and other terrorist inmates, increasing perimeter security at a number of key facilities.

Using New Tools

We have sought and received additional tools from Congress. Already, we have begun to utilize many of these tools. Within hours of passage of the USA PATRIOT Act, we made use of its provisions to begin enhanced information sharing between the law-enforcement and intelligence communities. We have used the provisions allowing nationwide search warrants for e-mail and subpoenas for payment information. And we have used the Act to place those who access the Internet through cable companies on the same footing as everyone else.

On December 5, 2001, at my request, the State Department designated 39 entities as terrorist organizations pursuant to the USA PATRIOT Act.

We have waged a deliberate campaign of arrest and detention to remove suspected terrorists who violate the law from our streets. Currently, we have brought criminal charges against 110 individuals, of whom 60 are in federal custody. The INS has detained 563 individuals on immigration violations.

We have investigated more than 250 incidents of retaliatory violence and threats against Arab Americans, Muslim Americans, Sikh Americans and South Asian Americans.

Since September 11, the Customs Service and Border Patrol have been at their highest state of alert. All vehicles and persons entering the country are subjected to the highest level of scrutiny. Working with the State Department, we have imposed new screening requirements on certain applicants for non-immigrant visas. At the direction of the President, we have created a Foreign Terrorist Tracking Task Force to ensure that we do everything we can to prevent terrorists from entering the country, and to locate and remove those who already have.

We have prosecuted to the fullest extent of the law individuals who waste precious law enforcement resources through anthrax hoaxes.[2]

We have offered non-citizens willing to come forward with valuable information a chance to live in this country and one day become citizens.

We have forged new cooperative agreements with Canada to protect our common borders and the economic prosperity they sustain.

We have embarked on a wartime reorganization of the Department of Justice. We are transferring resources and personnel to the field offices where citizens are served and protected. The INS is being restructured to better perform its service and border security responsibilities. Under Director Bob Mueller, the FBI is undergoing an historic reorganization to put the prevention of terrorism at the center of its law enforcement and national security efforts.

Outside Washington, we are forging new relationships of cooperation with state and local law enforcement.

We have created 93 Anti-Terrorism Task Forces—one in each U.S. Attorney's district—to integrate the communications and activities of local, state and federal law enforcement.

Answering the Critics

In all these ways and more, the Department of Justice has sought to prevent terrorism with reason, careful balance and excruciating attention to detail. Some of our critics, I regret to say, have shown less affection for detail. Their bold declarations of so-called fact have quickly dissolved, upon inspection, into vague conjecture. Charges of "kangaroo courts" and "shredding the Constitution" give new meaning to the term, "the fog of war."

---

2. In the fall of 2001 several anthrax letters were sent to major media outlets and two U.S. senators that resulted in five deaths and seventeen non-fatal infections. In October and November 2001 more than 750 "hoax" letters claiming to contain anthrax were sent worldwide.

Since lives and liberties depend upon clarity, not obfuscation, and reason, not hyperbole, let me take this opportunity today to be clear: Each action taken by the Department of Justice, as well as the war crimes commissions considered by the President and the Department of Defense, is carefully drawn to target a narrow class of individuals—terrorists. Our legal powers are targeted at terrorists. Our investigation is focused on terrorists. Our prevention strategy targets the terrorist threat.

> *"Those who pit Americans against immigrants, and citizens against non-citizens . . . only aid terrorists for they erode our national unity and diminish our resolve."*

Since 1983, the United States government has defined terrorists as those who perpetrate premeditated, politically motivated violence against noncombatant targets. My message to America this morning, then, is this: If you fit this definition of a terrorist, fear the United States, for you will lose your liberty.

We need honest, reasoned debate; not fearmongering. To those who pit Americans against immigrants, and citizens against non-citizens; to those who scare peace-loving people with phantoms of lost liberty; my message is this: Your tactics only aid terrorists—for they erode our national unity and diminish our resolve. They give ammunition to America's enemies, and pause to America's friends. They encourage people of good will to remain silent in the face of evil.

Our efforts have been carefully crafted to avoid infringing on constitutional rights while saving American lives. We have engaged in a deliberate campaign of arrest and detention of law breakers. All persons being detained have the right to contact their lawyers and their families. Out of respect for their privacy, and concern for saving lives, we will not publicize the names of those detained.

We have the authority to monitor the conversations of 16 of the 158,000 federal inmates and their attorneys because we suspect that these communications are facilitating acts of terrorism. Each prisoner has been told in advance his conversations will be monitored. None of the information that is protected by attorney-client privilege may be used for prosecution. Information will only be used to stop impending terrorist acts and save American lives.

We have asked a very limited number of individuals—visitors to our country holding passports from countries with active Al Qaeda operations—to speak voluntarily to law enforcement. We are forcing them to do nothing. We are merely asking them to do the right thing: to willingly disclose information they may have of terrorist threats to the lives and safety of all people in the United States.

The Limits of Congressional Oversight

Throughout all our activities since September 11, we have kept Congress informed of our continuing efforts to protect the American people. Beginning with a classified briefing by Director [Robert] Mueller and me on the very evening of September 11, the Justice Department has briefed members of the House, the Senate and their staffs on more than 100 occasions.

We have worked with Congress in the belief and recognition that no single branch of government alone can stop terrorism. We have consulted with members out of respect for the separation of powers that is the basis of our system of government. However, Congress' power of oversight is not without limits. The Constitution specifically delegates to the President the authority to "take care that the laws are faithfully executed." And perhaps most importantly, the Constitution vests the President with the extraordinary and sole authority as Commander-in-Chief to lead our nation in times of war.

Mr. Chairman and members of the committee, not long ago I had the privilege of sitting where you now sit. I have the greatest reverence and respect for the constitutional responsibilities you shoulder. I will continue to consult with Congress so that you may fulfill your constitutional responsibilities. In some areas, however, I cannot and will not consult you.

The advice I give to the President, whether in his role as Commander-in-Chief or in any other capacity, is privileged and confidential. I cannot and will not divulge the contents, the context, or even the existence of such advice to anyone—including Congress—unless the President instructs me to do so. I cannot and will not divulge information, nor do I believe that anyone here would wish me to divulge information, that will damage the national security of the United States, the safety of its citizens or our efforts to ensure the same in an ongoing investigation.

As Attorney General, it is my responsibility—at the direction of the President—to exercise those core executive powers the Constitution so designates. The law enforcement initiatives undertaken by the Department of Justice, those individuals we arrest, detain or seek to interview, fall under these core executive powers. In addition, the President's authority to establish war-crimes commissions arises out of his power as Commander in Chief. For centuries, Congress has recognized this authority and the Supreme Court has never held that any Congress may limit it.

In accordance with over two hundred years of historical and legal precedent, the executive branch is now exercising its core Constitutional powers in the interest of saving the lives of Americans. I trust that Congress will respect the proper limits of Executive Branch consultation that I am duty-bound to uphold. I trust, as well, that Congress will respect this President's authority to wage war on terrorism and defend our nation and its citizens with all the power vested in him by the Constitution and entrusted to him by the American people.

Militarism in Police Departments Encourages Police Brutality

by Diane Cecilia Weber

About the author: *Diane Cecilia Weber writes on law enforcement and criminal justice.*

One of the most alarming side effects of the federal government's war on drugs is the militarization of law enforcement in America. There are two aspects to the militarization phenomenon. First, the American tradition of civil-military separation is breaking down as Congress assigns more and more law enforcement responsibilities to the armed forces. Second, state and local police officers are increasingly emulating the war-fighting tactics of soldiers. Most Americans are unaware of the militarization phenomenon simply because it has been creeping along imperceptibly for many years. To get perspective, it will be useful to consider some recent events:

Blurring the Lines

- The U.S. military played a role in the Waco incident. In preparation for their disastrous 1993 raid on the Branch Davidian compound, federal law enforcement agents were trained by Army Special Forces at Fort Hood, Texas. And Delta Force commanders would later advise Attorney General Janet Reno to insert gas into the compound to end the 51-day siege. Waco resulted in the largest number of civilian deaths ever arising from a law enforcement operation.

- Between 1995 and 1997 the Department of Defense gave police departments 1.2 million pieces of military hardware, including 73 grenade launchers and 112 armored personnel carriers. The Los Angeles Police Department has acquired 600 Army surplus M-16s. Even small-town police departments are getting into the act. The seven-officer department in Jasper, Florida, is now equipped with fully automatic M-16s.

- In 1996 President Bill Clinton appointed a military commander, Gen. Barry R. McCaffrey, to oversee enforcement of the federal drug laws as the director of the Office of National Drug Control Policy.
- Since the mid-1990s U.S. Special Forces have been going after drug dealers in foreign countries. According to the U.S. Southern Command, American soldiers occupy three radar sites in Colombia to help monitor drug flights. And Navy SEALs have assisted in drug interdiction in the port city of Cap-Haitien, Haiti.
- The U.S. Marine Corps is now patrolling the Mexican border to keep drugs and illegal immigrants out of this country. In 1997 a Marine anti-drug patrol shot and killed 18-year-old Esequiel Hernandez as he was tending his family's herd of goats on private property. The Justice Department settled a wrongful death lawsuit with the Hernandez family for $1.9 million.
- In 1998 Indiana National Guard Engineering Units razed 42 crack houses in and around the city of Gary. The National Guard has also been deployed in Washington, D.C., to drive drug dealers out of certain locations.
- In 1999 the Pentagon asked President Clinton to appoint a "military leader" for the continental United States in the event of a terrorist attack on American soil. The powers that would be wielded by such a military commander were not made clear.

What is clear—and disquieting—is that the lines that have traditionally separated the military mission from the police mission are getting badly blurred.

Over the last 20 years Congress has encouraged the U.S. military to supply intelligence, equipment, and training to civilian police. That encouragement has spawned a culture of paramilitarism in American police departments. By virtue of their training and specialized armament, state and local police officers are adopting the tactics and mindset of their military mentors. The problem is that the actions and values of the police officer are distinctly different from those of the warrior. The job of a police officer is to keep the peace, but not by just any means. Police officers are expected to apprehend suspected law-breakers while adhering to constitutional procedures. They are expected to use *minimum* force and to deliver suspects to a court of law. The soldier, on the other hand, is an instrument of war. In boot camp, recruits are trained to

> *"Confusing the police function with the military function can have dangerous consequences."*

inflict *maximum* damage on enemy personnel. Confusing the police function with the military function can have dangerous consequences. As Albuquerque police chief Jerry Glavin has noted, "If [cops] have a mind-set that the goal is to take out a citizen, it will happen." Paramilitarism threatens civil liberties, constitutional norms, and the well-being of all citizens. Thus, the use of paramilitary tactics in everyday police work should alarm people of goodwill from across the political spectrum. . . .

The War on Drugs

Over the past 20 years there has been a dramatic expansion of the role of the military in law enforcement activity. In 1981 Congress passed the Military Cooperation with Law Enforcement Officials Act. That law amended the Posse Comitatus Act insofar as it authorized the military to "assist" civilian police in the enforcement of drug laws. The act encouraged the military to (a) make available equipment, military bases, and research facilities to federal, state, and local police; (b) train and advise civilian police on the use of the equipment; and (c) assist law enforcement personnel in keeping drugs from entering the country. The act also authorized the military to share information acquired during military operations with civilian law enforcement agencies.

As the drug war escalated throughout the 1980s, the military was drawn further and further into the prohibition effort by a series of executive and congressional initiatives:

- In 1986 President Ronald Reagan issued a National Decision Security Directive designating drugs as an official threat to "national security," which encouraged a tight-knit relationship between civilian law enforcement and the military.

> *"As the drug war escalated throughout the 1980s, the military was drawn further and further into the prohibition effort."*

- In 1987 Congress set up an administrative apparatus to facilitate transactions between civilian law enforcement officials and the military. For example, a special office with an 800 number was established to handle inquiries by police officials regarding acquisition of military hardware.

- In 1988 Congress directed the National Guard to assist law enforcement agencies in counterdrug operations. Today National Guard units in all 50 states fly across America's landscape in dark green helicopters, wearing camouflage uniforms and armed with machine guns, in search of marijuana fields.

- In 1989 President George Bush created six regional joint task forces (JTFs) within the Department of Defense. Those task forces are charged with coordinating the activities of the military and police agencies in the drug war, including joint training of military units and civilian police. JTFs can be called on by civilian law enforcement agencies in counterdrug cases when police feel the need for military reinforcement.

- In 1994 the Department of Justice and the Department of Defense signed a memorandum of understanding, which has enabled the military to transfer technology to state and local police departments. Civilian officers now have at their disposal an array of high-tech military items previously reserved for use during wartime.

All of those measures have resulted in the militarization of a wide range of activity in the United States that had been previously considered the domain of civilian law enforcement. As [reporter David C. Morrison] observed, "Not since federal troops were deployed to the former Confederate states during Reconstruction has the U.S. military been so intimately involved in civilian law enforcement."

The Emergence of SWAT Teams

Not only is the military directly involved in law enforcement; police departments are increasingly emulating the tactics of the armed forces in their everyday activities. This aspect of the militarization phenomenon has gone largely unnoticed. . . .

There is agreement in police literature that the incident that inspired the SWAT [Special Weapons and Tactics] concept occurred in 1966. In August of that year a deranged man climbed to the top of the 32-story clock tower at the University of Texas in Austin. For 90 minutes he randomly shot 46 people, killing 15 of them, until two police officers got to the top of the tower and killed him. The Austin episode was so blatant [writes Robert Snow] that it "shattered the last myth of safety Americans enjoyed [and] was the final impetus the chiefs of police needed," to form their own SWAT teams. Shortly thereafter, the Los Angeles Police Department formed the first SWAT team and, it is said, originated the acronym SWAT to describe its elite force. The Los Angeles SWAT unit acquired national prestige when it was used successfully against the Black Panthers in 1969 and the Symbionese Liberation Army in 1973.

Much like the FBI, the modern SWAT team was born of public fear and the perception by police that crime had reached such proportions and criminals had become so invincible that more armament and more training were needed. SWAT team members have come to consider themselves members of an elite unit with specialized skills and more of a military ethos than the normal police structure. Another striking similarity with the FBI is that SWAT units have gained their status and legitimacy in the public eye by their performance in a few sensational events.

The earliest SWAT teams consisted of small units that could be called into action to deal with difficult situations, such as incidents involving hostages, barricaded suspects, or hijackers. Early SWAT team members were not unlike regular police officers and were only slightly better equipped.

SWAT Teams Everywhere, Doing Everything

The 1980s and 1990s saw marked changes in the number of permanent SWAT teams across the country, in their mission and deployment, and in their tactical armament. According to a 1997 study of SWAT teams conducted by Peter

Kraska and Victor Kappeler of Eastern Kentucky University, nearly 90 percent of the police departments surveyed in cities with populations over 50,000 had paramilitary units, as did 70 percent of the departments surveyed in communities with populations under 50,000. Although the proliferation of those special units was slow in the late 1960s and early 1970s, their numbers took a leap in the mid-1970s, and growth has remained high since the 1980s. In fact, most SWAT teams have been created in the 1980s and 1990s. Towns like Jasper, Lakeland, and Palm Beach, Florida; Lakewood, New Jersey; Chapel Hill, North Carolina; Charlottesville, Virginia; and Harwich, Massachusetts, have SWAT teams. The campus police at the University of Central Florida have a SWAT unit—even though the county SWAT team is available. Kraska refers to the proliferation as the "militarization of Mayberry," and he is rightly alarmed that the special units are becoming a normal and permanent part of law enforcement agencies.

Under the Military Cooperation with Law Enforcement Officials Act, Congress directed the military to make equipment and facilities available to civilian police in the anti-drug effort. As a result, police departments began to acquire more sophisticated tactical equipment: automatic weapons with laser sights and sound suppressors, surveillance equipment such as Laser Bugs that can detect sounds inside a building by bouncing a laser beam off a window, pinhole cameras, flash and noise grenades, rubber bullets, bullet-proof apparel, battering rams, and more. The Boone County Sheriff's office in Indiana has acquired an amphibious armored personnel carrier. In Fresno, California, the SWAT unit has access to two helicopters equipped with night vision goggles and an armored personnel carrier with a turret. According to Cal Black, a former SWAT commander for the FBI, "The equipment SWAT teams use today is many times more sophisticated than it was when I began in SWAT in the 1970s. . . . Because of this high-tech equipment, the ability of SWAT teams has increased dramatically."

> *"SWAT team members have come to consider themselves members of an elite unit with specialized skills and more of a military ethos."*

The National Institute of Justice report on the DOJ-DOD [Department of Justice-Department of Defense] technology "partnership" boasted a number of high-tech items that SWAT teams now have at their disposal. Included among the showcase military technologies deemed applicable to law enforcement were "inconspicuous systems that can detect from more than 30 feet away weapons with little or no metal content as well as those made of metal." Other items in the pipeline include "a gas-launched, wireless, electric stun projectile"; a "vehicular laser surveillance and dazzler system"; "pyrotechnic devices such as flash-bang grenades [and] smoke grenades"; instruments of "crowd control"; mobile, even hand-held, systems to locate gunfire; and tagging equipment to locate, identify, and monitor the "movement of individuals, vehicles and containers." Special body armor and helmets are also under consideration. Nick Pastore, former police chief in New Haven, Connecticut, says: "I was offered tanks, bazookas, anything I wanted. . . . I turned it all down because it feeds a mind-set that you're not a police officer serving a community, you're a soldier at war."

An even more disturbing development reported in the Kraska-Kappeler study, however, is the growing tendency of police departments to use SWAT units in *routine* policing activity. The Fresno SWAT unit, for example, sends its 40-person team, with full military dress and gear, into the inner city "war zone" to deal with problems of drugs, gangs, and crime. One survey respondent described his department's use of SWAT teams in the following way:

> We're into saturation patrols in hot spots. We do a lot of our work with the SWAT unit because we have bigger guns. We send out two, two-to-four-men cars, *we look for minor violations* and do jump-outs, either on people on the street or automobiles. After we jump-out the second car provides periphery cover with an ostentatious display of weaponry. We're sending a clear message: if the shootings don't stop, we'll shoot someone.

A midwestern community with a population of 75,000 sends out patrols dressed in tactical uniform in a military personnel carrier. The armored vehicle, according to the SWAT commander, stops "suspicious vehicles and people. We stop anything that moves. We'll sometimes even surround suspicious homes and bring out the MP5s (machine gun pistols)."

Unfortunately, it is likely that the number of SWAT "patrols" will rise in the future. In their survey, when Kraska and Kappeler asked the question, Is your department using the tactical operations unit as a proactive patrol unit to aid high crime areas? 107 departments indicated that they were. Sixty-one percent of all respondents thought it was a good idea. In fact, 63 percent of the departments in that survey agreed that SWAT units "play an important role in community policing strategies." According to *Police* magazine, "Police officers working in patrol vehicles, dressed in urban tactical gear and armed with automatic weapons are here—and they're here to stay.". . .

A Warrior Mentality

With widespread political sanction, the military is now encouraged to share training, equipment, technology—and, most subtle, mentality—with state and local civilian police. SWAT team members undergo rigorous training similar to that given military special operations units. Training, as [the Kraska-Kappeler] study has noted, "may seem to be a purely technical exercise, [but] it actually plays a central role in paramilitary subculture" and moreover reinforces "the importance of feeling and thinking as a team." The research of Kraska and Kappeler revealed that SWAT units are often trained alongside, or with the support of, military special forces personnel. Of 459 SWAT teams across the country,

46 percent acquired their initial training from "police officers with special operations experience in the military," and 43 percent with "active-duty military experts in special operations." Almost 46 percent currently conducted training exercises with "active-duty military experts in special operations." Twenty-three respondents to the survey indicated that they trained with either Navy SEALs or Army Rangers. . . .

> *"Because of their close collaboration with the military, SWAT units are taking on the warrior mentality of our military's special forces."*

Because of their close collaboration with the military, SWAT units are taking on the warrior mentality of our military's special forces. SWAT team organization resembles that of a special combat unit, with a commander, a tactical team leader, a scout, a rear guard or "defenseman," a marksman (sniper), a spotter, a gasman, and paramedics. Moreover, SWAT teams, like military special forces, are elite units: Their rigorous team training; high-tech armament; and "battle dress uniforms," consisting of lace-up combat boots, full body armor, Kevlar helmets, and goggles with "ninja" style hoods, reinforce their elitism within law enforcement agencies. One commander—who disapproved of proactive SWAT policing and turned down requests from team members to dress in black battle dress uniforms while on patrol—nevertheless understood its attraction to team members: "I can't blame them, we're a very elite unit, they just want to be distinguishable."

The so-called war on drugs and other martial metaphors are turning high-crime areas into "war zones," citizens into potential enemies, and police officers into soldiers. Preparing the ground for the 1994 technology transfer agreement between the Department of Defense and the Department of Justice, Attorney General Reno addressed the defense and intelligence community. In her speech, Reno compared the drug war to the Cold War, and the armed and dangerous enemies abroad to those at home:

> So let me welcome you to the kind of war our police fight every day. And let me challenge you to turn your skills that served us so well in the Cold War to helping us with the war we're now fighting daily in the streets of our towns and cities across the Nation.

The martial rhetoric can be found in both political parties. Bill McCollum (R-Fla.), chairman of the Subcommittee on Crime of the House Judiciary Committee, has criticized the Clinton administration for not waging the war on drugs aggressively enough: "The drug crisis is a top—if not the top—national security threat facing our nation today . . . [the Clinton] administration's clear unwillingness to wage an all-out drug war cannot go unchallenged." In the current political climate, anyone who does not support an escalation of the drug war is condemned for being "soft on crime."

Departmental SWAT teams have accepted the military as a model for their behavior and outlook, which is distinctly impersonal and elitist; American streets are viewed as the "front" and American citizens as the "enemy." The sharing of training and technology by the military and law enforcement agencies has produced a shared mindset, and the mindset of the warrior is simply not appropriate for the civilian police officer charged with enforcing the law. The soldier confronts an enemy in a life-or-death situation. The soldier learns to use lethal force on the enemy, both uniformed and civilian, irrespective of age or gender. The soldier must sometimes follow orders unthinkingly, acts in concert with his comrades, and initiates violence on command. That mentality, with which new recruits are strenuously indoctrinated in boot camp, can be a matter of survival to the soldier and the nation at war.

Keeping the Peace?

The civilian law enforcement officer, on the other hand, confronts not an "enemy" but individuals who, like him, are both subject to the nation's laws and protected by the Bill of Rights. Although the police officer can use force in life-threatening situations, the Constitution and numerous Supreme Court rulings have circumscribed the police officer's direct use of force, as well as his power of search and seizure. In terms of violence, the police officer's role is—or should be—purely reactive. When a police officer begins to think like a soldier, tragic consequences—such as the loss of innocent life at Waco—will result.

After some controversial SWAT shootings spawned several wrongful death lawsuits against the police department of Albuquerque, New Mexico, the city hired Professor Sam Walker of the University of Nebraska to study its departmental practices. According to Walker: "The rate of killings by the police was just off the charts. . . . They had an organizational culture that led them to escalate situations upward rather than de-escalating." The city of Albuquerque subsequently hired a new police chief and dismantled its SWAT unit.

The tiny town of Dinuba, California (population 15,000), created a SWAT unit in the spring of 1997. A few months later an innocent man, Ramon Gallardo, was killed by the SWAT team when it raided his home looking for one of his teenage sons. The SWAT unit rushed into the Gallardo household at 7 a.m. wearing hoods and masks, yelling "search warrant." Gallardo and his wife were awakened by the ruckus, but before they could determine what was happening, Ramon was shot 15 times.

> *"When a police officer begins to think like a soldier, tragic consequences . . . will result."*

A police brutality lawsuit was later brought against the city. At trial, the police said they had to shoot in self-defense because Gallardo had grabbed a knife. Gallardo's wife testified that the knife on the scene did not belong to her husband and alleged that the police had planted it there to legitimize the shooting. The jury awarded the Gallardo family $12.5 million. Because the whopping verdict exceeded the small town's insurance coverage, the city is now in financial straits. After Gallardo's killing, the city fathers of Dinuba disbanded the SWAT unit and gave its military equipment to another police department.

Some local jurisdictions may wish to retain SWAT units for the special skills they possess, but the deployment of such units should be limited to *extraordinary* circumstances—such as a hostage situation. If a SWAT unit is created (or retained), the need for that unit should be assessed annually by locally elected officials. Policy-makers must be especially wary of "mission creep" and guard against it. Inactive SWAT teams have a strong incentive to expand their original "emergency" mission into more routine policing activities to justify their existence. In recent years, city officials in Dallas and Seattle have curtailed the activity of their SWAT units, taking them off drug raids and suicide calls. Other cities should follow their lead by curtailing the SWAT mission—or even dismantling the entire unit as was done in Albuquerque and Dinuba.

> *"Confusing the police function with the military function can lead to . . . unnecessary shootings and killings."*

The militarization of law enforcement in America is a deeply disturbing development. Police officers are not supposed to be warriors. The job of a police officer is to keep the peace while adhering to constitutional procedures. Soldiers, on the other hand, consider enemy personnel human targets. Confusing the police function with the military function can lead to dangerous and unintended consequences—such as unnecessary shootings and killings.

The proliferation of SWAT teams is particularly worrisome because such units are rarely needed. SWAT teams are created to deal with emergency situations that are beyond the capacity of the ordinary street cop. But, as time passes, inactive SWAT units tend to jettison their original, limited mission for more routine policing activities. Local jurisdictions should carefully assess the need for SWAT units and guard against the danger of mission creep. SWAT teams do possess specialized skills, but they should only be deployed on those extraordinary occasions when their skills are necessary—such as a hostage situation.

More generally, Congress should recognize that federal policies have contributed to the culture of paramilitarism that currently pervades many local police departments. Federal lawmakers should discourage paramilitarism by restoring the traditional American principle of civil-military separation embodied in the Posse Comitatus Act. The Military Cooperation with Law Enforcement Officials Act created a dangerous loophole in the Posse Comitatus Act. That loophole should be closed immediately. Congress should also abolish all military-civilian law enforcement joint task forces and see to it that all military hardware loaned, given, or sold to law enforcement agencies is destroyed or returned. Armored personnel carriers and machine guns, should not be a part of everyday law enforcement in a free society.

Aggressively Policing the Poor Leads to Abusive Police Practices

by Daniel HoSang

About the author: *Daniel HoSang is executive director of People United for a Better Oakland (PUEBLO), a grassroots social justice organization.*

[On January 6, 1994], an army of at least twenty federal and local cops descended on Melinda Cosby's house along a quiet residential street in working class East Oakland. They arrived at sunrise fully armed, a battering ram in hand and automatic weapons drawn, as if about to raid a hostile village. Their mission? To investigate what turned out to be false allegations of credit card fraud by Ms. Cosby. She was not home at the time, but her husband, Nathan, awoke to the sound of his front door crashing in. An instant later, he lay dead on his bedroom floor, shot in the back of the head through a window by an officer stationed in the backyard of the home.

Neither the officer who murdered Nathan Cosby nor the supervisors in charge of the mission were dismissed as a result of their conduct. The City of Oakland has yet to compensate Melinda Cosby for her loss. Church leaders, the school employees union that counted Nathan Cosby as a member, family members, and neighbors confronted the police chief at a community meeting. . . . They demanded to know how paramilitary forces could be deployed in a residential neighborhood with no repercussions. Who were the police accountable to?

An Occupying Army

To be sure, renegade police departments seem to have been the rule rather than the exception in the past few decades. In Philadelphia in the late 1970s and early 1980s, when police chief and then mayor Frank Rizzo reigned, the lines between civilian and military leadership were blurry at best. Likewise, in Los Angeles in the late 1980s and early 1990s, Chief Darryl Gates' LAPD seemed

Daniel HoSang, "The Economics of the New Brutality," *ColorLines*, vol. 2, Winter 1999–2000, pp. 21–26.

to many to be an army that existed to perpetuate its own power. And in 1996, the New Orleans police department was rocked by scandals in which four officers were charged with murder. Between 1993 and 1996, fifty New Orleans cops were arrested for felonies including bank robbery and rape.

[Writer] James Baldwin captured the sense of subjugation and domination wrought by this type of police conduct nearly forty years ago when he wrote that a police officer moves through Harlem "like an occupying soldier in a bitterly hostile country; which is precisely what and where he is, and is the reason he walks in twos and threes."

But while headline-grabbing incidents of police violence seem as common now as they were back then, the law enforcement strategies and priorities that underlie those incidents and the regulation of police officers themselves are changing. Over the last thirty years, many departments have increased training, education, and accreditation requirements for officers and enhanced police salary and benefits. Nationally, there has been nearly a ten-fold increase in the number of citizen police review agencies during the same period. . . .

The Department of Justice has launched probes into police practices in at least ten agencies, including the police departments of New York City, Los Angeles, Pittsburgh, and Buffalo. In response, some of the dirtiest police precincts in Philadelphia, New York, and New Orleans cleaned house. An increasing number of local, state, and federal law enforcement agencies have agreed to collect data to determine whether their departments use racial profiling to enforce traffic laws, resulting in the harassment of black and brown motorists. In New York City, shooting deaths of civilians by police have fallen from about 60 per year in the early 1970s to about 25 per year in the mid-1990s.

Yet on the streets of Harlem, East Los Angeles, or Indianapolis, people of color fear the police more than ever. A . . . *New York Times* survey revealed that nine out of ten black New York residents said they thought police often engaged in brutality against blacks, and nearly two-thirds said people of color in general experience police violence. Lawsuit settlements and judgments resulting from police misconduct are at an all-time high in New York City, reaching $27.3 million in 1996 alone. Ninety-eight percent of complainants to the Oakland Citizen Police Review Board are people of color, though whites comprise nearly forty percent of the city's population.

Which way, then, are the winds really blowing? Police are subject to more scrutiny and regulation than ever before, but police misconduct seems to grow unchecked. A new style of policing has emerged from changes in the political economy and shifts in the racial landscape.

Policing As Economic Development

Police strategies and roles are increasingly intertwined with economic development and private investment objectives. In the last thirty years, according to urban theorist David Harvey, the expansion of global capitalism and the mobility of capital has increased economic competition between different regions within the U.S. As cities and regions vie with one another to establish identities as safe, investment-friendly consumer centers, containment of all the "troublesome" poor folks and people of color become priority number one. Local police agencies regulate low-income communities with high unemployment and limit their access to public and private space.

> *"The enforcement priorities of the police illustrates a larger concern with the regulation and containment of immigrant communities of color."*

Eric Tang of the grassroots organization Committee Against Anti-Asian Violence observes that in New York City, police harassment of Asian Americans has taken a different bent. . . . "Police have shifted away from focusing on gangs and more towards regulating and controlling working and unemployed Asians, and containing them within Chinatown." Tang says police harass vendors who are moving to the northern borders of Chinatown, as well as the working poor that hang out in the parks and on the street corners throughout the neighborhood. Whether targeting workers in Chinatown or Southeast Asian youth in the Bronx, Tang says the enforcement priorities of the police illustrates a larger concern with the regulation and containment of immigrant communities of color in general.

New York City, in its effort to forge an identity as a safe cosmopolitan community welcoming to the professional and managerial class, has led the way . . . in criminalizing a broad swath of public activities that has led to unprecedented harassment and detention of poor, working class, and homeless people by the police. Civilian complaints for excess use of force have risen 41 percent since the New York City police began widespread arrests for minor violations.

Mayor Giuliani has been explicit in his intention to physically remove and contain any of the visible affects of poverty (i.e. homelessness) that dare to share space with gentrification and development initiatives. In 1997 and 1998, officers with the NYPD's street crimes unit frisked more than 45,000 people thought to be carrying guns, but they arrested fewer than 10,000. This policing strategy allows the police to detain, question, and thus regulate tens of thousands of mostly low-income people of color.

Indianapolis, Baltimore, New Orleans, San Francisco, Oakland, and Seattle have followed suit with similar "zero tolerance" policing strategies lifted directly from Giuliani's book.

Van Jones, executive director of the Ella Baker Center for Human Rights in San Francisco, observes that this strategy means that law enforcement is permeating the everyday life of many communities. "We see police involvement in the provision and regulation of social services, neighborhood development initiatives, and schools more than ever before." As circumstances within acutely poor neighborhoods worsen or remain the same while middle and upper class communities frolic in growing prosperity, police are charged with regulating the unrest these inequalities engender. To be sure, this is a highly racialized mandate.

Reclaiming the City

Urban scholar Neil Smith describes many Western cities at the dawn of the millennium as "revanchist," importing a term used to describe the reactionary movement in late 19th century France bent on retaliating against the French people following a working class uprising. Smith argues that the rightwing French movement, "built on popular nationalism and devoted to a vengeful and reactionary taking of the country," offers an appropriate framework to understand the U.S. today. In this context, the "taking back" of urban spaces for gentrification and development purposes, cloaked in the smug language of civic morality, seeks to exact revenge for the "theft" of the city by the poor, immigrants, and people of color during the last thirty years.

The frontier-like language of conquest and subjugation that underlies these strategies rationalizes a host of abusive police practices (the frontier is, after all, a violent and bloody space) meted out in the spirit of urban renewal. Mayor Jerry Brown's recent, highly racialized pledge to drive the "unemployed criminals" out of Oakland, coupled with his thesis that the surest path to economic development is through a dramatic reduction of crime, create a context that virtually necessitates a certain level of police brutality. Thus, [in 1998], when a freelance videographer captured police kicking an African American robbery suspect in the groin as he lay on the ground with seven police-inflicted bullet wounds, neither Brown nor any members of the City Council openly condemned the cops' behavior. These and other daily acts of violence are a central part of the police's role in the reclamation of the city.

> *"The 'taking back' of urban spaces for gentrification . . . seeks to exact revenge for the 'theft' of the city by the poor."*

Identifying an Enemy

Community policing and the neighborhood-cop partnerships they create allow a deeper penetration of vengeful philosophy into communities of color themselves. Nearly thirty percent of Latinos and 26 percent of African Americans report that they "very frequently" worry about getting beaten up, knifed, or shot. Only nine percent of whites report this same concern. U.C. Berkeley professor Ruth Wilson Gilmore writes that "crime is used to organize people's fears brought about by the vertigo of economic insecurity by identifying an enemy whose vanquishment will restore security." Communities of color and low-income communities are not exempt from this anxiety.

In this context, the "occupying army" metaphor invoked by James Baldwin forty years ago has shifted. Neighborhood watch programs, vehicle forfeiture measures aimed at regulating drug sales and prostitution, and anti-loitering measures that target young people are frequently cloaked in the notion that "good citizens" must "take back" and "reclaim" their communities from the lawless elements that have been permitted to run amok. Increasing schisms of generation and class within communities of color demarcate the boundaries between the "good guys" and the "bad guys."

The Miami Metro-Dade Tactical Narcotics Team (TNT) typifies many of these partnerships. Police confer with some community residents to identify the targets of the program and conduct intense, block-by-block sweeps, converging on neighborhoods with militaristic force and zealously prosecuting arrestees. The basis of the approach, according to Major Dan Flynn, is that "people

> *"[Aggressive policing is] frequently cloaked in the notion that 'good citizens' must 'take back' and 'reclaim' their communities from . . . lawless elements."*

want heavy-handed law enforcement that is aggressive, not abusive." Miami University professor Roger Dunham, who studied the TNT program, reveals the intent of the initiative: "Police are able to go into these neighborhoods, do intensive enforcement, and keep the people on their side."

From this perspective, the investigations of the Department of Justice, the expansion of police review boards, and the larger professionalization of policing are not insignificant. They are linked to an effort to win support for training the focus and attention of policing away from the unchecked and seemingly random racist thuggery of the past and towards a brutality specifically aimed at the poorest, most exploited sections of working class communities of color.

Security Without Brutality

Given the tacit support among many sectors of the middle and even working class for Giuliani's policing strategies (76 percent of whites and 52 percent of blacks recently polled support his crime policy), fundamental limits to police power and authority seem unlikely. But how can progressive forces present the most formidable challenge to the expanding police state? Two challenges are central.

First, the fear of crime has led some elements within working class communities of color (particularly older residents and property owners) to embrace the presence of police in their neighborhoods. Will Gonzalez of Philadelphia's Police-Barrio Relations Project argues that these communities must be presented with alternatives. "One of the challenges is to help people understand that you can have security without brutality," he says. "You can have public security with integrity." Jones and Gonzalez both point out that there exists no hardened consensus for police brutality and that this debate should not be conceded to reactionary forces.

Second, organizers must link their efforts to secure reform strategies (such as civilian police review boards and other accountability mechanisms) with broader efforts to confront gentrification and development strategies. Activists in New York City have successfully linked the police slaying of 23-year-old Guinean immigrant Amadou Diallo directly to the city's zero tolerance police strategy. For the time being, Giuliani has retreated to a more defensive posture in explaining his public safety policies.

In San Francisco, organizers have framed police harassment of the homeless, who are regularly cited or jailed during certain enforcement periods, in the context of the city's broader agenda to turn the entire city into a yuppie playground. These strategies require police accountability organizers to link with groups that have traditionally sat out confrontations over the role of the police—progressive labor unions, housing activists, and community development folks. To the extent that police conduct directly emanates from broad racial and economic imperatives, organizing to regulate that conduct must rally broader forces to its cause.

The War on Drugs Promotes the Unnecessary Use of Deadly Force

by Paul Armentano

About the author: *Paul Armentano is a senior policy analyst at the National Organization for the Reform of Marijuana Laws (NORML) Foundation in Washington, D.C.*

Few photos have inspired as many words as that of a young Cuban boy face to face with a MP-5 machine gun. The Associated Press photo of federal armed agents seizing Elián González from his Miami relatives aroused outrage among many Americans and—perhaps ironically—several congressional conservatives.[1] And while the photograph was unique, the act it captured was hardly unusual. Raids similar to the one on the González family home occur many times a day in the name of the War on Drugs, often with far more tragic results.

Tales of Tragedy

Take the case of Scott Bryant. Thirteen Wisconsin sheriff's deputies burst into the 29-year-old's trailer on the night of April 17, 1995, executing a no-knock warrant. Bryant, who was unarmed, was shot and killed during the assault while his 7-year-old son looked on. Police seized less than three grams of marijuana. On review, the county district attorney found that the shooting was "not in any way justified."

Robert Lee Peters had just settled down to watch a movie with his family when St. Petersburg police officers smashed through his front door unan-

---

1. In November 1999, Elián was rescued from a sinking Cuban refugee boat. His mother was killed in the incident. His father, Juan Miguel, who remained in Cuba, demanded that Elián be returned to him, claiming the Miami relatives who took him in were kidnappers. The relatives and their anti-Castro, Cuban American supporters claimed that to return him to Cuba would be cruel. The relatives dared the government to take Elián by force, which it did in a predawn raid on April 22, 2002. Elián was eventually returned to his father.

nounced with a battering ram in July 1994. Fearing that his home was being burglarized, Peters grabbed a gun and fired at his attackers. The officers returned fire, killing the 33-year-old father of two. Police confiscated two pounds of marijuana.

Sometimes victims possess no drugs at all. Just ask the family of Annie Rae Dixon, an 84-year-old grandmother shot and killed during a 2 a.m. drug raid of her east Texas home in 1992. No drugs were ever found on the premises. One officer later hypothesized that his pistol accidentally discharged when he kicked open Dixon's bedroom door. "[I] started throwing my guts up crying because I knew I had shot somebody that didn't have no reason to be shot," he said. No less vicious was the 1998 shooting death of Pedro Oregon Navarro by Houston police. Six officers stormed his home at 1:40 a.m. in a military-style raid after a man arrested for public drunkenness said Navarro was a drug dealer. Agents shot the bleary-eyed Navarro 12 times, killing him. A search of his residence produced no illicit drugs or weapons.

> *"Congress should address the broader issue of whether the escalating enforcement of drug prohibition threatens the right . . . to be secure in our homes."*

California rancher Donald Scott, 61, met a similar fate in 1992, when a team of local and federal agents burst into his mansion during a midnight raid, ostensibly to search for marijuana. When Scott reached for a pistol to defend himself, he was shot dead. An investigation by the Ventura County district attorney later revealed that the Los Angeles County Sheriff's Department had fabricated evidence that Scott was cultivating pot because it hoped to seize his property, which was adjacent to a federal park. Ventura County officials eventually agreed to pay the Scott family $4 million in damages; the federal government agreed to pay $1 million.

More recently, a SWAT team from El Monte, California, raided a home in neighboring Compton on the evening of August 9, 1999, killing retired grandfather Mario Paz by shooting him twice in the back. Police executing the search warrant said they believed the house was sometimes used as a mail drop by a local drug dealer. Although police found no drugs and filed no charges against any of the surviving family members, they refused to return an estimated $11,000 seized during the deadly raid.

Some victims are the victims of sheer error. Take the September 29, 1999, assault by Denver SWAT agents on the home of Ismael Mena. Mena, a 45-year-old father of nine, was shot eight times and killed by police in the unannounced raid. No drugs were found, and police now speculate that they may have had an incorrect address.

An equally vicious police blunder claimed the life of Reverend Accelyne Williams, a 75-year-old retired Methodist minister who suffered a fatal heart attack when Boston police broke into his apartment on March 24, 1994. Acting on false information provided by a confidential informant, anti-drug agents chased Williams to his bedroom, shoved him to the floor, and pointed guns at his head—inducing the heart attack that killed him. Boston Police Commissioner Paul Evans later admitted at a press conference that police likely raided the wrong apartment. "If that is the case, then there will be an apology," he said. Two years later, the city paid a $1 million settlement to Williams's widow.

William Pitt expressed the importance Americans once placed on the sanctity of the home from trespass when he said: "The poorest man may in his cottage bid defiance to all the forces of the Crown. It may be frail—its roof may shake—the wind may blow through it—the storm may enter—the rain may enter—but the King of England cannot enter—all his force dares not cross the threshold of the ruined tenement."

The fact that our government and law-enforcement personnel now view the sovereignty of the home as a quaint anachronism should disturb us all. In this regard, the photo of a terrified Elián González is a legitimate cause for congressional concern. However, rather than use this opportunity to attack the Clinton administration's handling of one, highly politicized case, Congress should address the broader issue of whether the escalating enforcement of drug prohibition threatens the right of all of us to be secure in our homes. To the families of the victims named above, the answer is all too clear.

Chapter 3

What Strategies Reduce Police Brutality?

CURRENT CONTROVERSIES

Chapter Preface

When police officers kill, public debate over the use of lethal force often follows. Some commentators suggest that the police should use alternatives to lethal force to reduce police brutality while others argue that current alternatives to lethal force are ineffective.

Research conducted by the International Association of Chiefs of Police (IACP) on the use and prevalence of deadly force shows that when given the choice, police officers are much more likely to use less-than-lethal means to handle a volatile situation. Data collected in 1999 from 319 police departments around the United States reveals that of the thirty-nine thousand calls received, police used force, including lethal force, only 3.41 times per ten thousand calls. "The image is that police use fatal force at higher rates," says John Firman, director of research for IACP. The data, he contends, proves otherwise. "Obviously," Firman maintains, "police are using a huge amount of discretion when encountering a resisting subject."

Despite evidence that the police do not abuse the use of lethal force, some experts argue that training in less-than-lethal methods would save lives. "We have a saying," explains Captain Sid Heal of the Los Angeles County Sheriff's Department, "'If the only tool you have is a hammer, you tend to think of every problem as a nail,' you don't really have any other way of solving the problem." If the police begin to see less-than-lethal force as another tool, supporters reason, fewer suspects will die. Major Steve Ijames of the Springfield, Missouri, police department claims, "There is enough anecdotal evidence to show that when police officers appropriately use nonlethal weapons such as pepper spray or find nonlethal ways to defuse a potentially deadly situation, the number of injuries and deaths—for both officers and others—decreases significantly." Since 1995, Captain Heal maintains, fifteen hundred to two thousand lives have been saved by the use of less-than-lethal weapons.

Other analysts suggest that an additional incentive for the use of less-than lethal force is to prevent the civil unrest and disorder that sometimes follow a fatal shooting. One tragic example of civil unrest followed the April 29, 1992, acquittal of three Los Angeles police officers accused of beating African American suspect Rodney King. Following the verdict, riots broke out in Los Angeles, and days later many of the city's minority communities lay in ruins. Sixty people lost their lives, hundreds were injured, and 850 buildings were set afire. Property losses exceeded 1 billion dollars. According to Rose M. Ochi, director of the U.S. Department of Justice's Community Relations Service, which helps state and local officials resolve and prevent racial and ethnic conflicts, the use of nonlethal weapons could prevent unnecessary civil unrest such as that which occurred in Los Angeles. "Incidents of police use of excessive and lethal force can be prevented, and the turmoil in the communities in the aftermath of such an incident can be reduced," says Ochi.

Other experts argue, however, that decisions about the conditions under which a police officer may use lethal force should not be based on public attitudes. Often, the public does not understand what really goes on in armed confrontations between suspects and police officers, these analysts argue. K-9 Officer Brad Smith of the West Covina Police Department explains: "Police officers are asked to make split second life or death decisions. We have to decide in a blink of an eye if we are going to shoot or not shoot." Even those who advocate less-than-lethal force advise caution. Retired police captain and weapons training instructor Cecil Pearson suggests, "When examining less-lethal options, we have to look and see where such tactics fit in around the concept and use of lethal force. . . . These devices should not be considered when facing any suspect that is armed with a firearm. Nor should they be considered in armed rapid intervention and hostage rescue. They are not designed for such use and are entirely inappropriate." The U.S. Circuit Court of Appeals supports this position. In *Plakas v. Drinski*, the court stated, "There is no precedent in this Circuit (or any other Circuit) which says that the Constitution requires law enforcement officers to use all feasible alternatives to avoid a situation where deadly force can justifiably be used."

Other critics of less-than-lethal force suggest that the alternatives are not effective to protect officers or suspects. British weapons expert and author Michael Yardley argues that "most of the systems so far tested have significant drawbacks." Bean bags—lead shot in a small bag—may be rolled up, placed in a shell case, and fired. The bag unrolls in flight and hits the target flat, thus causing less serious injury. However, if the bag does not unroll, it can penetrate the body, severely injuring or killing the suspect. Moreover, bean bags do not always incapacitate the suspect. Stun guns require officers to get very close to the suspect and are thus impractical in many situations. Air Tasers that use compressed air to fire darts at a suspect at a range of twenty feet are also often impractical and may cause the suspect unnecessary suffering. Chemical weapons such as pepper spray also require officers to be close to the subject. In addition, sprays do not always incapacitate suspects and raise health concerns for both the officer and the suspect. Tranquilizer darts take time to disable the suspect and have been known to kill. Devices that use light to illuminate and temporarily blind the suspect remain unproven, and officers must make contact with the suspect's eyes if the devices are to be effective. None of these methods guarantees that the suspect will be disabled and, Yardley concludes, "The application of anything, which cannot reliably achieve instant incapacitation, must be limited."

Whether using less-than-lethal force will reduce officer-involved deaths remains controversial. The authors in the following chapter recommend other strategies to reduce police brutality.

Public Protest Against Police Brutality Promotes Accountability

by Edward Lewis

About the author: *Edward Lewis is the publisher of* Essence, *an African American lifestyle magazine.*

We are entering a new millennium that will offer new opportunities and challenges. We must all realize that how we as a community take advantage of those opportunities and find solutions to those challenges is key to bringing us together to make our world a better place.

In nearly 30 years as a businessman, I have taken on many issues and supported many causes. I have gladly donated time and financial support to local and national small-business development and to educational and arts organizations—all in an effort to support those who may need assistance, encourage those who are taking steps toward a successful career, and provide a chance for those who want to further their learning.

But today I and millions of men and women across this nation are afraid—for ourselves, our fathers and brothers, our sons and daughters. What do we fear? Police brutality. This phrase, the ultimate contradiction, contains two words that should never be uttered together. Police in this country are sworn to protect the citizens. And yet in the last few years we've been sickened by highly publicized accounts of public servants brutalizing men—and women—in our communities. There are instances every day, I'm sure, we never hear about. But the stories that make the headlines—Rodney King, Abner Louima, Amadou Diallo—fill us with outrage, contempt and disbelief.[1]

---

1. King was beaten by three Los Angeles police officers as their supervisor watched on March 3, 1991. After the officers were acquitted of excessive force on April 29, 1992, rioting broke out in Los Angeles. Louima, a Haitian immigrant, was beaten and sodomized in a New York City police precinct house on August 9, 1997. Diallo, a West African immigrant, was killed after New York City police officers fired forty-one shots while he stood in his Bronx doorway on February 4, 1999.

As African-American men, we face enough daily challenges to try the patience of saints: inadequate opportunities for higher education; high unemployment rates; no guaranteed equal pay for equal work; limited economic empowerment; a constant struggle for social acceptance. We should not have to add to that list a fear that protectors of society may abuse us physically or treat us with disrespect and incivility.

> *"We must join to denounce police brutality and disrespect."*

It's most distressing that our concern is born out of the actions of those who are sworn to serve and protect us—those officers of the law whose salaries we pay.

We're in the midst of a tragic imbalance in our communities. We live in cities and towns that are divided, and we must make it known that we will do whatever it takes to balance the scales.

Denouncing Police Brutality

[In the spring of 1998], in New York I proudly joined a group of men—among them the Reverends Al Sharpton, Jesse Jackson and Jim Forbes of Riverside Church, former New York City mayor David Dinkins, Congressman Charles Rangel, Dennis Rivera of Local 1199, and publisher Earl Graves—in a rally against police brutality. We came together that day—businessmen, politicians, community leaders—as concerned American citizens.

We should not be afraid! We must join to denounce police brutality and disrespect. We must denounce the trampling of our civil liberties in the name of crime reduction. We must denounce abuse of power, and we must denounce the "us against them" attitude.

It's time to begin the healing process, time to bridge the gap of miscommunication, and time to cultivate an atmosphere of mutual respect between law enforcement and our communities. We must acknowledge that our streets are safer and agree that the majority of police officers do their jobs well.

But the leaders of our cities and communities must also acknowledge the problems. Until the mayors and the police commissioners—and all our elected officials—recognize these issues and work for the community instead of against it, we will live in fear. We should not have to wonder how many more Abner Louimas will suffer horrific pain and indignation. We should not be sickened by worry that another Amadou Diallo will needlessly, tragically lose his life. There must be no more victims.

I urge you to join me in this battle. The fight will not be won with words alone. Certainly our politicians, elected officials, and community leaders must be held accountable. But we must do our part first. If we do not exercise our right to vote, if we do not financially support those who help us in our cause, we are not waging a proper war.

But speeches and rhetoric aren't enough. We must back up our words with deeds. If we join as concerned citizens and do our part, small or large, our city halls will no longer turn a deaf ear. Our mayors will heed our calls for justice, our need for change, our demand for respect.

There's strength in combined effort. When our actions are noticed and the collective voice of Blacks, Hispanics, Asians and Whites is heard—and acted upon—we can take pride in ourselves as a true community—a community that should not have to live in fear.

Police-Brutality Protests Discourage Effective Policing

by Tamar Jacoby

About the author: *Tamar Jacoby, a senior fellow of the Manhattan Institute, a free-market policy center, is author of* Someone Else's House: America's Unfinished Struggle for Integration.

The march April 15, [1999] across the Brooklyn Bridge and into downtown Manhattan capped 10 weeks of demonstrations in New York, sparked by the police killing of 22-year-old West African street peddler Amadou Diallo. Now the protest is going national. Organizer Al Sharpton says he plans to accompany Diallo's mother on a 16-city tour, and the campaign is being celebrated as a triumph for decency and civil rights everywhere. Comparing the Diallo protesters to the followers of Martin Luther King Jr., civil rights veteran Rep. John Lewis of Georgia said . . . that "they, too, are standing up to gross injustice and saying, 'No more.'"

The comparison with King's movement could not be more misleading. Today, as in the '60s, there is a place for political protest. But as the Rev. Sharpton has proved often enough, it is easy to abuse King's great and glorious legacy.

The demonstrations in New York have caught the city's—and the nation's—attention. The arrests of nearly 1,200 protesters have prodded apathetic citizens to think about policing in minority neighborhoods and produced an apparent show of contrition by Mayor Rudolph Giuliani. But over the long run, these apparent benefits will come to look meager indeed, and the costs to the city—to blacks and whites and civic comity—will overshadow any gains.

The Costs of Police-Brutality Protests

The first cost is already obvious: The police are holding back. Pilloried by the demonstrators as racists and criticized across the city by whites as well as blacks, police officers are telling reporters that they can see the mistrust in people's eyes as they ride around town or walk the streets in uniform. In the toughest neighborhoods, they are openly taunted by defiant youths, and in response, some are less willing to risk their lives in doing their job. "It has put a second guess in the minds of officers. It is making them question their obligation." Patrick Lynch, an officer in Brooklyn, told a reporter. . . .

The number of stop-and-frisks by officers in the Street Crime Unit—the elite squad that has come under fire in the Diallo incident—has fallen precipitously. So have its arrests, which are down by more than half in the two months since the shooting. This new restraint may mute complaints that the cops are overly aggressive. But it is also likely to make them less effective, and evidence suggests that the streets are already less safe—particularly in poor minority neighborhoods. In the Brooklyn enclave of East New York, there were eight shooting incidents in March [1999], up from five in the same period [in 1998]. In the neighborhood of Bushwick, also in Brooklyn, the number jumped from two to six.

The second cost, and it affects both white and black New Yorkers, is the blow to truth and truth telling. Just what happened in the dark Bronx vestibule on the night the unarmed Diallo was killed is still unknown to anyone but the cops who shot him. Plainly enough, some sort of ghastly mistake occurred: An innocent man is dead, and with 41 bullets fired, no one can doubt that the four white officers used excessive force. The officers have been indicted on charges of second-degree murder. They have yet to tell their side of the story, though their lawyers say they thought Diallo was armed. But as the case goes to court, there has been no evidence yet that the cops were driven by racism, conscious or unconscious. [The officers were acquitted on all counts on February 25, 2000.]

This doesn't seem to matter—not to the demonstrators at police headquarters, anyway, or the thousands of people whose consciences have been pricked by the protests. Well-intentioned, middle-class people who would not dream of joining Sharpton on a picket line air their concerns at dinner parties and elsewhere. But many seem to care surprisingly little about the facts of the case, and when questions about the circumstances of the killing come up, they brush them away. "What do

> *"The costs [of demonstrations] to the city—to blacks and whites and civic comity—will overshadow any gains."*

you think actually happened that night in that vestibule?" I asked one man, white, well-heeled and politically astute. "I don't know." he answered, not even pausing, "but it doesn't really matter. The bigger truth is the truth that counts here—the way the mayor and other city authorities have signaled to the cops that racist behavior is okay."

There is no evidence of that either, though the protests—including placards comparing the mayor to Hitler—seem to have convinced the public that it must be so. Giuliani is a stubborn man, deliberately brash and often impolitic. He treats his political opponents, white and black, with a contempt guaranteed to backfire, and he makes no secret of his determination to keep the crime rate down—a determination that may breed occasional misjudgments.

The Race Question

But on race, the mayor has been resolute: Color should not and does not enter into city policy.

All New Yorkers, he has repeatedly insisted, must be treated similarly: no discrimination, no favors, no "special things," as he once put it, for any group, but rather the same "general things"—"safety, education and jobs"—for everyone. The dramatic drop in crime on his watch has benefited black and Hispanic New Yorkers more than anyone else, but not because he has ever singled them out.

The third cost—and perhaps the most tragic—is being borne by black New Yorkers: a growing sense of alienation and exclusion that risks becoming a self-fulfilling prophecy. You hear the anger and mistrust not just at the rallies, but also in classrooms, at impromptu campus meetings, in discussions among professionals. Spurred by the rhetoric of the demonstrations, many blacks have come to believe that not just the cops, but also ordinary New Yorkers and the "power structure" are irredeemably racist. Wounded and angry, they wonder if they will ever feel

> *"Angry, inflammatory protest ... will only make it harder for police to do their jobs in minority neighborhoods."*

safe or at home in New York—if they will ever feel that the city is their city, too. "How can you talk about blacks and whites coming together?" one student asked emotionally at a campus gathering. "We can't even walk in the same public spaces you do. This isn't our campus. This isn't our country. Diallo just proves what all of us have known in our hearts all along."

Meanwhile—and this is the last cost—concerned black and white New Yorkers have come no closer to the kinds of reforms that would improve the quality of policing in the city. Like any big urban force, the NYPD includes its share of rogue cups. Impulsive, even disturbed recruits slip through enlistment procedures designed to weed them out; power corrupts, and some brutality and graft are inevitable. The challenge for the department is to prevent abuses of power with tighter screening, better training and severe punishment in cases—such as the 1997 torture of Haitian immigrant Abner Louima—where the rogue elements turn criminal.

Misdiagnosing the Problem

Racially focused reforms of the kind called for by the protest coalition—sensitivity training, a residency requirement and the hiring of more minority officers—may or may not make the force more welcome in minority neighborhoods. But these changes do nothing to increase accountability or improve police judgment in dangerous circumstances, and they have proved no panacea in other cities. Public perceptions matter—in policing particularly—and city authorities must do their best to address them. By misdiagnosing what is wrong with the department—by mistaking a tragic killing for systemic racism—the demonstrators have only made it harder to achieve the kinds of reform that would make the city safer for everyone.

But the problem with Sharpton's protests—the difference between his movement and King's—goes well beyond a misdiagnosis, large or small. "It's open season on blacks," civil rights leader Jesse L. Jackson claimed . . .—an inflammatory exaggeration that would have been unthinkable under King's leadership. Dishonesty, demonization and political posturing had no place in King's historic crusade, not only because he was a man of integrity, but also because he knew that even a touch of bad faith would obliterate his only advantage: his moral power. Unlike the Diallo rallies, born of political calculation and fueled by rage, King's protests were driven by a basic faith that decent people everywhere would understand the justice of his cause and that the country could change for the better. His followers came out into the streets with a list of focused demands, and when authorities in a given city eventually agreed to address them, the protests stopped. Sharpton, in contrast, will not take yes for an answer. Nor does he grasp, despite the painful lessons of the civil rights era, the difference between conditions that authorities have the power to change—such as segregation and police practices—and those they cannot.

The tensions the Diallo incident have brought to light are neither new nor unique to New York. Every urban police force experiences complaints from minority citizens, and many, if not most, have a shameful, bigoted history to live down. But the truth, in New York and elsewhere, is often more complicated than simple racism.

Though no one likes to admit it, there is mistrust and stereotyping on both sides of the street—in minority communities as well as police officers. Teenagers blaring gangsta rap, acting "bad" and sporting loose clothing in imitation of what prisoners wear may not intend to signal a disrespectful attitude toward authority. But in bad neighborhoods, they draw the attention of officers who see them as potential troublemakers. As long as cops know that blacks account for a disproportionate share of arrests and convictions in the major crime categories, there will be more police activity—and more cop-community tensions—in those high-crime communities.

These inevitable strains ought to be of grave concern to everyone. But angry, inflammatory protest that distorts the problem and exaggerates the threat will not ease the animosity on either side of the color line and will only make it harder for police to do their jobs in minority neighborhoods.

The Police Must Discontinue the Practice of Racial Profiling

by David Cole

About the author: *David Cole, a Georgetown University law professor, is author of* No Equal Justice: Race and Class in the American Criminal Justice System.

Thanks to the New York police force, Abner Louima and Amadou Diallo have become household names.[1] Thanks to state police in New Jersey, Maryland and elsewhere, "Driving While Black" has entered the general lexicon. For the moment, the nation seems to be taking seriously the issue of racial bias in the criminal justice system. It's about time.

The issue is not new. Were it not for some of its dated rhetoric, the 1968 Kerner Commission Report, which discussed the causes of the urban riots of the mid- and late 1960s, could well be a description of many of our cities today.

"Negroes firmly believe that police brutality and harassment occur repeatedly in Negro neighborhoods. This belief is unquestionably one of the major reasons for intense Negro resentment against the police," the report said, adding:

"Physical abuse is only one source of aggravation in the ghetto. In nearly every city surveyed, the Commission heard complaints of harassment of interracial couples, dispersal of social street gatherings and the stopping of Negroes on foot or in cars without objective basis."

Creating the Perception of Bias

Often, the patterns of harassment were more than isolated incidents of sidewalk justice dispensed by rogue cops. In fact, they reflected a widespread pattern of police abuses rooted in departmental policies. In some cases, police de-

---

1. Louima, a Haitian immigrant, was beaten and sodomized in a New York City police precinct house, on August 9, 1997. Diallo, a West African immigrant, was killed after New York City police officers fired forty-one shots while he stood in his Bronx doorway on February 4, 1999.

partments created roving task forces that swooped down on high-crime neighborhoods and conducted indiscriminate street stops and searches.

"Police administrators, pressed by public concern about crime, have instituted such patrol practices often without weighing their tension-creating effects and the resulting relationship to civil disorder," the report said.

As the riots of the 1960s taught us, nothing corrodes public trust and faith in the criminal justice system like perceptions of bias. Unfortunately, those perceptions are as well-grounded today as they were then. Consider these facts:

- During a three-year period, from 1995 through 1997, 70 percent of those stopped on Interstate 95 in Maryland were black, though black motorists constitute only 17.5 percent of the speeders.
- During a 10-year period in Illinois, from 1987 to 1997, police in a special drug-interdiction unit stopped African-Americans at a rate double their presence on the roads, and Hispanics at a rate eight times greater than their presence on the road.
- [In April 1999], New Jersey Gov. Christine Todd Whitman admitted that state troopers there had been using a racial profile to stop motorists, and two troopers were charged with falsifying their records to hide their discrimination.
- Blacks are only 12 percent of the general population, but more than half of the nation's incarcerated population.
- One out of every three young black men from age 20 to 29 is under criminal justice supervision, either in prison or jail or on probation or parole.
- For every black man who graduates from college each year, 100 are arrested.

> *"The racial character of the prison population . . . leads police officers (and, indeed, all of us) to be more suspicious of minorities than of white citizens."*

Much of what drives these disparities is the war on drugs. According to the United States Public Health Service, African-Americans make up 14 percent of the nation's illicit drug users, roughly equal to their representation in the general population. Yet African-Americans are 35 percent of those arrested for drug possession, 55 percent of those convicted for drug possession, and 74 percent of those sentenced to prison for drug possession. Thus, for a crime they commit at a rate no greater than any other group, blacks are imprisoned at a rate six times their representation in the U.S. population (12 percent, in the 1990 Census).

Unacceptable Stereotypes

The racial character of the prison population, in turn, affects profiling. It leads police officers (and, indeed, all of us) to be more suspicious of minorities than of white citizens. For some crimes (although not for drug use), the greater suspicion is not entirely irrational, because there is evidence that minorities are more likely than whites to commit certain crimes, just as the young are more likely than the old, and men more than women. But the fact that such stereotypes might be minimally rational does not make them acceptable.

Relying on racial stereotypes is not necessary to good police work. The comparative statistics regarding blacks and whites are drawn from the very small subset of blacks and whites who engage in criminal conduct. Because most people of all races do not commit crimes, using race as a proxy

> *"Policies that tolerate racial profiling undermine the criminal law's legitimacy."*

for suspicion will necessarily sweep in large numbers of innocents. Every year, for example, approximately 98 percent of African-Americans are not arrested for any crime. And while officers are watching people of particular races, they will miss offenders of other races.

Most important, relying on race as a factor of suspicion violates the first principle of criminal law: individual responsibility. The state's authority to take citizens' liberty—and, in extreme cases, their lives—turns on the premise that all are equal before the law. Racial generalizations fail to treat people as individuals. As a result, policies that tolerate racial profiling undermine the criminal law's legitimacy.

How, then, do we restore legitimacy to a criminal justice system that has fostered so much skepticism and alienation among minorities?

First, government officials must make absolutely clear that racial profiling is unacceptable. Some police chiefs have said so, but others have tolerated the practice through their silence. Some courts have said racial profiling is unconstitutional, but others have said it's permissible as long as race is not the sole factor, a position that is indefensible as a matter of constitutional law. The Supreme Court has never addressed the question. So long as the practice is not clearly condemned, police officers will continue to do it, in part because it is not entirely irrational.

Second, police departments must be willing to lay bare the demographics of their enforcement tactics. The absence of publicly available data exacerbates the racial divisions on this issue. It allows many in the white majority to ignore or minimize the problem while leading many minorities to fear the worst. And without reporting, the police cannot be held accountable.

A Common Struggle

Third, police departments must be made more representative of the communities they serve. The NYPD street crimes unit that shot and killed Amadou Diallo was a mostly white force patrolling mostly minority neighborhoods. Increasing diversity is not sufficient in itself, but it increases the likelihood that communities and police will see themselves as friends in a common struggle, rather than enemies.

Finally, and fundamentally, we need to think beyond policing. It sometimes appears that the only public resources that the majority is eager to supply to the inner cities are more (and more aggressive) police officers. But, if similar levels of crime were occurring in white neighborhoods, and large numbers of white children were under criminal-justice supervision, isn't it likely that we would be hearing calls for different kinds of social investments, such as better schools, more job training, better after-care programs and drug treatment?

To restore legitimacy, the majority needs to show that it is willing to invest in something other than the strong arm of the law.

Unproven Accusations That the Police Use Racial Profiling Discourage Effective Policing

by William Norman Grigg

About the author: *William Norman Grigg is a senior editor of the* New American, *a conservative biweekly magazine.*

In major cities across the nation, criminals are winning the war for the streets—not because they are better armed or better organized than the police, but because the police have simply withdrawn from the battlefield. They have done so not out of cowardice or indifference, but because it has become all but impossible to enforce the law in predominantly black neighborhoods without incurring charges of "racism."

Avoiding Accusations

"I hear the same story from officers all across the country," reports James Carnell, a police officer from Boston who edits *Pax Centurion*, the publication of the Boston Police Patrolmen's Association. "They know that they're just one accusation away from losing everything," Carnell told *The New American.* "So many of them just figure that they get paid the same whether they enforce the law or not. These aren't bad cops. They have professional pride and they want to do their jobs. But they still are afraid that if they have a run-in with a member of an officially approved minority group, they'll be tagged as 'racists' and become the focus of a Justice Department investigation. So many of them just sit back and pretend that they don't see anything. It's a growing problem nationally."

"It's real. It's happening," veteran Seattle patrolman Eric Michl told the June 26, [2001] *Seattle Times.* "Parking under a shady tree to work on a crossword puzzle is a great alternative to being labeled a racist and being dragged through an inquest, a review board, an FBI and U.S. Attorney's investigation and a lawsuit." Michl described a traffic stop involving a black man whose erratic driving and antsy personal behavior suggested that he was high on cocaine. "Something was very suspicious," observed the 17-year police veteran. "If he were any other race, I would have probably arrested him on the spot. But then I started thinking, 'What if he's on cocaine, what if we get in a fight and he dies, and then we find out he's only guilty of a suspended license.' I don't want to see my name in the papers."

Defying his policeman's instincts, which dictated that he take the young man into custody, Officer Michl instead walked back to his cruiser to run a background check, which revealed that the vehicle had been stolen. By the time this was known, however, the suspect had gotten away. Although he was eventually caught, Michl—who, like most policemen, enlisted to protect the law-abiding against the lawless—believes that the incident illustrates the dangers that have resulted from the relentless demoralization of local police agencies. "There are a lot of us who are extremely frustrated about this," he observes.

Seattle Police Officer Al Warner reports similar frustrations. Warner describes a traffic stop near a bar in Seattle's Central Area during which four black men were arrested for smoking marijuana. Predictably enough, they accused Officer Warner of "racially profiling" them—a rather implausible charge to make, in light of the fact that Warner is black. "It's the catch phrase now," comments Warner. "If I were an African-American drug dealer here, that's the way I'd play the game. It intimidates officers."

Indeed, this is the way that street criminals, along with their political allies, are "playing the game"—and law-abiding black Americans are the most immediate victims. *Washington Times* police reporter Fred Reed points out that when police are intimidated by the prospect of professional and personal ruin, "the effect will of course be that black neighborhoods will get less law enforcement. Criminals won't know why life is suddenly easier, but they will notice that it is easier. They will become bolder. The quality of life in the neighborhood will go down. The papers will note that after a lull, crime is going up again. . . . There will be demands to hire more cops, who also won't do anything if they're smart."

> *"[Police officers] are afraid that if they have a run-in with a member of an officially approved minority group, they'll be tagged as 'racists.'"*

The cycle described by Reed is already well underway. It is most visible in Cincinnati, which was the scene [in early 2001] . . . of a destructive race riot that was supposedly triggered by the lethal police shooting of Timothy Thomas, a 19-year-old black man with numerous outstanding misdemeanor warrants. As black mobs tore apart neighborhoods, destroyed and pillaged businesses, and beat white pedestrians and motorists, radical attorney Ken Lawson applauded the rioters for giving "whites a better understanding of what it feels like to be a random target of violence just because of the color of your skin."

After a state of emergency and curfew were declared by Mayor Charles Luken, the riots subsided and a semblance of order was restored. But in a sense the riot was merely contained to predominantly black neighborhoods, where it actually gained intensity—in large measure because the city police were withdrawn. "In the weeks after the April [2001] riots, gunfire crackled at an alarming rate through Over-the-Rhine, West End, Avondale, Bond Hill and other predominantly African-American neighborhoods . . . neighborhoods that paid a toll in broken glass and looted buildings," reported the *Cincinnati Enquirer.*

The Demonization of the Police

In the aftermath of the riots and the successful campaign to demonize the police, observes Robert L. Woodson of the National Center for Neighborhood Enterprise, "crime is breaking records" in Cincinnati. "There have been a total of 74 shootings, leaving 86 people wounded or killed, compared with nine shootings and 11 victims for the same period [in 2000], . . ." wrote Woodson in an August 17, [2001] *Washington Times* commentary. As is the case elsewhere, the Cincinnati police "have decided that the risks of being pilloried as racists are so great, that they have pulled back in a process that can be clearly defined as police nullification."

Innocent black residents of inner-city regions are the primary victims of "police nullification," but they are

> *"When police are intimidated by the prospect of professional and personal ruin, . . . 'black neighborhoods will get less law enforcement.'"*

not the only ones. When riots erupted during . . . [the February 2001] Mardi Gras celebrations in Philadelphia and Seattle—much of it taking the form of racial attacks by black hoodlums upon white pedestrians—the police reaction was curiously subdued. The same was true during the early phase of the April [2001] riot in Cincinnati.

"If you want to make 20 traffic stops a shift and chase every dope dealer you see, you go right ahead," advised . . . [an] issue of the newsletter of the Cincinnati Fraternal Order of Police. "Just remember that if something goes wrong, or you make the slightest mistake in that split second, it could result in having your worst nightmare come true for you and your family, and City Hall will sell you out."

"Police nullification," "de-policing," "selective disengagement"—however the process may be packaged, what it amounts to is this: The "Thin Blue Line" separating the law-abiding from the lawless is being erased.

"The police can't win," wrote Fred Reed in the August issue of *Soldier of Fortune.* "They can, however, avoid losing. The answer is simply not to enforce the law against blacks, at least in black neighborhoods." Reed has received letters from police officers in Los Angeles, New York, Chicago, Nebraska, Pittsburgh, Indiana, and the Washington, D.C., area. "In sum, what they said was, 'if that's what the people want, that's what they'll get. Nothing.'"

"It's happening here," wrote a veteran officer. "Our mayor pretty much came out and said the department is full of racists and we [race] profile all the time. He didn't use those words. He didn't have to. So, many of us are opting out, myself included. . . . On our department we can't win at all. No support from even our own supervisor, nor the brass. So, what to do? Protect your [backside] and do as little as possible."

"Police officers are not robots, we are people, but we are people who can lose it all for trying to protect society," wrote another officer from Maryland's Prince George County, a predominantly black suburb of Washington, D.C. "In an instant your whole life's work can be gone, ruined after a grand jury, a Justice Department inquiry, or just Jack Johnson [a pious district attorney] prosecuting you in the court of public opinion."

Many other urban police departments are finding it all but impossible to recruit new officers. "Police departments in cities across the nation are facing what some call a personnel crisis, with the number of recruits at record lows, an increasing number of experienced officers turning down promotions to sergeant or lieutenant, and many talented senior officers declining offers to become police chiefs," reported the July 30, [2001], *New York Times*. Cynthia Brown, publisher of *American Police Beat* magazine, told the *Times* that [in 2001] . . . , for the first time, her publication ran "advertisements for police recruits from a dozen cities, including Portland, Oregon, and Seattle, and smaller cities like Santa Cruz, California, and Sheridan, Wyoming.". . .

Racial Profiling

The term "profiling," noted Officer James Carnell in an article for *American Police Beat* magazine, "began to appear in the media about five or six years ago. Some overzealous police used these 'profiles' as part of an effort to interdict the flow of drugs and guns into the inner cities. Some mistakes were undoubtedly made and some people were unfairly stopped, questioned and searched. Unfortunately, the nine justices of the Supreme Court and the staff of the ACLU [American Civil Liberties Union] are not always available at 2 AM for street corner consultation as to the fine differences between 'probable cause' and 'reasonable suspicion' versus common sense, police experience, and gut instinct.". . .

Not so much as a particle of evidence has been produced to document that police in any jurisdiction have followed *racial* profiles, as opposed to using *suspect* profiles in their pursuit of criminals. The term "racial profiling" is an invention of race-baiting leftist groups that seek to demonize police as bigots. "The media, wittingly or unwittingly in concert with anti-police activists, has employed the profiling accusation so carelessly that its existence and use by police has become an accepted fact," observes Officer Carnell. . . .

In his first address to a joint session of Congress, President George W. Bush insisted that "racial profiling . . . must end"—despite the fact that nobody can prove that it ever began. On February 27, [2001] he issued a directive to Attorney General Ashcroft ordering him to "work in cooperation with State and local law enforcement in order to assess the extent and nature of any such practices."

> *"Not so much as a particle of evidence has been produced to document that police in any jurisdiction have followed racial profiles."*

In a March 1, [2001] press conference announcing his intention to wipe out "racial profiling," Ashcroft recalled that as a senator he "had the happy privilege of working with Russ Feingold, [Democrat] senator from Wisconsin, toward legislation which would help us develop an understanding about the impact of racial profiling on American citizens." He expressed his willingness to implement legislation banning "racial profiling." In fact, he continued, if Congress does not produce satisfactory legislation soon, "I'll simply launch a study of my own, because I think this is an issue of such importance and magnitude. . . ." In this fashion, Ashcroft kept alive the [Bill] Clinton/[Janet] Reno tradition of defying Congress and ignoring constitutional limits on Executive Branch authority.

In 1999, the Clinton/Reno Justice Department filed suit against the New Jersey State Police, claiming that the agency was guilty of "racial profiling." As a result, notes [Heather] MacDonald, the administration of then-New Jersey Governor (and current Environmental Protection Agency Administrator) Christine Todd Whitman dismissed outright "drug and weapons charges against 128 defendants," who had insisted that police had pulled them over "merely because of race." New Jersey State Troopers are now required to "monitor the length of traffic stops that individual officers make and correlate it to the race of the motorist. [They] will also monitor by race the computer checks that individual officers run on license plates, on the theory that racist officers will spend more time bothering innocent black motorists and will improperly target them for background checks. Of course an officer's stop and arrest data will be closely scrutinized for racial patterns as well. And if in fact such investigatory techniques correlate with race because more minorities are breaking the law? Too bad for the cop. He will be red-flagged as a potential racist."

The outcome in New Jersey is just a foretaste of what police departments nationwide can expect if the Bush administration makes good on its stated intentions. According to Ralph Boyd Jr., the administration's assistant attorney general for civil rights, more lawsuits against state and local police departments may be necessary in order to eradicate the supposed scourge of "racial profiling." "There may be people we need to clobber over the head, and if we need to clobber people over the head, we'll do that," Boyd told the July 26, [2001], *Boston Globe*. According to the *Globe*, "Boyd said the Justice Department would collect racial data on policing, expedite individual complaints about alleged profiling and set up programs to train and monitor local police."

Although the New Jersey State Police were the targets of the only "racial profiling" suit filed against a police department by the Justice Department, more than a dozen other agencies were targeted for "pattern and practice" lawsuits during the Clinton/Reno reign. Such lawsuits lodge murky allegations of unspecified "civil rights" violations by police officers, and threaten severe civil penalties unless the affected city governments sign "consent decrees" effectively deeding control over their police to the Justice Department.

"What usually happens," explained Officer Carnell to *The New American*, "is that a city will sign off on a consent decree that police officers had nothing to do with and do not support. All they know is that they've been labeled 'racists' and left twisting in the wind." Such consent decrees, wherein the city agrees to submit to U.S. Justice Department mandates, have been forced upon New York City, Los Angeles, Pittsburgh, and Columbus, Ohio, and similar lawsuits have been filed against Dallas, Houston, and other cities. And, as noted above, the Bush administration is eager to continue this anti-police jihad.

Local, Independent, Accountable

With their every effort to enforce the law under the opportunistic gaze of race-obsessed radicals, and the federal government threatening to "clobber them over the head," it isn't a mystery why so many police officers are either acting as "tourists in blue" or investigating another line of work.

Under the Constitution, law enforcement was to be carried out almost exclusively by the individual states and their subsidiaries. As James Madison observed in *The Federalist*, No. 45, the "numerous and indefinite" powers reserved to the states would "extend to all the objects which, in the ordinary course of affairs, concern the lives, liberties, and properties of the people, and the internal order, improvement, and prosperity of the State." Keeping police locally accountable, and independent from federal control, would prevent the dangerous consolidation of power that is the hallmark of every tyranny—and this is particularly true of modern police-state monstrosities like Soviet Russia and Nazi Germany.

The "Thin Blue Line" exists not only to protect the property and persons of the law-abiding from the depredations of violent criminals, but also to act as an institutional impediment to the centralized consolidation of power. This is why the power elites have joined with the criminal class in a combined assault upon local police. And this is why it is more important than ever before that Americans support their local police, and work to restore their independence from federal control.

Early Warning Systems Reduce Police Misconduct

by Samuel Walker, Geoffrey P. Alpert, and Dennis J. Kenney

About the authors: *Samuel Walker is a professor of criminal justice at the University of Nebraska at Omaha, Geoffrey P. Alpert is a professor of criminal justice at the University of South Carolina, and Dennis J. Kenney is a professor of criminal justice at Rutgers University.*

It has become a truism among police chiefs that 10 percent of their officers cause 90 percent of the problems. Investigative journalists have documented departments in which as few as 2 percent of all officers are responsible for 50 percent of all citizen complaints. The phenomenon of the "problem officer" was identified in the 1970s: Herman Goldstein noted that problem officers "are well known to their supervisors, to the top administrators, to their peers, and to the residents of the areas in which they work," but that "little is done to alter their conduct." In 1981, the U.S. Commission on Civil Rights recommended that all police departments create an early warning system to identify problem officers, those "who are frequently the subject of complaints or who demonstrate identifiable patterns of inappropriate behavior."

An early warning system is a data-based police management tool designed to identify officers whose behavior is problematic and provide a form of intervention to correct that performance. As an early response, a department intervenes before such an officer is in a situation that warrants formal disciplinary action. The system alerts the department to these individuals and warns the officers while providing counseling or training to help them change their problematic behavior.

By 1999, .39 percent of all municipal and county law enforcement agencies that serve populations greater than 50,000 people either had an early warning system in place or were planning to implement one. The growing popularity of these systems as a remedy for police misconduct raises questions about their effectiveness and about the various program elements that are associated with effectiveness. To date, however, little has been written on the subject. This Brief

Samuel Walker, Geoffrey P. Alpert, and Dennis J. Kenney, "Early Warning Systems: Responding to the Problem Police Officer," *National Institute of Justice: Research in Brief*, U.S. Department of Justice, July 2001.

reports on the first in depth investigation of early warning systems. The investigation combined the results of a national survey of law enforcement agencies with the findings of case studies of three agencies with established systems.

How Prevalent Are Early Warning Systems?

As part of the national evaluation of early warning systems, the Police Executive Research Forum—funded by the National Institute of Justice and the Office of Community Oriented Policing Services—surveyed 832 sheriffs' offices and municipal and county police departments serving populations of 50,000 or more. Usable responses were received from 571 agencies, a response rate of 69 percent. The response rate was significantly higher for municipal agencies than for sheriff's departments.

Approximately one-fourth (27 percent) of the surveyed agencies had an early warning system in 1999. One-half of these systems had been created since 1994, and slightly more than one-third had been created since 1996. These data, combined with the number of agencies indicating that a system was being planned (another 12 percent), suggest that such systems will spread rapidly in the next few years.

Early warning systems are more prevalent among municipal law enforcement agencies than among county sheriffs' departments.

How Does an Early Warning System Work?

Early warning systems have three basic phases: selection, intervention, and postintervention monitoring.

No standards have been established for identifying officers for early warning programs, but there is general agreement about the criteria that should influence their selection. Performance indicators that can help identify officers with problematic behavior include citizen complaints, firearm-discharge and use-of-force reports, civil litigation, resisting-arrest incidents, and high-speed pursuits and vehicular damage.

Although a few departments rely only on citizen complaints to select officers for intervention, most use a combination of performance indicators. Among systems that factor in citizen complaints, most (67 percent) require three complaints in a given timeframe (76 percent specify a 12-month period) to identify an officer. The primary goal of early warning systems is to change the behavior of individual officers who have been identified as having problematic performance records. The basic intervention strategy involves a combination of deterrence and education. The theory of simple deterrence assumes that officers who are subject to intervention will change their behavior in response to a perceived threat of punishment. General deterrence assumes that officers not subject to the system will also change their behavior to avoid potential punishment. Early warning systems also operate on the assumption that training, as part of the intervention, can help officers improve their performance.

In most systems (62 percent), the initial intervention generally consists of a review by the officer's immediate supervisor. Almost half of the responding agencies (45 percent) involve other command officers in counseling the officer. Also, these systems frequently include a training class for groups of officers identified by the system (45 percent of survey respondents).

Nearly all (90 percent) the agencies that have an early warning system in place report that they monitor an officer's performance after the initial intervention. Such monitoring is generally informal and conducted by the officer's immediate supervisor, but some departments have developed a formal process of observation, evaluation, and reporting. Almost half of the agencies (47 percent) monitor the officer's performance for 36 months after the initial intervention. Half of the agencies indicate that the followup period is not specified and that officers are monitored either continuously or on a case-by-case basis.

The responses from the national survey should be viewed with some caution. Some law enforcement agencies may have claimed to have an early warning system when such a system is not actually functioning. Several police departments created systems in the 1970s, but none of those appears to have survived as a permanent program.

Findings from Three Case Studies

The research strategy for the case studies was modeled after the birth cohort study of juvenile delinquency conducted by Marvin E. Wolfgang, Robert M. Figlio, and Thorsten Sellin. They found that a small group within the entire cohort (6.3 percent of the total) were "chronic delinquents" and were responsible for half of all the serious crime committed by the entire cohort. The early warning concept rests on the assumption that within any cohort of police officers, a small percentage will have substantially worse performance records than their peers and, consequently, will merit departmental intervention. The research was designed to confirm or refute the assumption.

Three police departments were chosen for the case study investigation: Miami-Dade County, Minneapolis, and New Orleans. The three sites represent large urban areas, but the size of each police force varies considerably: At the time of the study, Miami-Dade had 2,920 sworn officers, New Orleans had 1,576 sworn officers, and Minneapolis had 890 sworn officers.

"The primary goal of early warning systems is to change the behavior of individual officers who have been identified as having problematic performance records."

The three sites were chosen for several reasons. Each has an early warning system that had been operating for at least 4 years at the time of the study. Also, the three systems differ from one another in terms of structure and administrative history, and the three departments differ in their history of police officer use of force and accountability.

One goal of the case studies was to evaluate the impact of early warning systems on the officers involved. In New Orleans, citizen complaints about officers in the early warning program were analyzed for 2-year periods before and after the initial intervention. Officers subject to early warning intervention participate in a Professional Performance Enhancement Program (PPEP) class; their critiques of the class were analyzed and a 2-day class was observed to determine both the content of the intervention and officer responses to various components.

Demographic and performance data were collected in Miami-Dade and Minneapolis on a cohort of all officers hired in certain years—whether or not they were identified by the early warning systems. The performance data included citizen complaints, use-of-force reports, reprimands, suspensions, terminations, commendations, and promotions. Other data were collected as available in each site.

These records were sorted into two groups: officers identified by the early warning system and officers not identified, with the latter serving as a control group. The performance records of the early warning group were analyzed for the 2-year periods before and after the intervention to determine the impact of the intervention on the officers' behavior. The analysis controlled for assignment to patrol duty on the assumption that citizen complaints and use-of-force incidents are infrequently generated in other assignments.

> *"Early warning systems appear to have a dramatic effect on reducing citizen complaints and other indicators of problematic police performance."*

Demographically, officers identified by the systems do not differ significantly from the control group in terms of race or ethnicity. Males, are somewhat overrepresented and females are underrepresented. One disturbing finding was a slight tendency of early warning officers to be promoted at higher rates than control officers. This issue should be the subject of future research, which should attempt to identify more precisely whether some departments tend to reward through promotion the kind of active (and possibly aggressive) behavior that is likely to cause officers to be identified by an early warning system.

The Impact of Early Warning Systems

Early warning systems appear to have a dramatic effect on reducing citizen complaints and other indicators of problematic police performance among those officers subject to intervention. In Minneapolis, the average number of citizen complaints received by officers subject to early intervention dropped by 67 percent 1 year after the intervention. In New Orleans, that number dropped by 62 percent 1 year after intervention. In Miami-Dade, only 4 percent of the early warning cohort had zero use-of-force reports prior to intervention; following intervention, 50 percent had zero use-of-force reports.

Data from New Orleans indicate that officers respond positively to early warning intervention. In anonymous evaluations of the PPEP classes, officers gave it an average rating of 7 on a scale of 1 to 10. All of the officers made at least one positive comment about the class, and some made specific comments about how it had helped them. Officers in the PPEP class that was directly observed were actively engaged in those components they perceived to be related to the practical problems of police work, particularly incidents that often generate complaints or other problems. Officers were disengaged, however, in components that they perceived to be abstract, moralistic, or otherwise unrelated to practical aspects of police work.

> *"The early warning systems ... studied operate in the context of a larger commitment to increased accountability on the part of the police department."*

This study could not determine the most effective aspects of intervention (e.g., counseling regarding personal issues, training in specific law enforcement techniques, stern warning about possible discipline in the future) or whether certain aspects are more effective for certain types of officers.

The original design of this study did not include evaluating the impact of these systems on supervisors. Nonetheless, the qualitative component of the research found that these systems have potentially significant effects on supervisors. The existence of an intervention system communicates to supervisors their responsibility to monitor officers who have been identified by the program. The New Orleans program requires supervisors to monitor identified officers under their command for 6 months and to complete signed evaluations of the officers' performance every 2 weeks. Officials in Miami-Dade think that their system helps ensure that supervisors will attend to potential problem officers under their command. In this respect, the systems mandate or encourage changes in supervisor behavior that could potentially affect the standards of supervision of all officers, not just those subject to early intervention. Furthermore, the system's database can give supervisors relevant information about officers newly assigned to them and about whom they know very little.

The original design of this study did not include evaluating the impact of these systems on the departments in which they operate. Nonetheless, the qualitative component identified a number of important issues for future research. The extent to which a system changes the climate of accountability within a law enforcement agency is not known, and identifying it would require a sophisticated research design. The qualitative findings suggest that an effective early intervention program depends on a general commitment to accountability within an organization. Such a program is unlikely to create or foster a climate of accountability where that commitment does not already exist.

The data developed as a part of an early warning system can be used to effect changes in policies, procedures, or training. Presumably, such changes help reduce existing problems and help the department maintain and raise its standards of accountability. Thus, these systems can be an important tool for organizational development and human resource management.

The Nature of Early Warning Systems

A second goal of the case studies was to describe the systems themselves. In all three sites, qualitative data gathered from official documents and interviews with key stakeholders yielded a description and assessment of the formal structure and administrative history of each program, along with an assessment of its place in the larger processes of accountability in the department.

In addition to finding that the early warning systems in the three sites vary considerably in terms of their formal program elements, the study documented that an effective system requires considerable investment of resources and administrative attention. Miami-Dade's program, for example, is part of a sophisticated data system on officers and their performance. The New Orleans program involves several staff members, including one full-time data analyst and two other full-time employees who spend part of their time entering data.

Early warning systems should not be considered alarm clocks—they are not mechanical devices that can be programmed to automatically sound an alarm. Rather, they are extremely complex, high-maintenance administrative operations that require close and ongoing human attention. Without this attention, the systems are likely to falter or fail.

> *"An early warning system is more likely to shield an agency against liability for deliberate indifference regarding police use of force."*

The findings regarding the impact of early warning intervention should be viewed with caution. As the first-ever study of such systems, this project encountered a number of unanticipated problems with the data. First, it was not possible to collect retrospectively systematic data on positive police officer performance (e.g., incidents when an officer avoided using force or citizens felt they had been treated fairly and respectfully). Thus, it is not known whether early intervention had a deterrent effect on desirable officer behavior.

Second, the early warning systems in each site studied operate in the context of a larger commitment to increased accountability on the part of the police department. Given the original research design, it is impossible to disentangle the effect of this general climate of rising standards of accountability on officer performance from the effect of the intervention program itself.

Finally, the early warning systems in two of the three sites experienced significant changes during the years for which data were collected. Thus, the intervention delivered was not consistent for the period studied. Significant changes also occurred in two sites immediately following the data collection period. In one instance, the system was substantially strengthened. In the other, it is likely that the administration of the system has deteriorated significantly; this deterioration may have begun during the study, affecting the data that were collected.

Policing Strategies and Legal Considerations

These intervention strategies are compatible with both community-oriented and problem-oriented policing. Community-oriented policing seeks to establish closer relations between the police and the communities they serve. Insofar as the systems seek to reduce citizen complaints and other forms of problematic behavior, they are fully consistent with these goals.

Problem-oriented policing focuses on identifying specific police problems and developing carefully tailored responses. Early warning systems approach the problem officer as the concern to be addressed, and the intervention is the response tailored to change the behavior that leads to indicators of unsatisfactory performance.

The issue of racial profiling by police has recently emerged as a national controversy. In response to this controversy, a number of law enforcement agencies have begun to collect data on the race and ethnicity of drivers stopped by their officers.

An officer who makes a disproportionate number of traffic stops of racial or ethnic minorities (relative to other officers with the same assignment) may be a problem officer who warrants the attention of the department. Traffic-stop information can be readily incorporated into the database and used to identify possible racial disparities (as well as other potential problems, such as disproportionate stops of female drivers or unacceptably low levels of activity).

Some law enforcement agencies may resist creating an early warning system for fear that a plaintiff's attorney may subpoena the database's information on officer misconduct and use that information against the agency in lawsuits alleging excessive use of force. Several experts argue, however, that in the current legal environment, an early warning system is more likely to shield an agency against liability for deliberate indifference regarding police use of force. Such a system demonstrates that the agency has a clear policy regarding misconduct, has made a good faith effort to identify employees whose performance is unsatisfactory, and has a program in place to correct that behavior.

Citizens Should Have Access to Accurate Data on the Use of Deadly Force

by James J. Fyfe

About the author: *James J. Fyfe, who served sixteen years on the New York City police force, is a professor of criminal justice at Temple University in Philadelphia, Pennsylvania.*

For most readers, I suspect, the most shocking aspect of *The Washington Post's* . . . series of articles on police use of deadly force was the discovery that, compared with other police forces, Prince George's County, Md., just outside Washington, D.C., officers have killed people so often.

And shocking it was. But what caught my attention, as well as that of other scholars of criminal justice, was the straightforward compilation of data on killings by officers in America's 51 largest law enforcement agencies. As hard as it is to believe, the list . . . is the most comprehensive accurate information on police killings in major U.S. cities that has appeared since 1981 and 1985, when the International Association of Chiefs of Police published federally funded reports on the subject.

An Absence of Accurate Information

In a nation that often seems obsessed with statistics on far less significant topics, this absence of information is bizarre—and dangerous. Deadly force is an inevitable component of police work. Excessive force, on the other hand, is a scourge that undermines a department's ability to do its job. But citizens who deserve responsive, nonaggressive police protection can't demand reforms unless they know what the facts are.

There is no federal agency that reports on killings or nonfatal use of deadly force by police. The FBI—which annually collects and publishes data on crime and on the assaults and murders of law enforcement officers—includes no infor-

James J. Fyfe, "When Cops Kill," *Washington Post*, vol. 18, July 6–22, 2001, p. 23. Copyright © 2001 by Washington Post Book World Service/Washington Post Writers Group. Reproduced by permission.

mation on violence committed by those officers in its Uniform Crime Reports.

Congress tried to correct this situation in 1994, passing a law ordering the Justice Department to report annually on the use of force, including excessive force, by police officers in America. The problem with this mandate is that Justice was given no real power to demand cooperation from state and local police departments—and, consequently, it doesn't get usable data. Instead it develops estimates by including in the National Crime Survey—a survey of citizens, rather than police—questions about how often the respondents have been subjected to police use of force. Since dead people can't participate in such a survey, this work tells us nothing about how often police kill.

In 1979, when I moved to Washington to teach at American University, a federal official told me that the FBI collected data on justifiable homicides by police. I questioned this because I had just left my job as a New York City cop, where I had spent the previous several years writing a doctoral dissertation on police use of deadly force there. During all that time, not one of the NYPD officials responsible for collecting information on shootings or for reporting crime figures to the FBI ever mentioned that these included a "justifiable homicide by police" category. I then checked with the FBI and was assured that it does collect these data, but it does not publish them because it cannot vouch for their accuracy. The FBI has good reason for its doubts: Whenever I have checked the FBI numbers for particular police departments against mortality figures obtained directly from the same agencies, they have differed.

Scholars once assumed that the Department of Health and Human Services's annual report on deaths in America—the report that gives information on deaths by cancer, automobile accident and so on—also provided accurate information on killings by police. During the 1970s, these reports typically indicated that about 250 Americans suffered "death by legal intervention of the police." Then the 1981 police chiefs' study showed that, just in the 54 cities with population greater than 250,000, the police were killing about 325 people every year. Since these cities accounted for only a quarter of all U.S. police officers, it was clear that the HHS data also were inaccurate—largely because local coroners were including most police killings in a general "death by gunshot wound" category, without specifying that the gunshot was from a police weapon.

What this means is that instead of judging police use of deadly force on the basis of systematic data, citizens must rely on anecdotal evidence—such as the 11 o'clock news. If the police shooting of an unarmed man in Cincinnati causes riots, people watching TV across America may conclude that the Cincinnati police are the worst of the worst. Are they? Nobody can tell, because the absence of data has meant that there has been no way to compare Cincinnati's experience with that of other cities. . . .

Similarly, when four New York City cops fired 41 shots, killing Amadou Diallo in his Bronx doorway, many Americans (who had already heard of Abner Louima, sodomized with a stick by a New York officer) regarded the NYPD with horror. But in this case there are some facts to challenge the popular image: the numbers collected by *The Post*. These show that New York ranked 43rd out of the 51 police departments in terms of fatal police shootings—0.71 such incidents per 1,000 officers.

Meanwhile, consider the Phoenix and San Diego city police departments—both excellent agencies, both regarded as models of successful, non-aggressive, community-oriented policing. *The Post*'s data show that their officers are nearly five times as likely as New York cops to shoot and kill people (the San Diego rate per 1,000 officers is 3.27; Phoenix's is 3.14). Shouldn't citizens of those cities have simple, official access to this kind of information?

Evaluating police restraint on the basis of anecdotes rather than systematic data has had consequences. Because so many media are based in New York, anything that goes wrong in that agency—Louima, Diallo—becomes a national, even international, story. Cops there are on alert that they will be held very publicly accountable for their mistakes.

> *"Citizens who deserve responsive, nonaggressive police protection can't demand reforms unless they know what the facts are."*

Here's a contrast: I testified as a defense expert on police practices in the Diallo case. Just a day earlier, I had completed an affidavit in a suit stemming from a police killing in Camden, N.J.

The Camden case involved a mentally disturbed man who, during the course of a long confrontation with the police, pulled from his pocket a talcum powder bottle wrapped in a sock. Eleven officers, some as far as 280 feet away, responded by firing at least 106 shots at him. The media coverage of this killing consisted of one small newspaper story. There was no discipline, no criminal trial, no outrage. In such places, where people are not paying attention, the need for change is not recognized and the police come to believe that such behavior is appropriate.

In order for the public to give police use of deadly force the attention it deserves, there must be data. We already know that when communities suffer disproportionately from crime, from cancer, from poverty, knowledge of the relevant statistics has empowered citizens and encouraged them to demand change. It is long past time that consistent, reliable data on deadly force—like *The Post*'s, which show that fatal shooting rates vary by more than tenfold across these 51 departments—were made available.

Only the federal government can make this happen. One way would be for Congress to put some muscle into the existing legislation by denying federal funds to jurisdictions that fail to collect and provide use of force data for inclusion in the FBI's Uniform Crime Report. However it is done, it is important that our government finds a way to assure us that the police we pay to protect us are mandated to tell us how often they kill.

Video Cameras Curtail Police Brutality

by Richard D. Emery

About the author: *Richard D. Emery is a civil rights lawyer who represents clients in suits against the New York City Police Department.*

Video cameras operating 24 hours a day in police precincts are the most important component of police oversight that is now missing in efforts to stem police brutality and abuse of authority. No other device or procedure can substitute for an instant replay of events that are alleged to constitute police misconduct. Only in this way can both the public and the accused police officers be more assured of a fair assessment of police actions.

Inevitably, every accusation of police misconduct includes ambiguous and confusing events. Police most often either deny that they abused a victim or claim that their physical actions were necessary as proper restraint of their accuser. Accusers invariably deny any improper conduct that warrants a physical restraint let alone abuse. And invariably the interactions between police officers and people in custody are ambiguous, subject to interpretation and, at a minimum, confusing in the sequence of events that led to physical injuries.

The result is that subsequent testimony of witnesses is often nearly useless. Witnesses contradict each other and allow emotions to color their interpretation of events. These events in normal time, happen very quickly and the mind is a fundamentally flawed recorder. Most often the victim does not even know exactly what happened, let alone nearby witnesses who are not part of the action. Of course the police officers involved are so biased by the fear of accusation and punishment that their story quickly becomes totally unreliable.

Put simply, the best way to sort these complicated confrontations is the same way we look at instant replays in slow motion for basketball and football. Often, with multiple parties coming in close physical contact to one another, the only way that a true version of events can be gleaned is painstakingly analyzing video

Richard D. Emery, "Cameras in the Station House," *Criminal Justice Ethics*, vol. 17, Winter 1998, p. 43.

tape. Certainly with a video tape more can be determined about who did what to whom than in any other after-the-fact method. Thus the value of video tape in sorting out police/citizens confrontations can not be overestimated. As we have learned repeatedly from events that were caught on video tape, far more can be determined in subsequent court proceedings than through witnesses whose memories are highly suspect even on day one, let alone months or even years after the event.

> *"The main value to video cameras is to assure the public that what their police do is legitimate."*

And even recorded corroborative activity that will show who was in the area, the witnesses' vantage points, and who was with whom, will be valuable in the event that the actual physical confrontation is not caught on tape.

No Expectation of Privacy

The question then is, "what is the cost of videotaping police activities?" The answer is: very little. Video cameras placed at locations in precinct houses that are not invasive of personal privacy—such as in locker rooms where personnel change or in the actual stalls of restrooms—do not trample expectations of privacy. In a public precinct, police officers who are public officials should not and can not have any expectation of privacy. After all, their superior officers at a minimum, and more likely even the press and public, have general access to these areas in precinct houses. Certainly any police officer knows that any other fellow officer would have an obligation to report misconduct that he or she saw in a precinct, to which all fellow officers presumably have full access in any event. Therefore, no police officer can argue that expectations of privacy within a precinct predominate over the value of video recordings of alleged police misconduct.

Similarly, police officers should have video cameras placed in police cars to record scenes of confrontation on the street or in the car itself. Certainly there can be no expectation of privacy that outweighs the value of a record of such confrontations that occur in the street or even in a police car where the interior can always be viewed from the outside anyway. Consequently, claims of expectations of privacy in these contexts are even slimmer.

Whether the same can be said for audio tape is a somewhat closer question. It may well be that police officers have a right to audio privacy even in a police precinct or in a police cruiser. But the simple fact is that audio recordings are far less important than video recordings. I for one would certainly advocate that audio recordings should be made along with video recordings both in police precincts and in police cars, notwithstanding that the intrusion into police privacy is somewhat greater in the context of audio recordings.

It is for this reason that police departments in Florida and California employ video cameras. We see them on television shows frequently and they are now commonplace as evidence in proceedings involving police chases, arrests, and precinct activities.

Of course the main value to video cameras is to assure the public that what their police do is legitimate. In all likelihood, in most instances, false accusations of police misconduct can be quickly disposed of by virtue of a video tape vindicating the version of events of a police officer wrongly accused. In those cases where police officers abuse their authority, of course the video tape is crucial to hold officers accountable, especially when they are presumptively thought to be innocent.

Finally, there may in fact be some modest deterrent effect on police officers if they do not become accustomed to constant video tape and ignore cameras as part of their every day life. However, all too often, police officers are not deterred whatsoever by video cameras when they abuse their authority and physically mistreat citizens. Nonetheless, many officers who would cross the line if no cameras were watching, may be restrained in the face of knowing that they will be caught red-handed.

In conclusion, it is hard to imagine a convincing argument that civil liberties expectations of privacy outweigh the value of video tape in what is essentially the recording of the public functions of police officers. Moreover, given the value and the accuracy of such video tapes in these highly publicized and hotly contested controversies, the case for installation of video cameras to record almost every aspect of police life is compelling.

Given the urgency of controlling police violence and assuring the public that their police operate humanely and fairly, video tape is our best weapon as a salutary response to the current police brutality crisis.

Chapter 4

Is Police Brutality Adequately Punished?

Chapter Preface

Civil rights activists working to stop police brutality often question why federal prosecutors do not automatically bring criminal charges against police officers for violating the civil rights of police brutality victims. Activists often cite the case of Amadou Diallo, a West African immigrant killed by four New York City Police Department officers on February 4, 1999, to support their argument that federal prosecutors sometimes fail in their responsibilities to victims.

On the evening of February 4, 1999, four officers approached Diallo as he stood outside his home in the Bronx. Believing that Diallo might be the rape suspect they were looking for, the officers, who were not in uniform, approached and announced themselves as the police. According to the officers, Diallo retreated into the vestibule and reached for an object in his pocket. Believing that Diallo was pulling out a weapon, one officer shouted, "Gun!" and the four officers began to shoot into the vestibule. One officer tripped, and believing their fellow officer had been shot, the other officers emptied forty-one bullets into the vestibule, nineteen of which hit Diallo, killing him.

After the officers were acquitted in state court on all counts from murder to reckless endangerment, some commentators questioned why the Civil Rights Division of the U.S. Department of Justice chose not to pursue criminal prosecution of the officers. Although the Civil Rights Division is responsible for the federal prosecution of police misconduct, federal prosecutors confront numerous obstacles in their efforts to punish police use of excessive and sometimes deadly force.

One obstacle to effective criminal prosecution of police officers is the federal grand jury, which is composed of citizens who are selected in the same manner as in a trial jury. To bring charges against officers for a criminal violation, the Civil Rights Division must persuade a federal grand jury to indict the individuals. Unlike a trial jury, which examines evidence and arguments presented during a trial, a grand jury examines evidence presented by federal prosecutors to determine whether the evidence is sufficient to make a case or whether "probable cause" exists to charge a police officer with a crime. According to law professor and former civil rights prosecutor Thomas Perez, the federal grand jury has several advantages. Grand juries, Perez explains, can issue subpoenas to demand the appearance of witnesses and the production of evidence. Suspected officers do not feel as if their department is betraying them, he explains, because the department has no choice but to hand evidence over to the grand jury. "Officers are understandably reluctant to provide inculpatory evidence against a fellow officer. A subpoena leaves them little choice but to testify," says Perez. The grand jury is also a secret proceeding. Testimony is not disclosed unless a case goes to trial. This secrecy, he argues, protects the target of the investigation if the allegations are false.

Law professor and former civil rights prosecutor Drew Days urges caution, however. Days believes that charges should be brought before the grand jury only if the civil rights division has strong evidence of wrongdoing. Pursuing the grand jury without strong evidence, he claims, unrealistically raises public expectations. "When these cases come back without an indictment, it reduces the credibility of the Civil Rights Division and the federal government. It makes people very cynical about asking us to come in on subsequent investigations," Days argues. Pursuing a weak case and losing, he reasons, may send a more dangerous signal to both officers and the community than not pursuing the case at all.

Another obstacle federal prosecutors face in police brutality cases is convincing trial juries that police officers should be convicted. "Prosecutors accustomed to benefiting from the sympathies of jurors for the police and against criminals here find these sympathies working against them," explains the Vera Institute of Justice in *Prosecuting Police Misconduct.* Former prosecutor Perez recalls a case in which the victim was an undocumented Mexican national who may have been involved in illegal drug trafficking. "Despite the fact that he was shot in the back and there were other egregious circumstances, we had difficulty obtaining a conviction," says Perez. "There is a war against drugs on the border and you're prosecuting the warriors?"

Meeting the legal requirement of "specific intent" is another hurdle that federal civil rights prosecutors face. In order to prosecute police officers for violations of civil rights laws, federal prosecutors must prove a defendant's specific intent to deprive a victim of his or her constitutional rights. Federal prosecutors must show that police officers not only used excessive force but *intended* to do so. The amount of proof necessary to obtain a conviction often depends on what some lawyers call "the blood-on-the-floor factor." "When you have a death or serious bodily injury involved, you up the chances of getting a conviction," Professor Days explains. "But if the case involves an altercation between a police officer and a citizen, and there is an injury such as a broken bone or missing teeth, it is unlikely that one will get a conviction."

Some argue that the "specific intent" legal standard should be interpreted more loosely. In fact, some federal courts have interpreted civil rights statutes to include prosecution of police officers for their "reckless disregard of the law." According to attorney Michael J. Pastor, "When officers such as those in the Diallo case act in reckless disregard of a suspect's constitutional rights, prosecutors should act to vindicate those rights." When police officers are forced to make quick use-of-force decisions, as they did in the Diallo case, officers will rarely specifically intend to violate the rights of the victim, Pastor claims; thus if officers know that the court applies only the stricter "specific intent" standard, officers can disregard the risk that they might violate a suspect's civil rights and act without fear of punishment. However, if the "reckless disregard of the law" standard were applied instead of "specific intent," Pastor argues, police officers would know that if they are reckless, they might risk violating a suspect's rights and face criminal prosecution.

Whether or not the obstacles faced by federal prosecutors deter the punishment of police brutality remains controversial. The authors in the following chapter debate whether police brutality is adequately punished.

Federal Lawsuits Against Police Departments Effectively Punish Police Brutality

by Alexis Agathocleous

About the author: *Alexis Agathocleous, an instruction assistant at Yale University Law School, writes for the Vera Institute of Justice, a research institute that makes policy recommendations for the criminal justice system.*

The 1970s saw the [U.S. Department of Justice Civil Rights] Division's first attempt to prosecute whole departments rather than individual officers. Division prosecutors became aware that even when individual criminal prosecutions were successful, they often failed to eliminate the larger culture of abuse and impunity that framed these cases. Drew Days was Assistant Attorney General for Civil Rights in the late 1970s. He remembers the prosecution of members of the Philadelphia homicide squad as "an object lesson on the limits of this enforcement mechanism." The defendants, he explains,

> were notorious for telling suspects in interviews that they would hit them so hard that their hearts would stop if they didn't cooperate. This was a squad that ultimately got a completely innocent civilian to confess to an arson-related murder of a family in North Philadelphia. It was quite a devastating bunch.

Failing to Promote Reform

The Division tried this case, and won. But Days recalls that the victory failed to spark any change in the department or prevent further abuse:

> After the officers were convicted, they took appeals. When Frank Rizzo, police chief in Philadelphia at the time, was asked whether he was going to suspend

Alexis Agathocleous, *Prosecuting Police Misconduct: Reflections on the Role of the U.S. Civil Rights Division*. New York: Vera Institute of Justice, 1998. The paper summarizes a roundtable discussion by eight former officials of the Civil Rights Division of the U.S. Department of Justice, including five former assistant attorneys general. From *Prosecuting Police Misconduct: Reflections on the Role of the U.S. Civil Rights Division*. Copyright © 1998 by Vera Institute of Justice. All rights reserved. Reproduced by permission.

the convicted officers, he said 'no.' He said that these officers were innocent until proven guilty by the U.S. Supreme Court, and that he was not going to do anything to violate that presumption of innocence. So we're talking about one of the most powerful tools the federal government possesses being essentially toothless when dealing with institutional and organic problems within a police department like Philadelphia's. It made no systematic change in the way that the police department functioned. Another group simply came forward, took over the homicide squad, and presumably did many of the same things.

Others agree that individual prosecutions often fail to produce the institutional changes needed to eliminate future abuse. John Dunne, Assistant Attorney General between 1990 and 1993, observes, "I really don't think that those few isolated successful prosecutions have had the trickle-down effect that you would hope on the common denominator of police misconduct."

In Philadelphia, violations of citizens' rights continued to occur and dozens of cases of misconduct remained unaddressed. Staff at the Civil Rights Division realized that

> *"Because pattern-or-practice suits would be aimed at entire law enforcement agencies, . . . they would enable the [Civil Rights] Division to target . . . problems."*

the incidents they had prosecuted were not isolated, but rather that the Police Department's management actually fostered misconduct and condoned cover-ups. In April 1979, the Police Project of the Public Interest Law Center of Philadelphia (PILCOP) confirmed the extent of the problem, publishing evidence that between 1970 and 1978, Philadelphia police officers killed 75 people who were not involved in a violent felony, were unarmed, and were running away when shot. They found that, on average, the police shot a civilian every week, and that two-thirds of those killed by police were African-American or Latino. Only nine of these incidents of deadly force resulted in disciplinary hearings.

Bringing Civil Actions

Faced with these facts, Drew Days remembers, federal prosecutors "began to think about what course of action might be available that hadn't yet been tried." In an unprecedented move, the Division decided to take civil action against the Philadelphia Police Department and key city officials—including the mayor, the medical examiner, the police commissioner, and 15 other police administrators.

Division prosecutors filed *United States v. City of Philadelphia* in August 1979, alleging systematic police abuse of civilians, and departmental policies and practices that deliberately encouraged such abuses. They introduced evidence of routine brutality; use of force to extract information and confessions; illegal stops, searches and seizures; and regular use of racial slurs by officers. They asserted that the defendants allowed the use of firearms in situations proscribed by state or federal law, condoned fragmented investigations into incidents of abuse, suppressed incriminating evidence of police wrongdoing, accepted implausible explanations for violent incidents caused by police, harassed complainants and witnesses, and terminated investigations of incidents of misconduct prematurely. They also accused the defendants of refusing to discipline officers for known violations, and ignoring the disproportionate victimization of racial minorities.

Drew Days remembers that the Division "put every resource into that case that we reasonably could. We had a prosecution team of six or seven lawyers, an ancillary support staff, and a special team of FBI agents. We had an amazing group working on the case."

The civil lawsuit significantly expanded the Division's previous action against individuals at the Philadelphia Police Department. Rather than targeting specific officers for specific criminal acts, the Division turned the spotlight onto institution-wide misconduct for the first time. But the defendants vigorously challenged the lawsuit's legality, arguing that the Attorney General had no standing to mount such a prosecution. Congress, they contended, had repeatedly denied the Attorney General the power to "seek to advance the civil rights of third persons," and the United States itself had no legal interests that had been affected by any actions of the Philadelphia Police Department. The defendants prevailed and the case was dismissed.

Pattern-or-Practice Lawsuits

Despite this setback, federal prosecutors and civil rights advocates continued to argue that federal civil cases should be allowed. If the law did not currently permit the Division to sue, then Congress should change the law. Using *United States v. City of Philadelphia* as a model, they proposed that the Civil Rights Division should be authorized to bring actions against departments that engage in a pattern-or-practice of depriving civilians of their rights. Because pattern-or-practice suits would be aimed at entire law enforcement agencies, proponents pointed out, they would enable the Division to target institutional and organic problems in a way that criminal prosecutions could not. These proposals were rejected by Congress in 1980 and again in 1991. But in 1994 Congress finally awarded the Civil Rights Division authority to bring these civil cases. . . .

Prosecutors and advocates have long argued that civil actions against departments—such as the one that the Division attempted to bring against the Philadelphia Police Department in 1979—should be made part of the federal government's arsenal against police misconduct. The beating of Rodney King[1] focused congressional attention on the problem of police misconduct, and in

---

1. King was beaten on March 3, 1991, by three Los Angeles police officers as their supervisor watched. After the officers were acquitted of excessive force on April 29, 1996, rioting broke out in Los Angeles. On April 16, 1993, a federal jury convicted two of the officers of violating King's civil rights.

1994—15 years after *United States v. City of Philadelphia*—the Violent Crime Control and Law Enforcement Act (the omnibus Crime Bill) included a provision that awarded "pattern-or-practice" authority to the Department of Justice for the first time.

When Civil Rights Division prosecutors gather sufficient evidence of systematic violations of constitutional rights or federal law by a police department, they may seek a judge's statement of the legal standards that govern that department (declaratory relief) and a court order that forces it to abide by those laws (equitable relief). This order can specify reforms that the department must implement in order to avoid further legal action.

> *"Pattern-or-practice suits force [police] departments to reassess and reform entire managerial, training, and disciplinary systems."*

Pattern-or-practice suits are pursued by the Division's Special Litigation Section. In order to obtain declaratory and equitable relief, the Section's prosecutors must prove in court that a law enforcement agency either has an illegal policy, or that a set of incidents constitute a pattern of unlawful conduct. The Division need not prove that discriminatory motives prompted the policy or conduct in question; but while in criminal cases evidence of misconduct must establish proof "beyond a reasonable doubt," in civil cases the proof must satisfy a lower standard of a "preponderance of the evidence." Conduct constituting a pattern or practice of misconduct can include excessive force, harassment, false arrests, coercive sexual conduct, and unlawful stops, searches, and arrests.

The Civil Rights Division used its new pattern-or-practice authority for the first time in 1996. Special Litigation Section prosecutors alleged that, since 1990, the police department in Pittsburgh, Pennsylvania had engaged in systematic violations of the law in its misconduct investigations and its training, supervision, and discipline procedures. They based these allegations on a long process of interviewing police officials and witnesses to alleged abuse, reviewing police records, and evaluating departmental policies with the help of experts.

The Consent Decree

The defendants—which included the Pittsburgh Bureau of Police (PBP) and the Department of Public Safety (DPS)—denied all the Division's allegations. However, they agreed that the best way to avoid the risk and costs of the federal suit, as well as future claims of systematic misconduct, was to reform their managerial practices and procedures. They therefore entered into a consent decree with the Division that established comprehensive and specific measures to improve their conduct. The consent decree was approved by the Court on April 26, 1997, and included the following reforms:

• The PBP must keep automated records on the performance of every officer. This includes an early warning system to identify problem officers.

- The PBP must implement a use of force policy that is in compliance with laws and professional standards. It must also develop a use of force reporting system.
- Only specially trained personnel are allowed to conduct strip searches, and only when authorized by a supervisor.
- The City must analyze reports of racial bias and use of racial epithets on a quarterly basis.
- Police officers who are arrested, charged, or accused of untruthfulness, physical force, racial bias, or domestic violence in a civil suit must notify their employers.
- Cultural sensitivity training must be expanded to include training in communications skills and avoiding improper racial, ethnic, and sexual communications.
- An independent auditor must prepare quarterly reports on compliance with all aspects of the order.

The consent decree is an order of the court with a five-year active life. The City of Pittsburgh must be in compliance with its demands within three years—that is, by April 2000—and must maintain these standards for two more. It can then petition to vacate the decree. The judge who approved the decree also determines whether the City is in compliance with its terms.

> *"Members of the public who are concerned about law and order may ultimately see institutional change as fairer than targeting the behavior of particular police officers."*

The Civil Rights Division entered into a similar consent decree on August 28, 1997 with the City of Steubenville, Ohio. Earlier that year, the Division had filed a civil suit against the Steubenville Police Department, accusing it of engaging in a pattern-or-practice of subjecting civilians to excessive use of force, false arrests, charges, and reports, and improper stops, searches, and seizures. Police officers in Steubenville reportedly beat witnesses of misconduct, falsified reports, and tampered with official police records in order to cover up misconduct. As in Pittsburgh, the department denied the allegations. But, among other reforms, the city agreed to improve training, implement use-of-force guidelines and reporting procedures, create an internal affairs unit, and develop a system to track civilian complaints and civil lawsuits against officers.

The Potential for Reform

Because pattern-or-practice authority is a relatively new development, scholars, prosecutors, and other observers are reluctant to draw firm conclusions about these federal civil actions at this point. But they note that these suits give the Division the considerable capability to open up an entire law enforcement organization to scrutiny. As the Pittsburgh and Steubenville consent decrees illustrate, pattern-or-practice suits force departments to reassess and reform entire managerial, training, and disciplinary systems.

Proponents of these suits believe that they can generate meaningful institutional reform in at least three ways beyond the detailed terms of the consent decrees themselves. First, they engage police leadership in the process, and it is they who set the tone on civil rights in their departments. As John Dunne explains,

> In going to speak to the National Police Academy as Assistant Attorney General, I was very troubled by remarks made by middle-level career police officers who were identified as prospective leaders. They showed very little interest in the work of the Civil Rights Division and the standards to which we believe their operations should be held. Like so many other things, this attitude starts at the top. Unless our message gets across to chiefs, mayors, and those who have ultimate responsibility, problems are going to continue.

Consent decrees are therefore particularly powerful, Dunne argues, because they force leaders and top-level officials to commit to reform:

> If you can get a police chief, a mayor, or a governor to be a signatory to a piece of civil litigation, I think you are going to achieve a great deal more in producing a proper standard of conduct throughout the department. It's got to start at the top.

Dunne also believes that pattern-or-practice suits are less threatening to the public than criminal prosecutions aimed at individual police officers. He explains, "As outrageous as an individual officer's conduct may be, deep down the average citizen may think, 'this cop in blue stands between me and the evil forces in the community.' On the other hand when the public sees a litany of stipulations to which a police department has agreed, it's palatable." Members of the public who are concerned about law and order may ultimately see institutional change as fairer than targeting the behavior of particular police officers. This may result, Dunne argues, in greater public support for efforts to reform the police.

Finally, reform packages that result from pattern-or-practice suits have a wider national impact than sanctions resulting from localized criminal cases. Although the consent decrees reached in Pittsburgh and Steubenville were tailored to problems within those specific departments, they have been used as models of reform by other law enforcement agencies. They offer those interested in remedying misconduct a tangible set of changes that can be effected in departments throughout the country.

Federal Intervention in Police Department Policies Discourages Effective Policing

by Darlene Hutchinson

About the author: *Darlene Hutchinson is publishing director of the Law Enforcement Alliance of America, a national coalition of law enforcement professionals.*

A legal battle is now being waged in U.S. District Court in Columbus, Ohio, pitting the legal weight and limitless financial resources of the U.S. Justice Department [DOJ] against that town's right to control its own police department.[1]

At stake is no less than the fate of local agencies everywhere to control their own destinies versus an emerging pattern by the [Bill] Clinton Justice Department aimed at federalizing municipal police departments, not to mention the states-rights concerns and the blurring division between the branches of government.

Unfortunately, Columbus isn't the first victim. Already federal takeovers of departmental policy have occurred in Steubenville, Ohio, and in Pittsburgh, Penn. The police administrators in these two cities were, more or less, forced to sign consent decrees admitting their departments had participated in a pattern of civil rights violations and therefore needed the federal government to come in and run all future operations.

Fighting Federal Control

What sets Columbus apart, what makes them different from these other two cities which acquiesced, is that this municipality has a contract with the local police union and can't make a deal with the devil without approval of FOP [Frater-

---

1. On September 4, 2002, a federal district court judge dismissed the federal lawsuit that accused the Columbus Police Department of civil rights violations.

Darlene Hutchinson, "Feds Threaten to Take over Ohio Police Department—Could Your Town Be Next?" *SHIELD*, Winter/Spring 2000. Copyright © 2000 by Law Enforcement Alliance of America, Inc. Reproduced by permission.

nal Order of Police] members—and thankfully they're fighting. The city's 30-year history of collective bargaining with rank-and-file legally forbids the city from exposing its officers to many of the changes demanded by the DOJ.

Therefore, since Columbus and the police union have decided not to sign the consent decree, the Department of Justice has filed a lawsuit against the city to recoup all federal grant money awarded over the years. Some would call this extortion.

Bill Capretta, president of the Capitol City Lodge No. 9 of the Fraternal Order of Police in Columbus, says the lawsuit is the "latest step in a Justice Department campaign to impose federal (law enforcement) standards on police departments nationwide."

Alleging a "pattern of civil rights abuses" by the Columbus police department, DOJ attorneys filed their suit on October 21, [1999], forcing Columbus to let the federal government implement their policy changes in the city's police department, which would include training and staffing reforms, as well as new disciplinary and reporting procedures. The suit was apparently the culmination of a two-year investigation.

The Justice Department alleges that its investigation uncovered "a pattern of abuses" by officers and that this pattern was tolerated by city administrators.

How Can This Be?

Many have asked how the federal government could threaten to recoup grant money spent years ago by local administrators; what authority do they have to extort the local police? In fact, these powers were vested in DOJ by the 1994 Omnibus Crime Act (the far-reaching law for which LEAA [Law Enforcement Alliance of America] was the only outspoken critic among police groups back then). Now in accordance with the authority derived from this act, the federal government has deemed the city of Columbus incapable of correcting such "wrongdoing."

So, essentially, any department which has accepted any federal grant money, and whose actions could be construed as inappropriate by a DOJ official (often a White House appointee), and who won't give in when faced with a "consent decree," may have to pay back the millions of federal dollars accepted and spent over the years (which could include

> *"It's bad for officer safety when bureaucrats play Monday morning quarterback with no real knowledge of the pressures on the street."*

everything from COPS [Community Oriented Policing Services] grants, to money from "violence against women" legislation, to victims funding, training money, etc.).

Incidentally, *The Columbus Dispatch* reports that no less than 12 other cities nationwide are the focus of similar investigations. . . .

The Content of the Consent Decree

The 48-page consent decree presented to Columbus officials by the Justice Department essentially says "The city denies all allegations and enters this Decree for the exclusive purpose of avoiding the risks and burdens of litigation. . . ." It seems this is yet one more indication of a pattern of how this Administration accomplishes its goals by backing its "victims" into a corner. Much like the pressure it's exerting on the gun industry, Clinton appointees are going after local police departments trying to impose their "style" of policing.

> *"The requirement that all complaints against personnel are investigated, even anonymous ones, . . . encourages bogus and unfounded accusations."*

Under the proposed consent decree in Columbus, a supervising lieutenant is required to review and/or discipline an officer who has "used force" five times in a one-year period. And the DOJ's consent decree defines "use of force" as follows: An effort by a Columbus officer to compel compliance from a civilian which elicits more than minimal resistance, including use of chemical spray, and aiming a firearm at a civilian. (It excludes mere presence of a police officer or police canines, police issuance of verbal commands, handcuffing with minimal or no resistance, a come-along grasp when the civilian is offering minimal or no resistance, the display or brandishing of a firearm, and aiming a firearm at a civilian when a supervisor orders guns drawn for purposes of a tactical entry.)

Obviously with such scrutiny, officers will be reluctant to act and use force when necessary, which could have a significant impact on the officers-killed and officers-injured rate which has decreased over the years. Officer Jim Gilbert reports that "after five uses-of-force in one year, officers may be counseled by a lieutenant and be retrained and possibly reprimanded or fired. This is unbelievable. I know for a fact in my precinct, I go on anywhere from 5 to 20 gun-runs or shots-fired calls in a week. The street officers here are just amazed and keep saying to ourselves, surely they wouldn't restrict or hamper something as important as officer safety, however, they are trying to do so."

Another item within the proposed "consent decree" is the creation of an "independent monitor [IM]." This independent monitor will report to a federal judge on whether the city is properly implementing the consent decree, and the IM can re-open any misconduct investigation or firearms-discharge investigation. Further, there is no time limit to file a complaint if the complainant alleges criminal behavior, excessive force, false arrest, unreasonable search/seizure, or discrimination.

The hiring of civilian auditors is also required, and the public will have input on crowd control policies if the provisions of this far-reaching consent decree are ever implemented.

Also, the consent decree requires that internal affairs investigators must follow-up on every complaint against officers, even anonymous ones. This way of thinking falls right in line with the initiatives the NAACP [National Association for the Advancement of Colored People] has been calling for the Administration to implement—a year ago the organization asked Clinton and [former Attorney General Janet] Reno to start withholding federal law enforcement dollars from departments with an unusually high number of excessive-force complaints (even before the complaints are proven!).

The Side Effects

There's an array of reasons why such federalization is unwise. First and foremost, it's bad for officer safety when bureaucrats play Monday morning quarterback with no real knowledge of the pressures on the street. Recently we've seen criticism of cops in [the management of the 1999 demonstrations at the World Trade Organization summit in] Seattle and at [the 1999 shootings at] Columbine [High School in Colorado] who "didn't act quickly enough." In contrast, the four NYPD [New York Police Department] officers who were pursuing a rapist when they encountered Amadou Diallo were charged with second-degree murder for responding too quickly when they opened fire on him after he suddenly reached for his waistband. Obviously, society is looking for infallible geniuses who will always make flawless split-second, life-and-death decisions in tough environments. Yet we pay surgeons 10 or 20 times as much as police to operate in pristine, controlled conditions.

With "independent monitors," civilian review boards and out-of-touch administrators scrutinizing their every move, morale among police officers is bound to plummet, which is exactly what has happened in Pittsburgh, after officials in that city signed a similar consent decree in 1997, allowing a federal takeover. Under these conditions, apathy is a certain by-product.

Officer Chuck Bosetti, of the Pittsburgh FOP, says "proactive policing" is discouraged under the DOJ consent decree. As a result, disorderly conduct arrests have dropped in that city 60 percent since the consent decree was signed in 1997, and gun-related arrests have dropped 22 percent. Obviously cops are becoming reluctant to enforce laws, and Bosetti points to complacency. "We're not the ones who are suffering," he says. "We're doing less and getting paid the same. It's the public who's affected." Smokey Hynes, FOP president in Pittsburgh, predicted in 1997 when the consent decree was signed that police would refuse to "take that extra step" when investigating suspected criminal activity out of fear of lawsuits and baseless allegations.

> *"'Isolated or accidental or sporadic discriminatory acts' do not fall under the 'pattern or practice' term."*

Conversely, Pittsburgh Police Chief Robert McNeilly seems happy to be operating under the feds' consent decree since he's been able to implement changes he had already envisioned for the police department when he was hired, but now he's having to hasten his reforms under DOJ's watchful eye. Incidentally, Pittsburgh must operate two full years at 100 percent compliance before the restrictions are lifted (and even after two and a half years, they still have not reached 100 percent compliance).

One of the biggest arguments by officers in Pittsburgh is the requirement that all complaints against personnel are investigated, even anonymous ones, which encourages bogus and unfounded accusations. Further, unproven complaints are left in an officer's file for three years after he leaves the force, and if an officer receives five similar complaints (even if all are anonymous), he may be counseled, transferred or sent for retraining. But the Pittsburgh chief doesn't seem to understand the officers' frustration and explains that investigating anonymous complaints against officers (even though it could be perceived as denying due process), reflects the model policies suggested by the International Association of Chiefs of Police. (Now it becomes clearer whose side the chief is on.)

Giving Cops a Voice

Ironically, the Clinton Administration, that openly acknowledged support by labor unions in securing the White House during the 1996 re-election campaign and continually claims to be supportive of law enforcement, is the force behind this effort that effectively crushes police collective-bargaining.

For instance, the consent decree's "independent monitor" could make decisions in Columbus which would supersede and negate the present collective-bargaining process. What's worse is that the city and DOJ were negotiating for more than a year about the proposed consent decree, more or less behind closed doors, and the FOP was barred from attending or commenting on those proceedings. [In the summer of 1999], the police union and its officer-members were notified that the federal takeover of the department was underway.

Further proof of the Justice Department's arrogant and dismissive attitude toward officers' participation in determining their own fate was evident in the request made by DOJ to the presiding court to postpone deliberation on the suit until December 20, 1999. Police observers believe that date was selected as a blatant move to deny officers a role in the court proceedings since it came one week after the expiration of the FOP contract with the city of Columbus, and therefore the union could have been precluded from having a say in the matter.

Nonetheless, officers in Columbus are demanding to be heard. Shortly after the DOJ filed suit against the city (when the city failed to concede), the FOP filed a 19-page motion asking U.S. Judge John D. Holschuh to include the organization as a defendant in the DOJ lawsuit. FOP President [William] Capretta claimed in the motion that the union is best able to defend itself and rank-and-file officers against the federal claims and protect their reputations, because the city has its own separate interests to look out for. Moreover, James E. Phillips, an attorney for the FOP, has demanded that the Justice Department divulge the specifics behind the alleged widespread abuse of civil rights by Columbus police, and if the FOP is approved as a defendant in the case, they can compel the DOJ to divulge evidence and specifics. "There are only three cases we've heard about," says Phillips.

Three cases? Another source cites a dozen incidents of wrongdoing since 1993. This is amazing considering the literally millions of contacts between police and the public, and is hardly indicative of a "pattern." Columbus officer James Scanlon said it best in a September 1999 letter-to-editor: "I want police officers held to a higher standard. Nothing is worse than a dirty cop. Let's continue to bust them on a case-by-case basis and let their guilt or innocence be determined by facts instead of innuendo."

But as this saga unfolds, at issue will be the definition of "pattern or practice" as given in the 1994 Omnibus Crime Bill. [In 1998] the U.S. Supreme Court interpreted the same phrase as used in the 1964 Civil Rights Act, saying that the matter at hand had to be the "standard operating procedure—the regular, rather than unusual practice. . . . [That] isolated or accidental or sporadic discriminatory acts" do not fall under the "pattern or practice" term. The three cases the FOP has been told about hardly fall under this definition.

Civilian Oversight Promotes Impartial Investigation of Police Misconduct

by Emma Phillips and Jennifer Trone

About the authors: *Emma Phillips is a program analyst and Jennifer Trone is a senior writer and editor for the Vera Institute of Justice, a research institute that makes policy recommendations for the criminal justice system.*

In both new and more mature democratic societies, citizens are putting increased pressure on police not only to control crime but also to treat everyone they contact fairly and with respect. A continuing challenge, therefore, is to create practical mechanisms for citizens to routinely oversee and influence the conduct of law enforcement, including the manner in which police exercise their powers to arrest, interrogate, and use lethal and non-lethal force.

Responding to a Crisis in Confidence

In countries, states, or cities where there is a commitment to democratic governance, civilian oversight appears to arise in response to a specific crisis of confidence in the police. Until such a crisis occurs, democratic societies tend to leave police to look after themselves. The crisis in confidence may take the form of a specific and highly publicized event or trend. The prototypical example in the United States was the Rodney King incident in 1991, where officers of the Los Angeles Police Department were recorded on a bystander's videotape beating an African-American motorist senseless with their batons. The incident launched a decade of focused attention and action on police reform in the United States. Similarly, in Brazil public outrage over the large number of

Emma Phillips and Jennifer Trone, *Building Public Confidence in Police Through Civil Oversight.* New York: Vera Institute of Justice, 2002. The paper summarizes remarks at an international meeting on civilian oversight of police sponsored by the Police Assessment Resource Center, the Vera Institute of Justice, and the Ford Foundation. The meeting brought together police officials and those who oversee their work. From *Building Public Confidence in Police Through Civil Oversight.* Copyright © 2002 by Vera Institute of Justice 2002. All rights reserved. Reproduced by permission.

deaths in police custody, particularly in the states of Rio de Janeiro and São Paulo, led to the creation of *Ouvidorias de Polícia* (Police Ombudsmen's offices) in nine Brazilian states.

A crisis in confidence may also come, as in Peru, in reaction to a period of undemocratic rule in which the authority of the police was abused for political ends. Officers functioning under the authoritarian government of President [Alberto] Fujimori were successful in combating the Shining Path [a Peruvian terrorist group]. But according to General Enrique Yépez Dávalos, the militaristic policing style they adopted to fight terrorism left local citizens equally vulnerable to crime and abuse by the officers who should have been protecting them. As a result, the police have found it difficult to shed this negative image and to gain the trust and confidence of the public. To address the problem, the Ministry of the Interior began a radical reorganization of the police in October 2001 that includes establishing ombudsmen's offices and creating neighborhood committees to improve public security. Similarly, in Nigeria the transition from military dictatorship to democracy has required changing the image of the police from a tool of an oppressive government to a public service agency. To facilitate this shift, national lawmakers reconstituted the Police Service Commission. Most governments have two unconnected agencies—one to punish misconduct and one to reward good performance—but the commission has both responsibilities, making it unusual and potentially a very effective form of civilian oversight.

> *"Where there is a commitment to democratic governance, civilian oversight appears to arise in response to a specific crisis of confidence in the police."*

In South Africa, the constitutional mandate for the Independent Complaints Directorate (ICD) was a central component of the country's transition to democracy. According to ICD Executive Director Karen McKenzie, the history of the South African police as a key instrument in enforcing apartheid means that the ICD has an obligation to provide all members of previously disenfranchised communities with an opportunity to report any insult or injury suffered at the hands of the police and to know that their complaints will be taken seriously.

Creating Civilian Oversight

In some contexts, mechanisms for civilian oversight may develop outside government. The Kenyan Human Rights Commission, a non-governmental organization [NGO] that currently monitors some aspects of police behavior, is a typical example. But civilian oversight can also arise organically from the concerns of even a small group of citizens. In Russia, for example, widespread police involvement in drug-trafficking spurred residents in one city to take on the problem themselves. They created a special foundation called A City Without Drugs, bought television cameras, and drove through the streets filming officers in the process of selling drugs. Then they showed the films to members of the National Anti-Drug Committee. With the committee's support, the films aired on national television, sparking demands for parliamentary hearings and focusing attention on the problem of narco-corruption in other cities.

Pramod Kumar, of the Institute of Communication and Development in Chandigarh, India, describes this kind of citizen organizing as "incident-related mobilization," in which a specific event creates a ground swell of interest and energy, but one that dissipates over time. Yet before the Russian citizens lost interest in the problem of narco-corruption, the campaign begun by A City Without Drugs evolved into a mechanism that engages citizens across the country in holding officers accountable for misconduct. Hotlines in four regions of the country—several more are in the works—give citizens a safe means to report officers who are selling drugs. These reports go to the police and to a nongovernmental organization.

If mechanisms for civilian oversight develop in response to particular historical and political conditions, their role and priorities also evolve as these conditions change. In the absence of a specialized civilian oversight institution in Kenya, for example, the Kenyan Human Rights Commission (KHRC), a nongovernmental advocacy organization with a broad mission, has been documenting complaints against the police, running public campaigns to promote police reform, and educating officers about human rights. According to Deputy Director Wambui Kimathi, these activities ensure that institutions like the police submit to what's known in Kiswahili as "kiti moto"— public scrutiny, or literally, the "hot seat."

> *"Some people [are convinced] that civil society should play an active role in strengthening law enforcement's own controls, rather than attempting to supplant them."*

Kenya's current process of constitutional review provides an opportunity to establish an organization dedicated solely to police oversight with the authority and resources to investigate complaints against the police, something the KHRC cannot do. Fundamental political shifts like those taking shape in Kenya offer opportunities for citizens and police leaders to jointly develop new, more efficient forms of civilian oversight.

Blending Internal and External Oversight

By definition, civilian oversight involves people outside the police gaining access to previously non-public or secret internal police processes in order to hold law enforcement accountable for its actions, policies, and priorities. In practice, however, there is always a division of responsibility between *external* review and law enforcement's own *internal* review systems. According to Merrick Bobb, director of the Police Assessment Resource Center (PARC) in Los Angeles and monitor of the Los Angeles County Sheriff's Department, there may even be aspects of the oversight process that police departments are better equipped to handle than non-police organizations. He observes, for example, that while agencies outside the police can be capable of investigating low-level complaints, reviewing fatalities and other serious incidents requires the greater resources, expertise, and structure that a police agency's internal affairs division offers. Yet because it's always difficult for any police officer to judge another officer—making internal investigations susceptible to bias and distortion—Bobb argues that these investigations in particular should be carefully reviewed and judged for objectivity, thoroughness, and fairness by an agency or group operating outside the police.

> *"To be accepted as legitimate by both the police and the public, the oversight agency must be widely regarded as impartial and objective."*

Bobb's example illustrates the relative strengths and weaknesses of internal and external review, which, when fostered appropriately, can complement each other. Equally important, many advocates of civilian oversight argue that there will never be enough resources to support external oversight alone. Creating false expectations about what an oversight agency can achieve only leads to public frustration and disenchantment. These concerns have convinced some people that civil society should play an active role in strengthening law enforcement's own controls, rather than attempting to supplant them.

David Bruce, a researcher at the Centre for Studies in Violence and Reconciliation in South Africa, believes this task is particularly important in emerging democracies where police typically have very poor controls over their own behavior and external oversight mechanisms are generally under-funded. Rather than trying to become an alternative to internal review, Bruce argues, oversight mechanisms that operate outside the police should use their limited resources to help law enforcement agencies establish systems to monitor and control their own behavior. The challenge, he adds, is to form civilian oversight mechanisms that acknowledge and respect the expertise of police and the complex challenges of fighting crime.

An interesting experiment along these lines is taking place in Los Angeles. The County Board of Supervisors recently created the Office of Independent Review, staffed by a group of six civil rights lawyers who are empowered to participate in and help direct the sheriff department's internal investigations of complaints against its officers. The lawyers then recommend a disposition to the sheriff and can also recommend discipline if warranted. The Office of Independent Review was proposed initially by Sheriff Lee Baca. Policing experts in the United States are closely watching this unusual blend of internal and external review to see if it succeeds. . . .

Civilian agencies that oversee the police differ widely in terms of their involvement in the process of investigating complaints against officers and determining punishment. Choices about how involved to be in the investigation are influenced by the agency's capacity and legal authority—whether it has the power to subpoena witnesses and documents, hold public hearings, and provide legal advice to complainants. Some agencies assume primary responsibility for conducting investigations. At the other extreme are agencies that lack the authority or resources to conduct any investigations. But perhaps most common are agencies that monitor the police department's investigations and only occasionally launch their own inquiries—usually in response to allegations of very serious misconduct or when the department's investigation appears incomplete or faulty. Similarly, some oversight agencies have no influence over how misconduct is punished, while others can make recommendations, and a few have even more authority.

The state ombudsmen in Brazil represent one extreme. None of the nine ombudsmen are permitted to investigate alleged incidents of misconduct, and they have no influence over whether and how to discipline officers who engage in misconduct. They do, however, review investigations conducted by the police *corregedorias* (internal affairs divisions) and can press for additional fact finding. According to Julita Lemgruber, director of the Center for Studies of Public Security and Citizenship and former ombudswoman for the state of Rio de Janeiro, these restrictions undermine public confidence in the ombudsmen and severely limit their ability to respond effectively to complaints. For Lemgruber, the next logical step in Brazil is giving ombudsmen a bigger role in investigating complaints and punishing officers. Specifically, she and the center have recommended that the ombudsmen be given the legal authority and resources to set deadlines for internal investigations, determine when an investigation is complete, investigate serious cases of misconduct, and recommend punishment.

> *"One of the major goals of civilian oversight is to make law enforcement more transparent."*

At the other extreme in terms of investigations is South Africa's Independent Complaints Directorate (ICD). The ICD is required to investigate all deaths that are related to police action and may investigate any other alleged misconduct. In addition to other legal powers, ICD investigators can make arrests. While the ICD currently refers many less serious complaints back to the police for investigation, ICD director Karen McKenzie hopes that by 2005, her agency will be able to investigate all complaints. Her plans have been challenged by those who believe the ICD will never have enough funding to conduct a large number of investigations in an efficient manner. Following an investigation, the ICD may refer the case to the prosecutor's office, which decides whether to file criminal charges. The ICD may also recommend how the police department should discipline the officer involved.

The Human Rights Commissions (HRCs) in India represent a middle course.

159

They monitor the investigations that law enforcement conduct and launch their own investigations only when the police department's inquiry is inadequate. The HRC then recommends punishment for the officer and/or interim compensation for the victim.

A Need for Objectivity

Merrick Bobb, monitor of the Los Angeles County Sheriff's Department and director of PARC, has pointed out that when oversight agencies get involved in investigating allegations of misconduct and determining punishment, they are required to make judgments about both the officers and the citizens involved. In order for those judgments to be accepted as legitimate by both the police and the public, the oversight agency must be widely regarded as impartial and objective. And to achieve such status, the agency has to function in a deliberate and pragmatic fashion, resisting impulses to advocate wider social change or to amplify the public outrage that led to its creation.

The moral authority of the oversight entity is partly derived from the experience and integrity of its members. The "Protection of Human Rights Act 1993," which constituted the national and state Human Rights Commissions in India, states that the chairperson of the national HRC must be a retired chief justice of the Supreme Court and the chairperson of a state HRC must be a retired chief justice of a high court. Members of the national and state HRCs are appointed by the president of India and by the governor of the state, respectively. According to Mr. Sankar Sen, senior fellow at the Institute of Social Sciences in New Delhi, the HRCs have sufficient moral and political sway to be effective. Experience in West Bengal provides good evidence for his claim. According to B.P. Singh, additional director general of the West Bengal Human Rights Commission, 97 percent of that commission's recommendations have been implemented.

One of the major goals of civilian oversight is to make law enforcement more transparent, particularly in how these agencies respond to officers who abuse their authority. The ability of a civilian oversight agency to effectively communicate the investigation of an allegation and the results of that process to the complainant and the public—and to the police if the oversight agency is conducting the investigation—could be just as important as the actual resolution. In a survey of residents of Rio de Janeiro and São Paulo who filed complaints against the police, 62 percent were not satisfied by the work done by the ombudsmen's office. This is hardly surprising since 56 percent of the people surveyed didn't even know the results of their complaint. By keeping complainants informed about the status of their cases, the ombudsmen's offices might be able to significantly improve how the public views their work and the police.

Civilians Cannot Objectively Oversee Police Practices

by Bill Rhetts

About the author: *Bill Rhetts—a retired police officer who served in Fontana, Los Angeles, and Riverside, California—was the sole police officer sitting on the* Police Policy Review Commission, *a citizens review board in Riverside.*

The people who press for "civilian review boards" are always those who have a "bone to pick" with the police: either disgruntled former police "experts" or those associated with those who feel they've been "done wrong" by officers.

The first issue to consider, is what would the purpose of a "civilian review board" (CRB) be? The Riverside Police Department currently has a police advisory committee, [Law Enforcement Political Action Council] (LEPAC.)

If it is to review specific police actions, this purpose is flawed in several areas. First, all police actions are presently subject to review by the citizen complaint process, internal review—triggered by concerns of co-workers or supervision/management, the District Attorney, the Grand Jury, the CA DOJ [California Department of Justice], the CA DFEH [California Department of Fair Employment and Housing], the US DOJ [United States Department of Justice] / FBI, etc. A CRB is clearly redundant.

Who Should Evaluate Police Officers?

A secondary issue would be, what would qualify members of a board to investigate and evaluate police actions? In the profession of law enforcement, we do not consider a police officer to be a "seasoned veteran" until he or she has "five years patrol experience." In other words, even a newly sworn police officer who has completed the police academy is not even qualified to pass judgment as a Police Review Board member.

Several difficulties are encountered here. Lay persons lack a sufficient understanding of police practices and operating conditions to knowledgeably perform a meaningful evaluation. This would be similar to an automobile mechanic being chosen to evaluate the work of a surgeon. Having currently serving law enforcement personnel would achieve no benefit above present processes. Often cities using CRBs pay more dollars in civil law suits, simply because the CRB did not agree with the Officer's tactics. . . .

Even having former law enforcement personnel would present several different problems. Counter productive to the notion of having "knowledgeable" people involved in the process is the problem of "perishable skills" and "stale" knowledge. Police work is a dynamic process, which is impacted by continuously evolving tactics, equipment, theories, statutory law, case law, policies, and other variables. The final option would be to train/educate civilian board members or investigators, to a level comparable to sworn officers/investigators. This too is flawed, however, as it is ludicrous to suggest that a student is qualified to accurately evaluate the performance of a practitioner. In short, only those who are contemporary police practitioners are qualified to accurately evaluate contemporary police actions. The fact that some people do not trust the police does not change this fact. Complaints against medical professionals are investigated by qualified medical personnel. Complaints against mechanics are investigated by persons with a qualifying mechanical background. Financial audits are performed by accountants.

And as to the question of how can the officer's own department be trusted to address complaints or objectively investigate misconduct, consider this: Have you ever in ANY business or service operation seen it suggested that "If you have a complaint, please do not disturb the manager. We ask that you immediately bring any problems to the attention of our competition." Of course not! Who is more qualified to satisfy a complaint than the supervisor or manager of the person who delivered the service at issue? NO ONE!

Unrealistic Expectations

Lastly, let us consider what a CRB would accomplish with their findings. Would it have the ability to terminate an officer? Obviously not. Would it have the ability to prosecute an officer? Obviously not. Would it have the ability to otherwise sanction an officer? Obviously not. Would its role be strictly advisory? Yes, obviously. What impact or influence would this advice carry? If it cannot, under existing state and federal law and labor contracts, cause sanctions on the basis of its own findings, would it be in a position to return the work of a departmental investigation for "additional work?" If so, would it have the ability to continue to direct reconsideration, until the department's findings mirrored its own opinions? That would not exactly constitute an objective process. It would simply provide "teeth" for an unnecessary, unqualified body to impart its own "feelings" as to the appropriateness of police action. Unfortunately, we are already well aware that there is a difference of opinion with regard to almost ALL police actions. Those who receive service or protection, may or may not be satisfied. Their satisfaction may be influenced by past experiences, expectations influenced by media portrayals, both fictional and non-fictional personal prejudices, drug/alcohol influence, mental stability, personal relationship to parties involved in the incident (including officers), and innumerable other factors. And then of course, the recipient of enforcement action is only happy with the officer in the rarest of situations.

Police work became the domain of professionals when the general populace found it was no longer able or willing to protect itself, person by person. Police officers are uniquely charged with performing a myriad of services and upholding volumes upon volumes of laws, as modified by even more volumes and volumes of case laws. They are expected to do so flawlessly, each and every time. They are expected to bring the unwilling into compliance and/or custody, without injury, or violent appearance. They are expected to master weapons and defensive arts, but never employ them against aggressors. In short, they are expected to fulfill the expectations of everyone, every time, in spite of the fact that nothing will satisfy most of those who call upon them because an overwhelming majority of those they contact created the situations they find themselves in by their own choice.

> *"Lay persons lack a sufficient understanding of police practices and operating conditions to knowledgeably perform a meaningful evaluation."*

Discouraging a Noble Profession

A civilian review board is an absolutely IDEAL way to discourage those few members of our society who have chosen a noble profession, followed an anointed calling, and performed invaluable service to their fellow man, by second guessing and sanctioning them for actions based upon a pure heart, sound training, established law, and well-thought policy. We police officers are not against citizens, the citizens are the reason we took that oath of office, and that is to protect & serve them. The word IDEAL above is written in upper case for a purpose. Ideally, we would all hope the best for our community, but realistically there is evil in our society. Many citizens want us to do our job, but they seem to not like the way it sometimes has to be done. As a former veteran of the Los Angeles Police Department, I have experienced that a CRB is idealistic and not realistic. . . . We can not be idealists in a real real world. Therefore, we must be realists.

I have often observed that there are essentially only two things that a police officer can do wrong . . . ANYTHING or NOTHING. A CRB would be a most effective way of proving out my observation.

My request in closing? In the time of an emergency don't call us, call the CRB members; so that when somebody needs saving from an armed criminal, or any other conceivable human service, at any hour, or any day, people will know there are a handful of PERFECT PEOPLE ready to respond. Let's just hope that the decision doesn't have to be made in a split second, under stressful conditions . . . CRB's do much better taking such matters under submission for resolution by committee.

Police Chiefs Should Be Given the Authority to Discipline Officers

by Anonymous

About the author: *An anonymous police chief responds to police-accountability recommendations in the* Connection, *a newsletter of the California Association of Human Relations Organizations, an organization that promotes human and civil rights.*

I agree with the premise that more needs to be done to ensure police are accountable to the community they serve. There are a number of impediments that discourage this from occurring.

The Bias of External Controls

Binding arbitration is a labor tool that impedes accountability. The reality of binding arbitration is that decisions regarding management of a police department are removed from the Chief and put into the hands of a third party that is NOT accountable to the community. I can give you countless horror stories of employees who won their jobs back, with back pay due to an arbitrator's ruling. The nature of binding arbitration, in practice, seems to be such that it is in the interest of the arbitrator to make both parties happy. I once read a study that revealed most arbitrators "split the baby", and render decisions that give something to both parties irrespective of the evidence. This is typically done to ensure that they will be selected to handle future arbitrations. Arbitration is one of the tools used to prevent the chief of police from having the final call on matters of discipline, promotion, reassignment and other matters necessary to manage a complex organization.

Civil service boards (personnel commissions) are another tool used to impede accountability. Most civil service boards are filled with members of the community picked by the mayor and city council. As such, they owe their allegiance to the politicians who appointed them. I am aware of notable cases where the boards have rendered politically expedient decisions to placate specific interest groups at election time. I have seen boards that have been totally co-opted by a police officer association that donated time and money to elect the political candidates who appointed them.

The Impediments to Justice

Personally, I would like to see the laws addressing confidentiality of internal investigations revised. As it stands now, virtually nothing surrounding a citizen complaint can be shared with the public or even the person who filed the complaint. This is extremely frustrating since the public has a right and a need to know whether their police department is being run in a professional manner. The existing blackout of information frustrates not only the citizen, but also the police administrator who is trying to inspire public confidence in the department.

Similarly the Peace Officers' Bill of Rights can be a significant hindrance to accountability. Under this legislation, police officers are afforded rights above and beyond what other public employees receive. In fact, . . . legislation establishes a statute of limitations on complaints by insisting that a department can't discipline an officer for an act that occurred more than a year ago.

Additionally, police officer associations were successful in getting a law enacted that forces persons seeking to file a complaint to read and sign an admonition acknowledging that they will be criminally prosecuted for filing false and malicious police misconduct complaints. One should consider that it is also a crime for police officers to falsely and maliciously file crime reports, yet we don't require police officers to read and sign a similar admonition every time they write a crime report.

Some agencies have gone so far as to wait 48 hours after a fatal use of force incident before they even attempt to interview the officer to find out what happened. And of course, the Peace Officers' Bill of Rights requires the interview to take place with the officer's attorney present and after they have had ample opportunity to review and dissect the evidence already brought to light. One should consider the fact that if we encountered a civilian who had shot and killed another person and refused to give a statement or cooperate with the investigation, we would probably arrest them at the scene absent evidence to suggest the shooting was justifiable.

Civilian review boards are only rarely effective for a variety of reasons. Much like civil service boards, they tend to be populated by appointees of elected officials who may have agendas that are not consistent with the search for truth. Civilian review boards are not exempt from being co-opted by the police officer association. Too often, they overrule recommendations of the chief and allow officers to return to work despite evidence of wrongdoing.

Another big factor undermining most efforts by civilian review boards efforts is the lack of resources and qualified staff allotted to them. Most boards do not have a sufficient number of investigators to effectively investigate the number of complaints. If the personnel on the board lack credibility, skill, and judgment, the whole process suffers. Review board investigations I have been involved with lack the detail and thoroughness to survive rigorous review of a Police Officers Association attorney.

I remember one case from an agency I used to work for that really highlighted the shortsightedness of review board actions. A Caucasian officer was charged with excessive force and racial slurs. The officer showed up at the hearing arm in arm with an African-American woman, who sat prominently in the front row. Sufficient evidence was presented to sustain at least some of the allegations, but the review board absolved the officer. I discussed the decision with some of the board members and they told me that they didn't feel the officer was "guilty of racism because he had a black girlfriend." In some jurisdictions, rank and file police officers actually prefer the civilian review process because they know it is not effective.

> *"The police chief should have the authority to hire, investigate, reassign, and discipline his/her personnel."*

The ultimate tool to discipline officers for criminal conduct is the district attorney. However, even the district attorney cannot always be relied upon to be the objective prosecutor of criminal violations committed by police officers. There is an almost incestuous relationship between the police and prosecutors. Each party knows they need the other to accomplish their normal missions. In most instances, the prosecutors are reluctant to prosecute officers for fear of damaging this relationship. This is particularly evident during election time, when the district attorney is seeking the endorsements of the police officers association.

However, I have also witnessed instances where the district attorney has sought to prosecute an officer to make it appear that he is tough on police misconduct. This typically occurs in real liberal communities where the endorsement of police associations carries no weight. I like the proposed idea of a special prosecutor who police chiefs can take charges of criminal conduct to for the prosecution of police officers.

The Value of Internal Control

The police chief should have the authority to hire, investigate, reassign, and discipline his/her personnel. If the chief is not performing his duties in a satisfactory manner, he or she should be removed and replaced with someone who will. I have a problem with the effort to create "shadow systems" of accountability. Chiefs of police and sheriffs get paid well to manage their departments. Why not hold them accountable for results? If the CEO of a major corporation is promoting conduct that results in millions of dollars of liability or produces a product that their customers are not satisfied with, the CEO is removed. Regrettably, in law enforcement the CEO keeps his/her job or is promoted and frequently has the responsibility to ensure the actions of his/her staff do not expose the city or county to costly lawsuits removed from his/her shoulders.

I think every law enforcement agency should have a mechanism for conducting proactive integrity investigations. Large departments should have full-time units that continually conduct audits, inspections and sting investigations on department personnel to ensure compliance with policy and ethical directives. Every department should have some mechanism to identify and address problem employees through an early warning system. As far as I am concerned, an officer who has racked up a significant number of unsustained complaints is as much a liability as an officer with a lot of sustained findings.

Law enforcement agencies should not only be allowed to share information about former employees . . . , but the California Commission on Peace Officer Standards and Training (POST) should be given the power to revoke peace officer certificates for misconduct. As it stands now, the POST certificate is a lifetime certificate, even if the recipient has been convicted of a felony and is legally prohibited for being a sworn officer. The Police Officer Research Advisory Committee (PORAC) is fighting efforts to give POST the authority to revoke peace officer certificates.[1]

Departments should also invest in technology to address police accountability. For example, officers can be mandated to use digital audio recorders and videos to record all contacts with citizens. My own experience, and that of many of my peers, is that the use of these types of technology significantly reduce the number of complaints against officers and assist in clarifying what actually transpired during a situation where a complaint has been filed.

---

1. A bill to give POST the power to revoke certificates failed in the California Senate on August 21, 2001.

Police Culture Makes It Difficult to Prosecute Police Brutality

by Jerome H. Skolnick

About the author: *Jerome H. Skolnick, a law professor at the Center for the Study of Law and Society at the University of California at Berkeley, coauthored with James J. Fyfe* Above the Law: Police and the Excessive Use of Force.

Police work in an unpredictable, sometimes violent, sometimes deadly environment. The potential danger of their workplace and their authority to use force to overcome resistance make it unsurprising that police actions can have brutal, even fatal, consequences—sometimes for innocent people, as Amadou Diallo's family knows all too well. It's also not surprising that, to cope with such violence and danger, police have developed a very close-knit culture that has its own set of norms. A policeman understands that his fellow officers might, in the heat of the moment, do things that they wouldn't want brought to light later on. Maybe they administered a "tune-up" to teach compliance to a suspect. Or maybe they visited a "beat wife," or prostitute, while on duty. A cop learns to back up the stories colleagues tell to superiors and investigators; in turn, he is confident colleagues will back him up.

The Blue Wall of Silence

This makes it very hard to investigate and prosecute cases of police misconduct. It may even encourage misconduct. Officers in the New York City Police Department's [NYPD's] 70th precinct did not protest when [on August 9, 1997] they saw Abner Louima being marched around the station house with his pants down to his ankles. Officer Justin Volpe proudly showed off the results of his sadistic anal assault. He waved a broken broomstick stained with blood and feces around [for] his fellow officers to see, even bragging to Sergeant Kenneth

Jerome H. Skolnick, "Code Blue," *American Prospect*, vol. 11, March 27, 2000, pp. 49–53. Copyright © 2000 by The American Prospect, Inc., 5 Broad Street, Boston, MA 02109. All rights reserved. Reproduced by permission.

Wernick that "I took a man down tonight." Yet no police officer came forward that night to report Volpe. Why not?

"Cops don't tell on cops," explained Officer Bernard Cawley in his testimony before the 1993 Mollen Commission, which investigated various cases involving police corruption:

> And if they did tell on them, just say if a cop decided to tell on me, his career's ruined. He's going to be labeled as a rat. So if he's got 15 more years to go on the job, he's going to be miserable because it follows you wherever you go. And he could be in a precinct—he's going to have nobody to work with. And chances are if it comes down to it, they're going to let him get hurt.

This is the famous "blue wall of silence," and it helps explain how it is that to the sodomizing of Abner Louima, the 56 blows inflicted upon Rodney King [on March 3, 1991], and the perjury of Detective Mark Fuhrman[1] we must now add both the growing corruption scandal in the Los Angeles Police Department [LAPD], the 41 bullets pumped into Amadou Diallo [on February 4, 1999], and the conspir-

> *"To cope with . . . violence and danger, police have developed a very close-knit culture that has its own set of norms."*

acy to obstruct justice of three officers found guilty of making up a story to cover up the role of one of them—Charles Schwarz—in the bathroom attack on Abner Louima. The LAPD corruption scandal—which includes allegations of shooting, beating, stealing and selling drugs, evidence planting, false arrests, and perjury—was fueled by the testimony of ex-LAPD antigang Officer Rafael Perez, who is cooperating with authorities to obtain a lighter sentence for his theft of cocaine placed in evidence. Since September 1999, when the scandal broke, more than 20 police officers have been relieved of duty, forced to quit, or fired. Dozens of criminal convictions have been overturned because of perjured testimony, and every day seems to bring new and increasingly damaging revelations. And while police in the Diallo trial were acquitted by a responsible jury, the fact that the defendants didn't come forward with their stories until the trial led some critics to suspect that the cops had used this time to construct a narrative relieving themselves of criminal responsibility. After all, the only witness who could contradict their account was no longer alive.

Policing Police Brutality

In its colloquial sense, the term "police brutality" suggests that police are deliberately teaching the recipient a lesson of compliance not sanctioned by any legitimate legal authority. Except in instances like Louima's, where the victim's

---

1. Fuhrman, a former police officer with the Los Angeles Police Department, was convicted of perjury for denying that he had used racial slurs while a witness during the course of the criminal trial of O.J. Simpson for the murder of his wife Nicole Brown Simpson and her friend Ron Goldman.

injuries are difficult to cover up, or like Rodney King's, when a bystander videotapes the beating, cases of police brutality in which the victim is a drug dealer, or is on parole or probation, rarely come to public attention. Some police consider the administration of a bit of vigilante justice to be nobody's business but their own. Had the police beaten Louima in a patrol car and nowhere else, the abuse would likely have passed unnoticed.

Even police who do end up accused of assaulting persons of low character, drug dealers, or ex-cons are hard to convict. For one thing, "police brutality" has no real meaning in court; it is a newspaper term, not a legal one. It is understood that police are trained and authorized to use force, even deadly force, when it is needed to arrest or apprehend someone who has probably committed a crime. Also, New York City has a "48 hour rule," negotiated by the Policeman's Benevolent Association (PBA), which gives police 48 hours to consult with PBA representatives before higher-ranking officials can talk to them. After the Diallo shooting, Internal Affairs investigators could not separate the four officers and immediately ask each of them what happened, which would have provided the best evidence. Instead, the police had ample time before the trial to consult with their lawyers and to develop a compelling story. Finally, judges and juries are reluctant to send otherwise seemingly unblemished police to prison, especially for inflicting punishment on "lowlifes." In the King case, the officers tried to persuade a Simi Valley jury that 56 powerful strokes were necessary to apprehend King—and they were acquitted. (They were later retried in a federal court in Los Angeles, where King testified, and they were convicted of violating King's civil rights.)

When specific charges are brought in police brutality cases, they are usually grounded in a bright legal line police are never supposed to cross: Once police have a suspect safely in custody, they are not allowed to use retributive force, no matter how heinous the crime they believe the suspect to have committed. In the Louima case, Officer Volpe believed—mistakenly, as it turns out—that Louima had assaulted him. The standard street punishment for such disrespect is a beating. Volpe shoved a broomstick up Louima's rectum and then broke front teeth with the feces-laden end of the stick to teach him to respect and fear police. (Volpe, the rare police officer convicted of assault, is now serving time.)

> *"The police had ample time before the trial to consult with their lawyers and to develop a compelling story."*

In the Diallo case, police argued that Diallo acted suspiciously, ignored their commands, and reached for a wallet that one of them thought was a gun—and that, consequently, they were justified in shooting to defend themselves. The claim that a suspect was "resisting"—in effect, the defense in the Diallo case—is the standard justification against accusations of brutality. (Police executives sometimes review the "resisting arrest" cases of police officers to determine whether a cop inclines toward administering vigilante justice.) But as the first King trial—and . . . , in a way, the Diallo trial—makes clear, the resisting-arrest defense often works for police.

Facing a Dilemma

As anyone who watches police movies knows, even "good cops" are presented with a real dilemma when they witness police misconduct. Police are caught between the imperatives of the blue wall of silence and police department rules compelling a cop who knows of police misconduct to notify Internal Affairs investigators immediately. If the officer promptly reports an incident, he's labeled a "rat" or a "cheese eater" by other cops. Thus police usually lapse into silence and talk about the misconduct of other cops only when pressured by Internal Affairs investigators or by threat of prosecution.

Clearly, the blue wall of silence can conceal (and possibly encourage) egregious violations of civil rights, not to mention less extreme incidents of unwarranted violence and abuse. But how do we break down the blue wall of silence without undermining necessary solidarity—a culture of "I'll watch your back and you watch mine" that often extends far beyond any literal line of fire—that is essential to police work? The first crack in the wall needs to be made by top police officials, prosecutors, and judges who have winked at and tolerated police perjury—"testalying"—for years.

The Official Corruption Unit

I have . . . been studying the Official Corruption Unit (OCU) of Manhattan District Attorney Robert M. Morgenthau, an office that is authorized to investigate the corruption of any public official but concentrates mainly on police cases. It maintains a regular, sometimes rocky relationship with the Internal Affairs Bureau of the NYPD. In some instances William Burmeister, who . . . was the OCU director, has felt that Internal Affairs moved too quickly to expose the names of officers being investigated, alerting other guilty cops to be on their guard. However honest and diligent Internal Affairs investigators might be, their organizational imperatives differ from the OCU's. While the NYPD's Internal Affairs Bureau wants to cut off scandals and their related publicity as quickly as possible, the district attorney's office, via the OCU, wants to see how far the corruption has spread, by turning crooked police into undercovers who wear "wires" to collect evidence to be used in courtroom prosecutions. Hence the tension: Do you allow the misconduct to continue in order to catch all the perpetrators while subjecting the public to the ongoing crimes of crooked and brutal police? Or do you arrest and charge quickly, understanding that other bad cops will be alerted to the investigation and get away?

The OCU was founded in 1991 when Governor Mario Cuomo disbanded New York State's Special Prosecutor's Office and redistributed its authority to local district attorneys. Morgenthau, a Manhattan icon, brought in Burmeister, a former assistant district attorney, to head the new unit. Burmeister's past prose-cutorial positions in the Manhattan District Attorney's Office and the New York State Organized Crime Task Force didn't prepare him for the levels of corruption, brutality, and perjury he discovered in the NYPD. His awakening came when he was investigating Manhattan's 30th precinct, located in Washington Heights, a heavy drug-dealing neighborhood in north Manhattan. Burmeister says that his investigation (which eventually led to the Mollen Commission Report) was prompted by a conversation he had with a defense attorney who, while acknowledging that his client was guilty, revealed that his client had had in his possession at the time of arrest three kilos of cocaine, not two as the police had charged. The police, the lawyer claimed, had stolen one kilo. Burmeister investigated; the lawyer was right.

Investigating Bad Cops

OCU investigations are often secret, employing tactics—stings, wires, wiretaps—familiar to organized-crime investigators. Burmeister showed me a "sting" video on which two officers stop a Dominican-looking driver—actually an undercover agent for the OCU—who has a brown paper bag on the front seat, containing several thousand dollars in marked money. One of the officers discovers the bag and then stuffs money into his pants. The thief was later apprehended and agreed to wear a wire for the OCU to help root out corruption in exchange for leniency.

To maintain the secrecy of the investigations, Burmeister asked Morgenthau to move the OCU's team of seven prosecutors, six investigators, several paralegals, and a receptionist out of the main Manhattan Criminal Courts building where police routinely meet with prosecutors. (A cop who agrees to wear a wire doesn't care to be seen by other cops, and the investigators don't want him to be seen.) The office is now located in a remodeled Soho loft, with no name on the downstairs buzzer, on a street featuring fashionable clothing stores. Burmeister was so concerned with secrecy that he usually brought a sandwich to lunch with staff in his office, fearing that a conversation in a neighborhood restaurant might be overheard by crooked police or their friends.

> *"Police usually lapse into silence and talk about the misconduct of other cops only when pressured by Internal Affairs investigators or by threat of prosecution."*

The Case of Norman Batista

The most challenging cases to prosecute are those that fall into the category of retributive beatings, or tune-ups, administered under cover of "the suspect was resisting arrest." I have been following such a case prosecuted by the OCU against officers of the Manhattan North Drug Initiative (MNDI), a highly touted

NYPD effort to rid Washington Heights of drug trafficking. The incident occurred less than a month after officers from Brooklyn's 70th precinct were arrested and charged with brutalizing Abner Louima. Though the MNDI case received far less publicity than the sensational misconduct in the Louima case, the MNDI case is far more typical.

The facts are roughly as follows: A drug dealer, Jose Polanco, sold illegal drugs out of an apartment on West 172nd Street. Five officers, two of whom were supervisors, had obtained a warrant to search the apartment. One of the officers, a sergeant, testified that it took several minutes to gain entry into the well-barricaded apartment. Polanco, who was given immunity to testify, said he had flushed all his drugs down the toilet when he'd heard the police pounding on the door. By doing so, he had undercut any criminal case that might be made against him or the buyer, since neither had any drugs in their possession and the police had not witnessed a sale. (After searching the apartment, the police could find only a minute amount of cocaine residue on the tip of a screwdriver.)

Polanco testified that he and the drug buyer, a middle-aged Dominican man who had moved to New York 19 years earlier and had worked for 16 years as a busboy, were ordered to their knees and searched. Then, he testified, the police began to beat them and told them to shut up and take the beating and not to scream. Polanco, an experienced drug seller with the sturdy build of a defensive back, testified that he had complied. He also testified that he could hear loud cries of pain as the buyer, Norman Batista, was further beaten. Polanco and Batista curled into fetal positions to protect themselves; for this reason, neither could later on identify which officers had administered the blows and the kicks. After being taken into custody, Batista experienced severe pain for several hours, and the police offered to cut him loose. He refused their offer and was eventually transported to an emergency room at Metropolitan Hospital. The emergency room physician found that Batista had seven broken ribs, four on one side and three on the other, where he had been kicked while lying on the floor. Batista spent the next six days in the hospital with additional injuries to his chest, sternum, cheek, testicles, and knees.

> *"The most challenging cases to prosecute are those that fall into the category of retributive beatings . . . administered under cover of 'the suspect was resisting arrest.'"*

The doctor was shocked by Batista's condition. He also didn't believe that Batista had resisted arrest—no charges were ever filed—and alerted a friend who was an assistant DA in the Manhattan District Attorney's Office. The case was assigned to Burmeister's OCU because of the unit's experience in prosecuting police. Two officers, Detective Olga Vazquez and Officer Richard Thompson, who had been on the force seven and five years, respectively, were charged with first-degree assault, which carries a potential sentence of 25 years.

Vazquez and Thompson were tried together and waived a jury trial, as defendants are permitted to do in New York state court but not in federal court. . . . Police usually waive a jury trial in New York City where jurors are likely to be people of color and where they believe judges will be sympathetic to police officers. (Had the officers in the Diallo case been tried in the Bronx, the judge would have been a black woman not known for her sympathy to police. Since, as defendants, they were entitled to a trial by jury, they asked for a change of venue to Albany.)

No Witnesses

The defense attorneys for Vazquez and Thompson—one of whom was Marvin Kornberg, a veteran lawyer who has defended many police officers, including Justin Volpe—argued in summation that even though five officers were present, none of them saw which officer or officers did the beating—and that therefore there was no compelling eyewitness testimony to prove assult. The defense attorneys argued that without eyewitnesses, the state had not met the burden of proof; besides, they argued, it doesn't make sense to send good police officers to prison when the alleged victim is a person who buys drugs.

Since no police came forward to testify, Assistant District Attorney Diane Kiesel, who was trying the case (and who is now a state judge), argued that Batista's injuries proved that he had without doubt been criminally assaulted in that apartment. Even if the prosecution couldn't prove that these two police defendants had actually administered the beating, the police nevertheless had a duty to prevent the crime. Since they did not, the prosecution argued, they were accessories to a crime. But Judge Ronald Zweibel acquitted the police defendants, even though one or more of the officers must have inflicted the injuries, and one or more of them must have seen it happening. . . .

On the day of the acquittal, approximately 75 off-duty police officers jammed into the courtroom. They applauded loudly and embraced each other with evident joy when the acquittal was announced. The blue wall of silence had been vindicated.

The Problem of Aggressive Policing

The Diallo shooting was clearly different. The case against the officers was weak from the start. If they had legitimately made a mistake—an argument they made persuasively at the trial—they were justified in using deadly force. The number of shots mattered little. As the defendants testified, officers are trained to shoot at the "center mass," the center of the chest. This is a polite way of saying that police are taught to shoot to kill, which is how they should be taught. Unless they are prepared to kill, they should never shoot. Only the Sundance Kid can shoot a gun out of someone's hand. (Of the 41 shots at Diallo, more than half of them missed.)

But the Diallo case highlights two additional issues. First, would the officers have mistaken a wallet for a gun if Diallo had been white? Imagine the outcry if four black cops had shot an unarmed white man in Howard Beach, Queens. Race was the elephant in the living room that nobody introduced at the Diallo trial, but it is a policing issue that public officials ignore at their peril, and it's not an easy one to remedy. Following the Louima affair, the mayor and police commissioner transferred white officers from the 70th precinct and replaced them with black officers who, ironically, are suing the city on grounds of improperly using race as a criterion for assignment. And as tensions grow between minority communities and the police, it is ever more difficult to recruit minorities into the NYPD—which, in turn, makes it harder to answer critics who call for more minorities in policing.

> *"[Reports] show just how far police supervisors' tolerance of tune-ups and perjury can go."*

Something like the Diallo shooting was likely to happen eventually, as a result of New York's aggressive approach to street policing. The Street Crimes Unit was seen by the mayor and Commissioner Howard Safir as the driving force behind the city's crime reduction, reportedly stopping and frisking 27,061 people in 1998 and making 4,647 arrests. (These figures are from a study critical of the NYPD by Attorney General Elliot Spitzer, which acknowledges that not all stops are actually reported.) Most of these stops are in high-crime, heavily minority areas of the city, which means that enormous numbers of innocent young black men—like Diallo—are subject to being stopped, questioned, and frisked. Moreover, many of the actual arrests are for minor offenses, such as drinking beer in the street, resulting in a critical overloading of the criminal courts in New York City. Even if the Diallo shooting was legally justifiable, it nevertheless raised serious questions about the policies and training of the NYPD, some of which have been remedied.

But of the Diallo, Louima, and Batista cases, the Batista case is most typical. It may also be the most troubling since it reflects a "culture war" between those who believe it's okay to punish the enemy, without regard to the Constitution, and those who believe police should play by the rules of law and procedure, even when that can make securing criminal convictions more difficult. As I watched the trial, I began to see the police and the judge on one side, and the emergency room doctor and the prosecutors on the other. The police who showed up to hear the verdict clearly supported their fellow officers. In their view, a drug dealer and a buyer had frustrated good cops by disposing of drugs. Since the criminals could not legally be punished, the police had administered a well-deserved beating, something the police watching from the gallery could easily imagine having done themselves. Judge Zweibel may have felt the same way, which is perhaps why he was not inclined to imprison police officers for this offense.

By contrast, the emergency room physician was appalled by the brutality of the beating and referred the case to the prosecutor's office. In the minds of the prosecutors, the beating had crossed way over the line of acceptably tough policing: This beating was a criminal assault, no matter that the victim had been buying drugs. The Batista case shows how difficult it can be to prosecute police, who rely on counsel funded by the PBA, who coordinate their defense. "Prosecuting police is like prosecuting the Mafia, with their lawyers," Burmeister told me.

The Batista case highlights something else as well. Teaching a lesson of compliance with a tune-up is most likely to occur in specialized units, like the MNDI police or the Los Angeles CRASH antigang unit. These "elite" units often compete to be the toughest or have the best arrest statistics. They are reminiscent of the elite, corrupt detectives memorialized in *Prince of the City* or the detectives for whom "the pad" was a way of life in *Serpico*. Like them, the CRASH cops and drug enforcers accused in the Batista case thought they could count on the code of silence to frustrate the efforts of even the best prosecutors. The crimes of the CRASH unit and those of New York City's "Dirty 30" detailed in the Mollen Commission Report show just how far police supervisors' tolerance of tune-ups and perjury can go.

In a sense, though, these scandals are our own fault, the outcome of the "war on drugs" and the "tough on crime" initiatives demanded by voters. In a war, the enemy is not entitled to constitutional protections and the rule of law. The police scandals in New York and Los Angeles are the most visible symbols of what warlike policing is all about. Investigators independent of police departments— like the OCU—are a necessary but insufficient counter to police lying, corruption, and brutality. Cops and politicians listen to the messages sent by the voters. If we, as voters, publicly support "wars" on drugs and crime, we shouldn't be surprised when soldiers occasionally mistreat the enemy, do a bit of looting on the side, and lie about what really happened.

The Courts Do Not Adequately Punish Police Departments That Use Racial Profiling

by David Cole

About the author: *David Cole, legal affairs correspondent for the* Nation, *is the author of* No Equal Justice: Race and Class in the American Criminal Justice System.

It's no mean feat to find an issue on which President Bill Clinton, the Rev. Al Sharpton, Attorney General Janet Reno, many of the nation's police chiefs and NAACP [National Association for the Advancement of Colored People] president Kweisi Mfume agree, but at a Washington conference in June [1999], they all expressed the view that racial profiling—the practice of targeting citizens for police encounters on the basis of race—needs to end. Clinton proclaimed profiling "wrong" and "destructive," and ordered federal agencies to gather data on the demographics of their law enforcement patterns. The consensus on profiling was underscored in August [1999], when the National Association of Police Organizations, which staged a debate on the subject at its annual meeting in Denver, had to rely on a white separatist, Jared Taylor, to defend the practice.

Evidence of Racial Profiling

Given the mountain of evidence that has piled up recently on racial profiling, the consensus is not surprising. Studies in Maryland, New Jersey, Illinois, Florida, Ohio, Houston and Philadelphia have confirmed that minorities are disproportionately targeted by police. On April 20 [1999], the New Jersey Attorney General's office issued a 112-page mea culpa admitting that its state troopers had engaged in racial profiling, offering statistics to support the claim and advancing a sophisticated analysis of the nature and scope of the problem. The next day North Carolina—yes, North Carolina—became the first state to pass a law requiring troopers to record and make public the racial patterns of their traffic stops. Connecticut followed suit with its own reporting law in June, and most recently, Florida Governor Jeb Bush has directed the Florida Highway Patrol to begin collecting similar data on January 1, 2000.

The press has covered the subject widely, recounting tales of black professionals stopped for petty traffic violations and investigating the arrest patterns of offending cops. While police departments are obviously at the heart of the problem, the crucial role that courts have played in protecting and sustaining widespread racial profiling has been overlooked. The courts have not only failed to recognize that racial profiling is unconstitutional, but they have effectively insulated it from legal challenge. Where lawsuits challenging profiling have succeeded, it is only because political pressures compelled the police to settle.

Court Support for Racial Profiling

The legal case against profiling should be easy to make. Defenders of the practice argue that it makes sense to target minorities because they are more likely than whites to commit crime. But the Constitution forbids reliance on racial generalizations unless they are the only way to achieve a "compelling purpose." Law enforcement is undoubtedly compelling, but racial stereotypes are hardly the only way to go about it. In fact, race is a particularly bad basis for suspicion, since most black people, like most whites, don't commit any crime. Annually at least 90 percent of African-Americans are not arrested for anything. On any given day, the percentage of innocent African-Americans is even higher. Thus, racial profiles necessarily sweep in a large number of innocents. In addition, when officers target minorities they miss white criminals. One need only recall the [late-night television comedy] *Saturday Night Live* skit in which the black actor Garrett Morris and the white actor Chevy Chase walk through Customs. Morris, carrying nothing, is immediately surrounded by multiple Customs agents, while Chase pushes through an open wheelbarrow full of powder cocaine without a hitch.

Yet the Supreme Court has all but invited racial profiling. In 1996 the Court upheld the practice of "pretextual traffic stops," in which police officers use the excuse of a traffic violation to stop motorists when they are investigating some other crime. The same year, the Court allowed the police to use the coercive setting of a traffic

> *"The Court has erected major barriers to lawsuits challenging profiling as racial discrimination."*

stop to obtain consent to search. Together, these rules allow the police to stop and search whomever they please on the roads, without having to demonstrate probable cause. And where the police are freed from the need to justify their actions, they appear to fall back on racial stereotypes. In Maryland, for example, blacks were 70 percent of those stopped and searched by Maryland State Police from January 1995 through December 1997, on a road where 17.5 percent of the drivers and speeders were black. New Jersey reported that 77 percent of those stopped and searched on its highways were black or Hispanic, even though only 13.5 percent of the drivers were black or Hispanic.

At the same time, the Court has erected major barriers to lawsuits challenging profiling as racial discrimination. Dismissive of statistical evidence, the Court requires proof that individual officers acted out of racist motives in each case. Thus, the array of recent studies showing that minorities are disproportionately targeted do not establish a violation of the Constitution's equal protection guarantee. In fact, unless the police admit to racial profiling, the Court's intent standard is nearly impossible to meet.

Even when a party can prove that he was profiled, the Court has made it very difficult to obtain a remedy that addresses the practice of profiling systemically. In *City of Los Angeles v. Lyons*, the Court ruled that victims of past police misconduct cannot obtain court injunctions against future misconduct unless they can prove that they will be personally subjected to the practice in the future. In 1994, a federal court in Florida dismissed a racial-profiling suit on these grounds even as it complained that the Supreme Court's *Lyons* decision "seemingly 'renders [the federal courts] impotent to order the cessation

> *"Faced with stark evidence, [the Courts] would rather deny than confront discrimination."*

of a policy which may indeed be unconstitutional and may harm many persons.'"

An ACLU [American Civil Liberties Union] case . . . in Illinois illustrates just how difficult the courts have made it to challenge racial profiling. The Illinois State Police don't record the race of the drivers they stop, so the ACLU sought to obtain copies of ticketed motorists' license applications, from which they then planned to use Social Security or address information to develop racial data. The court ruled that the ACLU would have to pay Illinois $160,000 for that information.

Using last names as a rough proxy for ethnicity, the ACLU then showed that although Hispanics compose less than 8 percent of the state's population, they were 27 percent of those stopped and searched by a highway drug interdiction unit. The court replied that statistics aren't enough. The ACLU showed that the state police permit consideration of race, that their training materials focus on Hispanics as drug couriers and that state troopers admit they consider race. The court replied that the ACLU's claim still failed because the plaintiffs did not identify specific "similarly situated" white motorists who were not stopped and ticketed. When the ACLU pointed to a white lawyer who had been following a Latino motorist the day he was stopped, the court said the lawyer wasn't similarly situated, because her car was a different color and her license plate was from a different state.

Lawsuits have played an important role in the campaign against racial profiling, but not through any actions of the courts. The single most significant development to date on the profiling front was Robert Wilkins's decision in 1992 to sue when a Maryland state trooper illegally stopped and searched him and his family. Because Wilkins, a Harvard Law School graduate and prominent public defender, was such a sympathetic plaintiff, Maryland quickly settled, agreeing to record the race of those it stopped and to provide that data to the court and the ACLU. That led to the first systematic evidence of a problem that until then had been largely a matter of anecdotes.

Another settlement, in Philadelphia, was also crucial. In 1996, civil rights attorney David Rudovsky and the ACLU threatened the Philadelphia police with a lawsuit sparked by media revelations of rampant police abuse. The city settled before the suit was filed, allowing plaintiffs access to racial breakdowns of police stops. There, as in Maryland, the data have provided critical evidence for charges of racial profiling.

Despite the courts, more progress has been made on racial profiling than on any other issue of racial inequality in criminal law enforcement in the [1990s]. There are many reasons for this. The issue has tremendous organizing appeal and has captured the attention of mainstream civil rights groups, such as the NAACP and the Urban League, which have all too often shied away from criminal justice issues. Unlike most law enforcement victims, innocent victims of racial profiling elicit public sympathy. The practice targets not just the disfranchised poor but rich and middle-class minorities, who are much more likely to have their complaints taken seriously.

Everyone who drives understands the ultimate arbitrariness of who gets pulled over. And because most people see the world to one degree or another through racial stereotypes, it is easy to believe that police officers act on these bases.

Equally important, the relief that activists have requested, at least at this stage, seems nonthreatening: They ask principally for the collection and reporting of data. How police departments and the public will respond when the results come in remains to be seen. Profiling is not the work of a few "bad apples" but a widespread, everyday phenomenon that will require systemic reform.

It also remains to be seen whether the advances made on racial profiling will prove to be a wedge for more deep-rooted and lasting reforms directed at racial disparity in criminal justice, or merely an exception to the rule of laissez-faire. But one thing is certain: The courts will not lead. At one time, one could have looked to the federal courts, protectors of individual rights and leaders in the fight against racial discrimination, to play a significant role in the battle. But today's courts are cut from a different cloth. Faced with stark evidence, they would rather deny than confront discrimination.

Civil Lawsuits Rarely Lead to the Punishment of Police Brutality

by Human Rights Watch

About the author: *Human Rights Watch is a worldwide nongovernmental organization that makes public its research on human rights abuses.*

Civil lawsuits against police officers and departments have become a common way of seeking "accountability" of a sort, with larger municipalities paying victims and their families tens of millions of dollars, through either pre- or mid-trial settlements or civil jury awards following judgments against officers and/or the police department. While victims certainly deserve compensation when officers violate their human rights, civil remedies are never a sufficient form of accountability because they almost never address flawed management, policies, or patterns of abuse, nor do they hold an individual officer financially responsible. And settlements in particular are problematic, especially in high-profile cases, by leaving responsibility for an abuse incident unresolved in the minds of both the community and police department.

Under Title 42 U.S. Code Section 1983, the federal civil rights civil statute, individuals may file lawsuits against an offending officer, police department, or jurisdiction. Although the federal law, Section 1983, is used most frequently, plaintiffs may also use state-level statutes in bringing abuse lawsuits. The statute mandates that:

> Any person who, under color of any statute, ordinance, regulation, custom, or usage, of any State or Territory or the District of Columbia, subjects or causes to be subjected, any citizen of the United States or other person within the jurisdiction thereof to the deprivation of any rights, privileges, or immunities secured by the Constitution and laws, shall be liable to the party injured in an action at law, suit in equity, or other proper proceeding for redress. . . .

Success rates in bringing civil lawsuits against officers vary dramatically

Human Rights Watch, *Shielded from Justice: Police Brutality and Accountability in the United States.* Washington, D.C.: Human Rights Watch, 1998. Copyright © 1998 by Human Rights Watch. Reproduced by permission.

from city to city, with some cities settling early and quietly while others vigorously fight brutality suits. If a case goes to trial, some juries have shown a predisposition to believe police officers' accounts, particularly when the victim has a criminal record. The strongest cases presented by victims of serious abuse are often settled by a city to avoid embarrassing attention; in such settlements, the department rarely acknowledges that an officer was in the wrong. Often, parties are sworn to secrecy regarding the amount of the settlement or information about the officer that may have been disclosed during the process.

The Price of Civil Actions

The amounts paid in civil lawsuit settlements and following judgments in police brutality cases varied greatly in the cities examined by Human Rights Watch. In New York City, taxpayers paid plaintiffs about $70 million in settlement or civil jury awards in claims alleging improper police actions between 1994 and 1996. In Los Angeles, the city paid approximately $79.2 million in civil lawsuit awards and pre-trial settlements against police officers (not including traffic accidents) between 1991 and 1996. In other cities, the amounts paid were quite small. In Atlanta, where the city "litigates aggressively" to defend itself against police abuse lawsuits, the city paid just over $1 million between 1994 and 1996, although in June 1997 the city paid out $750,000 in a single case—one of the largest single payouts in Atlanta's recent history. Between 1994 and 1996, Indianapolis paid approximately $750,000 total in police misconduct lawsuits, pre-trial and post-verdict.

Of the cities examined, Philadelphia was among those paying the largest amounts to settle civil lawsuits alleging police misconduct. Between July 1993 and November 1996, the city agreed to pay $32.6 million in settlements and civil jury awards arising from lawsuits alleging police misconduct. The former deputy city solicitor (and newly appointed anti-corruption director) stated. "This is not Monopoly money. This is real money. How do we save the taxpayers millions of dollars?" The *Philadelphia Inquirer* estimated in 1996 that the year's payouts would fund 250 police officers for a year.

Washington, D.C. paid $4 million in settlement or post-verdict payments in police misconduct suits by individuals claiming false arrest/assault during a three-year period between 1993 and 1995. This amounted to four times the budget of the city's Civilian Complaint Review Board [CCRB]; the board was abolished in 1995, in part due to budgetary constraints. In Detroit, the police department announced new training programs for recruits in April 1997 in an attempt to stem the enormous amounts paid by the city's taxpayers in civil lawsuits alleging po-

> *"Civil remedies are never a sufficient form of accountability because they almost never address flawed management, policies, or patterns of abuse."*

lice misconduct. Between 1987 and 1994, the city reportedly paid $72 million in settlements or jury awards stemming from police misconduct lawsuits (excluding claims based on vehicle accidents and chases), and in the twenty-two-month period between July 1, 1995 and April 1997, the city paid just under $20 million in cases involving alleged police brutality, police chases and minor accidents.

The New Orleans Law Department resisted providing any information regarding payouts in civil cases to individuals alleging police abuse. Between 1994 and 1996, the city reported paying approximately $1

> *"Because attorneys choose the strongest cases to pursue, some of the most important abuse complaints may not be filed with external or internal review units."*

million for excessive force and wrongful death suits. According to local attorneys who represent plaintiffs in these cases, the state has not actually paid on a police misconduct claim since mid-1995.

Taxpayers in some cities, such as New York and Philadelphia, are paying three times for officers who repeatedly commit abuses: once to cover their salaries while they commit abuses; next to pay settlements or civil jury awards against officers; and a third time through payments into police "defense" funds provided by the cities. For all of the coverage, city residents get in return an erosion of standards and heightened tension in poor and minority neighborhoods.

Undermining Monetary Compensation

The positive aspects of civil lawsuits, which provide some plaintiffs or their families with compensation, are undermined by several factors. In many instances, an attorney representing a police abuse victim will instruct him or her not to file a complaint with citizen review agencies or internal affairs units for fear of making a statement that may be unhelpful in pursuing the civil case or in defending the client of criminal charges that are pending against him or her. Therefore, because attorneys choose the strongest cases to pursue, some of the most important abuse complaints may not be filed with external or internal review units. Since these units are complaint-driven, no investigation will ensue.

Another problem in most cities is that civil settlements paid by the city on behalf of an officer usually are not taken from the police budget but are paid from general city funds. In larger cities, even significant payouts in these cases do not have much of an effect on the city's operations, and only lead to change when they become an embarrassment. In Philadelphia, for example, civil lawsuits on behalf of victims of police misconduct made headlines after they reached record highs in 1995 and 1996. Eventually, the threat of more lawsuits that could significantly affect the city's budget forced city officials to accede to a reform plan backed by community leaders. But that was an exceptional case; other cities continue to pay large amounts without examining, acknowledging, or correcting the police activities that led to the lawsuits.

The individual officer who is the subject of a police misconduct lawsuit found in favor of the plaintiff is rarely forced to pay the victim. In fact, an officer who is the subject of a successful lawsuit alleging abuse may escape any sanction. Most of the departments examined by Human Rights Watch did not initiate an internal affairs or review agency investigation when a civil claim or suit alleging serious abuse is filed or a settlement or award is made favoring the plaintiff. There are notification systems in some cities whereby the city attorney's office informs the relevant internal affairs unit that a suit has been filed or resolved, but that information is not necessarily used in evaluating the officer; indeed, some internal affairs units investigate complaints made in civil lawsuits only in order to assist the city in defending itself against plaintiffs' claims.

Some internal affairs investigators—in defending their inaction when civil suits alleging misconduct are filed or decided in favor of the plaintiff—state that plaintiffs' attorneys will not allow them to interview the alleged victim. Yet there is no reason why they could not use the information developed through a lawsuit, including names of witnesses and officers present, to begin an investigation even without a formal complaint or direct statement from the alleged victim. As it is, a city may pay hundreds of thousands, or millions, of dollars on behalf of a brutal officer, yet the officer pays no price whatsoever.

Disconnected from Internal Investigations

Even in cities where some type of early warning system is utilized to identify potential problem officers—as in Boston, Los Angeles, New Orleans, New York, and Portland—civil lawsuits filed against officers are not monitored the way complaints filed with citizen review agencies or internal affairs units are. This is so even though civil suit complaints include detailed information about serious violations that should be investigated. While clearly frivolous cases should not be used in assessing an officer's performance, this disconnect between lawsuits and internal investigations is baffling, because the suits could be used as a management tool; they should also be monitored by prosecutors in case criminal acts are credibly alleged.

> *"A city may pay hundreds of thousands, or millions, of dollars on behalf of a brutal officer, yet the officer pays no price whatever."*

Yet, most internal affairs staff interviewed by Human Rights Watch made statements such as "civil cases are not our problem," or asserted that the settled suits do not indicate the "guilt" of an officer, disregarding the important information that citizen-initiated lawsuits could provide. City attorney offices seemed to share this perspective; for example, the New York City Law Department wrote to Human Rights Watch, "concerning notification procedures where a lawsuit alleges police misconduct, the Law Department does not have a formal procedure for notifying IAB [Internal Affairs Bureau] or the CCRB of such lawsuits."

In Portland, the police chief [Charles Moose] explained why "risk management data" (civil lawsuit information) are not used as a tool in reviewing officers, as suggested by Portland's citizen review agency: "I have not been able to determine a way to utilize Risk Management Information to label employees as problem officers. Tort claim notices do not contain all of the facts and I do not think it is fair to attempt to determine the involvement of an individual without examining all of the facts." Like many other high-ranking police officials, the chief fails to recognize that the information in such lawsuits could be valuable, at a minimum, in determining whether to launch an investigation.

> *"Civil remedies must always be available, but they cannot be a substitute for police department mechanisms of accountability or prosecutorial action."*

Gannett News Service published a series of investigative articles in March 1992 examining the fate of police officers named in one hundred civil lawsuits in twenty-two states in which juries ordered $100,000 or more to be paid to plaintiffs between 1986 and 1991. The awards from the lawsuits totaled nearly $92 million dollars. Of 185 officers involved in these cases, only eight were disciplined. No action was taken against 160, and seventeen were promoted. The reporter concluded, "[T]axpayers are penalized more for brutality than the officers responsible for the beatings."

The Christopher Commission examined eighty-three civil cases with settlements, judgments or jury verdicts of more than $15,000 between 1986 and 1990 against officers with the Los Angeles Police Department. During this period, Los Angeles paid more than $20 million in over 300 lawsuits alleging excessive force through judgments, settlements and jury verdicts. A majority of cases involved clear and often egregious human rights violations committed by officers, resulting in the victim's serious injury or death. The commission found the department's investigation of these cases deficient in many respects and noted that discipline against the officers involved was frequently light or nonexistent. Eighty-four percent of the officers investigated received positive ratings in their personnel evaluations, and 42 percent were promoted following the incident. The commission recommended establishing procedures to monitor results of civil litigation and to make use of the information obtained. It called on the city attorney to notify promptly the Police Commission and the department when lawsuits are filed alleging police misconduct, and called on the Internal Affairs Division to investigate every "significant" claim. In its November 1997 report, the Office of the Inspector General (OIG) of the Los Angeles Police Commission reviewed 561 civil claims for damages involving department employees forwarded from the City Attorney's office to the department in 1995.

The department did not sustain a single allegation of misconduct against a sworn employee, of the 561 claims reviewed. While the City Attorney's office does notify the department when a claim is filed in state court, the OIG found that there has been no procedure in place for the City Attorney to notify the department of federal lawsuits.

As with most aspects of police abuse, data collection on lawsuits is inadequate. Some cities do not distinguish amounts paid in cases of misconduct, including excessive force, from damages arising because of mishaps such as traffic accidents. Others compile statistics that combine information on wholly different issues, such as false arrest and excessive force. In Atlanta, because it claimed no data had been collected in a systematic manner, the city attorney's office provided Human Rights Watch with some information by asking its staff the amounts they remembered the city having paid. Despite repeated letters and telephone calls from Human Rights Watch, no civil lawsuit data relating to police misconduct were provided by Chicago or Philadelphia.

The city of Boston is unique among the cities examined in that it apparently does not compile, or acknowledge compiling, amounts paid in police abuse lawsuit settlements or jury awards. Nine months after Human Rights Watch's initial inquiry, we received a letter from the staff attorney with the Office of the Legal Advisor of the police department, stating: "[N]either the Department, nor the City of Boston, maintain records in a form responsive to your request, i.e., a list or compilation of the amount of money paid to settle police brutality cases."

What Civil Suits Can Do

Although they usually do not affect policies, civil lawsuits have led to reform occasionally. In *Tennessee v. Garner* (1985), the U.S. Supreme Court held that police shootings under the authority of laws and policies that allowed officers to use deadly force to apprehend nonviolent fleeing suspects violated the Fourth Amendment of the U.S. Constitution, which protects against unwarranted search or seizure. As a result, police departments were compelled to formulate more restrictive policies on the use of deadly force or face future liability for officers' exercise of the broad - and unconstitutional - discretion allowed them by state legislation. Decisions in other cases under Section 1983 (the federal civil statute commonly used by individuals alleging police abuse) have held police agencies liable for inadequate policy and training regarding nonlethal force, strip searches, and vehicle pursuits. As described below in the chapter on Philadelphia, the threat of overwhelming civil lawsuits filed on behalf of victims of police abuse and court-ordered reforms in that scandal-ridden department forced police officials to agree to wide-ranging reforms.

Civil lawsuits also can lead to the disclosure of information—particularly when a case goes to trial—that otherwise would not have been available. Even initial complaints filed by alleged victims or their families provide information of interest to police abuse monitors.

Citizen review agencies generally do not utilize civil lawsuits, instead relying on individuals to come to the agency to file a complaint. Some agencies are overburdened and hardly interested in seeking out additional complaints. Others have respected concerns voiced by attorneys representing plaintiffs who prefer that their clients not speak to any investigator. A more proactive approach, however, is that of San Francisco's Office of Citizen Complaints, which has established a new procedure: once it is notified of police abuse lawsuits by the city attorney's office, it sends the plaintiff an OCC complaint form, explaining how the OCC works, and suggesting that the victim file a complaint.

Civil suits should be used in addition to, not instead of, other accountability avenues. When police departments or criminal prosecutors deflect criticisms by stating that victims of abuse can always sue, they forsake their responsibilities. Civil remedies must always be available, but they cannot be a substitute for police department mechanisms of accountability or prosecutorial action.

Juries Are Reluctant to Convict Police Officers

by Scott Turow

About the author: *Scott Turow, an attorney, is the author of several novels in-cluding* Presumed Innocent *and* Personal Injuries.

Americans are right to be disturbed by the [February 2000], acquittals in the . . . criminal trial of four white New York City police officers who gunned down Amadou Diallo, a West African immigrant, as he reached for his wallet in the vestibule of his apartment building in the Bronx. But there is much about the intense public discussion—the recriminations against the prosecutors and the jury, and the fury about racial profiling—that strikes me as naive, or even delib-erately coy.

A Typical Outcome

This verdict is not an anomaly. I have been on the ground in the criminal jus-tice system for more than 20 years, first as an assistant U.S. attorney in Chicago, later as a defense lawyer; I was even hired once as a special prosecu-tor to investigate a suburban police department. And my experience is that ju-ries are notoriously reluctant to convict cops for doing their jobs.

Catch a cop using his power for himself—taking bribes, selling drugs, stealing recovered property, extorting sexual favors from prisoners—and juries will cut him little slack. But when a police officer is trying to do what he's been sworn to do, which is to corral bad guys, even if he has gone about it overzealously or stupidly, juries often refuse to convict. Consider the first Rodney King trial, where the Los Angeles police officers accused of beating the black motorist faced state charges for the assault. Despite a videotape that plainly portrayed the fallen man being clubbed repeatedly, the jury in Simi Valley, Calif., set all the of-ficers free. (It was only after that verdict set off furious rioting in L.A. that fed-eral civil rights charges were brought and the officers were convicted.)

In my eight years as an assistant U.S. attorney, police beating cases—prosecutions for a cop's use of excessive force—were the only class of crimes for which our office had a losing record in court. To be sure, the government wins these cases now and then, especially when there are police witnesses for the prosecution, as in the trial of the New York City officers who brutalized Haitian immigrant Abner Louima in a police precinct men's room. But over time, I have watched fine prosecutors bring—and more often than not lose—these cases in front of juries.

I once conducted a long-running investigation of an officer in a Chicago suburb who was known, in the parlance, as a "hitter." Along with other officers, he'd beaten a burglar so forcefully that the baton marks on the young man's back looked like the

> *"Jurors are loath to convict because they know that cops on the job are trying to protect not only themselves but, more importantly, us."*

spokes of a wagon wheel; he'd also smacked around two other citizens during their arrests. Despite the pattern, this was the only case of my career in which I had to argue furiously to persuade the grand jury to indict. And I regarded it as a moral victory when the petit jury hung at trial, rather than rendering an outright acquittal.

More recently, I watched with a sense of doom when four police officers and three prosecutors were tried for conspiring to obstruct justice in the trials of Rolando Cruz, who'd spent nearly 12 years in Illinois prisons, most of it on death row, for a murder that, ultimately, he was found not guilty of committing. I had a rooting interest in the case, since for many years I'd represented Cruz's co-defendant, who, like Cruz, was freed after two wrongful convictions. I had no doubt that the evidence fully supported the grand jury's decision to indict the so-called DuPage 7, [the law enforcement officers accused of the wrongful conviction of Rolando Cruz]. One officer had already admitted that he had testified to events that never happened, and the principal evidence against Cruz, a supposed confession, had emerged only days before Cruz's first trial. Somehow it had never been reduced to a written police report or recorded in the minutes of an 18-month grand jury investigation. Nonetheless, knowing the predilections of juries, the acquittals of all the accused did not surprise me. I was taken aback, however, when several jurors joined the defendants at a party after the verdict.

Unsettling Attitudes

As a young prosecutor, I was outraged by what I viewed as the unwillingness of citizens to enforce the law when the police are the defendants. And now, I find myself unsettled by the latitude the Diallo jury seemed to have given the four officers in that case, particularly because their testimony seemed to be suspiciously orchestrated at points. None, supposedly. could remember which of them had shot first—that is, who was responsible for setting off the chain reaction that led to Diallo's death—and they denied disturbing Diallo's body after the shooting, when common sense tells me that their first thought had to have been to search him for the gun they all said they believed he had.

And it is probably true, in retrospect, that the Diallo prosecutors made mistakes. For example, New York law permitted an instruction requiring the jury to find that each of the 41 shots fired was justified before they could acquit. The DAs did not ask the judge to give those directions, apparently preferring to argue that no shots were reasonable, and fearing, perhaps, that such an instruction would invite the jury to convict only the two officers who had each emptied their 16-shot clips; no doubt, the prosecutors would be pleased to have only two convictions today.

But no matter how perceptive the Monday-morning quarterbacking is, history would indicate that the prosecution faced a steep hill from the start of that case.

With time—and more than a decade on the defense side—I've come to terms with the kind of justice juries apply in police cases. Jurors are loath to convict because they know that cops on the job are trying to protect not only themselves but, more importantly, us. The jurors. Their families. Yes, some cops are bullies; some want the job so they can handle a gun. But most are decent, well-intentioned folks who have taken up a calling that is not particularly well-paid and in which, for our benefit, they face risks every day far greater than those most of us confront when we leave for the office.

> *"Jurors cannot help thinking that the alleged victim got what he was asking for."*

Beyond that, these cases often present situations where jurors cannot help thinking that the alleged victim got what he was asking for. Rodney King led police on a 100-mph car chase before he caught his beating; Rolando Cruz admitted that in his pursuit of a reward, he told the police a series of whoppers about the murder for which he was convicted.

That factor, of course, is what distinguishes Diallo. Defense arguments notwithstanding, he did nothing to invite what happened to him. The horror that a person in this country could be gunned down by police merely for retreating to his home and reaching for his wallet outlasts the verdict and clearly motivates the Justice Department's agreement to review the case for possible civil rights prosecution. [The Justice Department did not pursue a civil rights prosecution.] . . . In spite of the jurors' resistance to affixing criminal blame to individual cops, no one ultimately wants to defend Diallo's death.

The Race Question

Like many others, I find it hard to imagine the police shooting 41 times at a white man in a middle-class area standing peaceably in his doorway. Yet it is that comparison which invites—and also begs—many of the questions about racial profiling that have swirled about the Diallo case. It is a primal indignity to any human being to be suspected on the basis of something as meaningless as flesh tones. But there are also uncomfortable realities that are being politely banished from most public discussions about crime and race.

Nearly a third of African American males between the ages of 20 and 29 are under some type of correctional control—imprisoned, or on probation or parole—compared with one in 15 whites of the same ages. In the 1990s, a black person was four to five times more likely than a white to be arrested for a weapons offense. And African American males have a 29 percent chance of serving time during their lives, more than seven times the figure for whites.

This staggering disproportion represents a failure of the American political majority to come to terms with the plight of the poor, and probably also reflects some degree of bias in the justice system. But we are living in a wonderland if we expect the overriding realities of those numbers to be forgotten on the street. Thus, no one is more victimized by the crimes of minorities than other minorities, not only because those crimes are most often committed against them, but also because so much of the shadow of that lawlessness falls on the vast preponderance of Americans of color who lead law-abiding lives.

Yet who among us, white or black, doesn't cross the street at night when we see a group of teens in gang attire down the block? In Washington, D.C., taxicab commissioner Sandra Seegars, an African American, caused a stir recently by defending the nighttime practice of Washington's overwhelmingly black taxi drivers' refusal to pick up young African American males "dressed in the tough-guy street look."

In Chicago, we've had a case strikingly similar to Diallo, involving LaTanya Haggerty, an unarmed auto passenger who was killed by a police officer who claims to have mistaken a padlock for a gun. The case has rightly stirred indignation about police practices, but, there are none of the racial overtones of the Diallo case. That is because the officer who shot Haggerty was, like Haggerty herself, an African American female.

Media reports tend to indicate that the Diallo jury did not discuss racial issues. But I believe that these realizations live in the minds not only of most police officers, but of many other Americans who find themselves torqued between self-protective impulses that lead them to play crude odds on the street, and a recognition of the bedrock injustice of making judgments about human beings on the basis of race. In the end, the Diallo jury capitulated to the usual reluctance to convict cops for their conduct on duty. But it also seems to have decided not to hold four officers responsible for an American dilemma that we all too often feel helpless to change.

Organizations to Contact

The editors have compiled the following list of organizations concerned with the issues debated in this book. The descriptions are derived from materials provided by the organizations. All have publications or information available for interested readers. The list was compiled on the date of publication of the present volume; the information provided here may change. Be aware that many organizations take several weeks or longer to respond to inquiries, so allow as much time as possible.

American Civil Liberties Union (ACLU)
125 Broad St., 18th Floor, New York, NY 10004-2400
website: www.aclu.org

The ACLU is a national organization that works to defend Americans' civil rights guaranteed in the U.S. Constitution. Among other services, the ACLU provides legal assistance to victims of police abuse. The ACLU publishes *Fighting Police Abuse: A Community Action Manual* and the New York Civil Liberties Union report *Arresting Protest*, which are available on its website.

Amnesty International (AI) USA Office
322 8th Ave., New York, NY 10001
(212) 807-8400 • fax: (212) 627-1451
e-mail: admin-us@aiusa.org • website: www.amnestyusa.org

Amnesty International is a worldwide campaigning movement that works to promote human rights and opposes cruel treatment of prisoners. Its reports *Police Brutality and Excessive Force in the New York City Police Department, Rights for All: Police Brutality in the USA*, and *Cruelty in Control? The Stun Belt and Other Electro-Shock Equipment in Law Enforcement* are available on the AI website.

Collective Opposed to Police Brutality (COBP)
c/o Alternative Bookshop
2035 St-Laurent, 2nd Floor, Montreal, Quebec, Canada H2X 2T3
(514) 859-9065
e-mail: cobp@tao.ca • website: www.tao.ca

COBP is a collective of people concerned about police brutality and other abuses perpetrated by the police. COBP's goal is not just to denounce police abuses but also to offer support to victims as well as inform citizens. The collective publishes *Info-bavures*, a bulletin that documents police abuses in Montreal and elsewhere in Quebec, and the pamphlet *Neighborhood Policing: Caressing the Community with an Iron Fist*.

The Heritage Foundation
214 Massachusetts Ave. NE, Washington, DC 20002-4999
(202) 546-4400 • fax: (202) 546-8328
e-mail: info@heritage.org • website: www.heritage.org

The Heritage Foundation is a conservative public policy research institute that advocates strengthening law enforcement to stop crime. It publishes position papers on a broad range of topics, including police issues. Its regular publications include the monthly *Policy Review*, the *Backgrounder* series of occasional papers, and the Heritage Lecture series. Selected articles are available on its website, including "Twenty-One Steps Officials Can Take to Support Their Local Police" and "Turning a Dangerous City into a Safe One."

Human Rights Watch
350 Fifth Ave., 34th Floor, New York, NY 10118-3299
(212) 290-4700 • fax: (212) 736-1300
e-mail: hrwnyc@hrw.org • website: www.hrw.org

Human Rights Watch monitors and reports human rights abuses in the United States and internationally. It sponsors fact-finding missions, disseminates results, and publishes the bimonthly *Human Rights Watch* newsletter. The report *Shielded from Justice: Police Brutality and Accountability in the United States* is available on its website.

International Association of Chiefs of Police (IACP)
515 N. Washington St., Alexandria, VA 22314
(703) 836-6767 • toll free: (800) THE IACP • fax: (703) 836-4543
website: www.theiacp.org

IACP consists of police executives who provide consultation and research services to and supports educational programs for police departments nationwide. The association publishes the monthly *Police Chief* magazine, which covers all aspects of law enforcement. Selected articles and reports are available on its website, including "Policies Help Gain Public Trust: Racial Profiling" and *Police Use of Force in America 2001*.

Law Enforcement Alliance of America (LEAA)
7700 Leesburg Pike No. 421, Falls Church, VA 22043
(703) 847-COPS
website: www.leaa.org

LEAA is a coalition of law enforcement professionals, crime victims, and concerned citizens united to fight for legislation that reduces violent crime while preserving the rights of all citizens, particularly the right of self-defense. LEAA publishes the magazine *SHIELD* and the newsletter the *LEAA Advisor*, recent issues of which are available on its website.

National Association for the Advancement of Colored People (NAACP)
4805 Mt. Hope Drive, Baltimore, MD 21215
(877) NAACP-98
website: www.naacp.org

The NAACP is a civil rights organization that works to end racial discrimination in America. It researches and documents police brutality and provides legal services for victims of brutality. The NAACP publishes the book *Beyond the Rodney King Story: An Investigation of Police Misconduct in Minority Communities*, the magazine *Crisis* ten times per year, and *Police-Citizen Violence: An Organizing Guide for Community Leaders*.

National Black Police Association (NBPA)
3251 Mt. Pleasant St. NW, 2nd Floor, Washington, DC 20010-2103
(202) 986-2070 • fax: (202) 986-0410
e-mail: nbpanatofc@worldnet.att.net • website: www.blackpolice.org

The association is a nationwide organization of African American police associations dedicated to the promotion of justice, fairness, and effectiveness in law enforcement. The NBPA serves as an advocate for minority police officers. The association publishes "Police Brutality: A Strategy to Stop the Violence" on its website.

National Center for Women and Policing (NCWP)
433 S. Beverly Dr., Beverly Hills, CA 90212
(310) 556-2526 • fax: (310) 556-2509
e-mail: womencops@feminist.org • website: www.womenandpolicing.org

A division of the Feminist Majority Foundation, the NCWP promotes increasing the numbers of women at all ranks of law enforcement as a strategy to improve police response to violence against women, reduce police brutality and excessive force, and strengthen community policing reforms. The report *Gender Differences in the Cost of Police Brutality & Misconduct: A Content Analysis of LAPD Civil Liability Cases 1990–1999* is available on its website.

National Coalition on Police Accountability (N-COPA)
59 East Van Buren, No. 2418, Chicago, IL 60605
(312) 663-5392 • fax: (312) 663-5396
e-mail: nkrhodes@mailbox.syr.edu • website: http://web.syr.edu/~nkrhodes/N-COPA.html

N-COPA is an organization of religious, community, and legal groups, and progressive law enforcement representatives working to hold police accountable to their communities through public education, community organization, legislation, litigation, and promotion of empowered independent oversight. The coalition publishes the bimonthly journal *Policing by Consent.*

National Institute of Justice (NIJ)
National Criminal Justice Reference Service (NCJRS)
PO Box 6000, Rockville, MD 20850
(301) 519-5500 • toll free: (800) 851-3420
e-mail: askncjrs@ncjrs.org • website: www.ojp.usdoj.gov/nij

A component of the Office of Justice Programs of the U.S. Department of Justice, NIJ supports and conducts research on crime, criminal behavior, and crime prevention. NCJRS acts as a clearinghouse for criminal justice information for researchers and other interested individuals. It publishes and distributes the following reports from the Bureau of Justice Statistics: *National Data Collection on Police Use of Force, The Role of Psychology in Controlling Excessive Force*, and *Understanding the Use of Force by and Against the Police.*

National Organization of Black Law Enforcement Executives (NOBLE)
4609 Pinecrest Office Park Dr., Suite F, Alexandria, VA 22312-1442
(703) 658-1529 • fax: (703) 658-9479
e-mail: noble@noblenatl.org • website: www.noblenatl.org

NOBLE serves the interests of black law enforcement officials. It works to eliminate racism, increase minority participation at all levels of law enforcement, and foster community involvement in working to reduce urban crime and violence. NOBLE condemns the use of excessive force by police. Its publications include the quarterly magazine *NOBLE National* and the newsletter *NOBLE Actions.*

October 22nd Coalition
P.O. Box 2627, New York, NY 10009
(212) 477-8062 • toll free: 1-888-NO BRUTALITY • fax: (212) 477-8015
e-mail: Office@October22.org • website: http://October22.org

The coalition is a diverse group of activist organizations and individuals concerned about police brutality. October 22nd is the date of the coalition's annual "National Day of Protest Against Police Brutality, Repression, and the Criminalization of a Generation," which is intended to raise awareness about police misconduct. The coalition publishes a newsletter, available on-line, as part of its efforts to organize protest activities.

It also coordinates the Stolen Lives Project, a report that documents the names of those who have been brutalized and killed by the police since 1990. The coalition also publishes the newsletter, *Wear Black!*

Police Executive Research Forum (PERF)

1120 Connecticut Ave. NW, Suite 930, Washington, DC 20036
(202) 466-7820 • fax: (202) 466-7826
e-mail: perf@policeforum.org • website: www.policeforum.org

PERF is a national professional association of police executives that seeks to increase public understanding of and stimulate debate on important criminal justice issues. PERF's numerous publications include the book *And Justice for All: Understanding and Controlling Police Abuse of Force*, and the papers *The Force Factor: Measuring Police Use of Force Relative to Suspect Resistance* and *Police Use of Force: A Statistical Analysis of the Metro-Dade Police Department.*

Police Foundation

2101 Connecticut Ave. NW, Washington, DC 20036
(202) 833-1460 • fax: (202) 659-9149
e-mail: pfinfo@policefoundation.org • website: www.policefoundation.org

The foundation conducts research projects on police activities and aims to improve the quality of police personnel. It publishes the report *Officer Behavior in Police-Citizen Encounters: A Descriptive Model and Implications for Less-Than-Lethal Alternatives* and the books *Police Use of Force: Official Reports, Citizen Complaints, and Legal Consequences* and *The Abuse of Police Authority: A National Study of Police Officers' Attitudes.*

Bibliography

Books

William J. Bratton with Peter Knobler	*Turnaround: How America's Top Cop Reversed the Crime Epidemic.* New York: Random House, 1998.
Ronald G. Burns and Charles E. Crawford	*Policing and Violence.* Upper Saddle River, NJ: Prentice-Hall, 2001.
John L. Burris with Catherine Whitney	*Blue vs. Black: Let's End the Conflict Between Cops and Minorities.* New York: St. Martin's, 1999.
Agnes Callamard	*Monitoring and Investigating Excessive Use of Force.* Amsterdam: Amnesty International, 2000.
Dean J. Champion	*Police Misconduct in America: A Reference Handbook.* Santa Barbara, CA: ABC-CLIO, 2001.
Norman Dennis, ed.	*Zero Tolerance: Policing a Free Society.* London: IEA Health and Welfare Unit, 1998.
Christopher Dunn, et al.	*Arresting Protest: Special Report of the New York Civil Liberties Union,* April 2003.
Terence J. Fitzgerald	*Police in Society.* New York: H.W. Wilson, 2000.
Victor Kappeler, Richard Sluder, and Geoffrey Alpert	*Forces of Deviance: Understanding the Dark Side of Policing.* Prospect Heights, IL: Waveland Press, 1998.
Regina Lawrence	*The Politics of Force: Media and the Construction of Police Brutality.* Berkeley: University of California Press, 2000.
Stephen Mastrofski	*Community Policing in Action: Lessons from an Observational Study.* Washington, DC: U.S. Department of Justice, 1998.
Andrea McArdle and Tanya Erzen, eds.	*Zero Tolerance: Quality of Life and the New Police Brutality in New York City.* New York: New York University Press, 2000.
Michael J. Palmiotto	*Police Misconduct: A Reader for the 21st Century.* Upper Saddle River, NJ: Prentice-Hall, 2001.
Jeffrey Ian Ross	*Making News of Police Violence: A Comparative Study of Toronto and New York City.* Westport, CT: Greenwood, 2000.

Katheryn K. Russell	*The Color of Crime: Racial Hoaxes, White Fear, Black Protectionism, Police Harassment, and Other Macro-aggressions.* New York: New York University Press, 1998.
Jeff Slowinkowski and Helen Connelling	*Community Policing and Youth.* Washington, DC: U.S. Department of Justice, 1999.
William Terrill	*Police Coercion: Application of the Force Continuum.* New York: LFB Scholarly, 2001.
U.S. Department of Justice	*Mental Illness: Police Response.* Washington, DC: Police Executive Forum, 1998.
Samuel Walker	*Police Accountability: The Role of Citizen Oversight.* Belmont, CA: Wadsworth Thompson, 2001.

Periodicals

Terry Carter	"Cops in the Cross Fire," *ABA Journal*, October 2000.
Alexander Cockburn	"Crazed Cops, 'Fallen Heroes,'" *Nation*, February 14, 2000.
David Cole	"We Need to Take the Unnecessary Force out of Law Enforcement," *Liberal Opinion Week*, May 31, 1999.
Charles P. Connolly	"In Defense of Police," *National Executive Institute Associates Leadership Bulletin*, November 2001.
Larry Ellis	"The Jonny Gammage Law: Federal Prosecution of Police Brutality," *Synthesis/Regeneration*, Fall 2000.
Joe Fortunato	"Brutality, Repression and Criminalization of a Generation," *Synthesis/Regeneration*, Winter 2000.
William Norman Grigg	"Militarizing Mayberry," *New American*, October 7, 2002.
Sidney L. Harring	"The Diallo Verdict: Another 'Tragic Accident' in New York's War on Street Crime?" *Social Justice*, 2000.
Tom Hayden	"LAPD: Law and Disorder," *Nation*, April 10, 2000.
Bob Herbert	"Riots, Then and Now," *New York Times*, April 19, 2001.
Derrick Z. Jackson	"Injustice, American Style," *Boston Globe*, March 1, 2000.
Tamar Jacoby	"Restoring Trust Is a Two-Way Street," *New York Post*, February 28, 2000.
William F. Jasper	"Local Police Under Siege," *New American*, May 11, 1998.
James Kilpatrick	"How Much Force Is Too Much for Police Officers?" *Conservative Chronicle*, February 10, 1999.
Robert W. Lee	"Police, Race and Cincinnati's Riots," *New American*, May 21, 2001.
Heather MacDonald	"N.Y. Press to NYPD: Drop Dead," *American Enterprise*, September 2000.
Heather MacDonald	"Stop Persecuting the Police," *Wall Street Journal*, February 5, 2001.

Bibliography

Timothy W. Maier   "'Fed' Up Police," *Insight*, July 3–10, 2000.

Sheryl McCarthy   "Cops Can't Shoot People for Talking Back," *Liberal Opinion*, April 10, 2000.

Lucas Miller   "Culture of Complaint: What Happened When I Was Accused of Police Brutality," *Slate*, September 21, 2000.

Frank Morales   "The Militarization of the Police," *Covert Action Quarterly*, Spring/Summer 1999.

Salim Muwakkil   "No Cop Accountability," *In These Times*, April 11, 1999.

Michael Novick   "Demonstrate Against Police Brutality and for Community Control of the Police!" *Turning the Tide*, Winter 2000.

Clarence Page   "From Brutality to Inaction, New York Police Lack Right Response," *Liberal Opinion Week*, July 3, 2000.

Michael J. Pastor   "A Tragedy and a Crime: Amadou Diallo, Specific Intent, and the Federal Prosecution of Civil Rights Violations," *Legislation and Public Policy*, 2002.

Richie Perez   "The Inner Cities Feel the Billy Club," *Rights*, July/September 1998.

Neal Pollack   "Uncivil Action: Why the Convention Police Deserve Protest," *New Republic*, August 28, 2000.

Bobby L. Rush and   "Symposium: Should Washington Step in to Curb Police
James J. Fotis   Brutality in the States?" *Insight*, May 17, 1999.

Rowan Scarborough   "Dangerous Alliances," *Insight*, October 25, 1999.

Al Sharpton   "Making Local Police Misconduct a Federal Case," *Essence*, June 1999.

Esmeralda Simmons   "Police Brutality in New York City Revisited: One More Time," *Poverty & Race*, May/June 1998.

Jeffrey Toobin   "The Unasked Question: Why the Diallo Case Missed the Point," *New Yorker*, March 6, 2000.

Turning the Tide   "Demilitarize and Democratize the Police!" *Turning the Tide*, Fall 1998.

Daniel B. Wood   "Why the Police Are Hard to Police," *Christian Science Monitor*, September 27, 1999.

Index

Index